The Making of Economic Policy

The Making of Economic Policy

Theory and Evidence from Britain and the United States since 1945

Paul Mosley

READER IN ECONOMICS, SCHOOL OF HUMANITIES AND SOCIAL SCIENCES, UNIVERSITY OF BATH

DISTRIBUTED BY HARVESTER PRESS

First published in Great Britain in 1984 by
WHEATSHEAF BOOKS LTD
A MEMBER OF THE HARVESTER PRESS GROUP
Publisher: John Spiers
Director of Publications: Edward Elgar
16 Ship Street, Brighton, Sussex

British Library Cataloguing in Publication Data

Mosley, Paul
The making of economic policy.
1. Economic policy 2. Macroeconomics
I. Title
339 HD82

ISBN 0-7108-0144-0
ISBN 0-7108-0215-3 Pbk

Typeset in 11 point Times by Thomson Press (I) Limited, New Delhi
and printed in Great Britain by
Biddles Ltd, Guildford and King's Lynn

THE HARVESTER PRESS PUBLISHING GROUP
The Harvester Press Publishing Group comprises Harvester Press Limited (chiefly publishing literature, fiction, philosophy, psychology, and science and trade books), Harvester Press Microform Publications Limited (publishing in microform unpublished archives, scarce printed sources, and indexes to these collections) and Wheatsheaf Books Limited (a wholly independent company chiefly publishing in economics, international politics, sociology and related social sciences), whose books are distributed by the Harvester Press Limited and its agencies throughout the world.

In memory of my father
Eric Samuel Mosley, 1904–76

Contents

Tables

Figures

Preface

In this book I try to explain the making of macro-economic policy since the war in a way which is consistent with our available knowledge concerning the manner in which such decisions actually are taken. There has been a welcome tendency in recent years amongst economists to accept that governments' economic policy actions are not taken in a random and unpredictable manner but are, logically enough, guided by their self-interest and by their perception of the state of the economy at the time. But economists, almost instinctively, reach for maximising models whenever they try to incorporate a new aspect of reality into their own picture of the world, and nearly all the formal models of macro-economic policy-making constructed in the last fifteen years have been of a kind in which 'the government', conceived as a unitary body, maximises a 'social welfare function' subject to a 'constraint' imposed by the estimated behaviour of the economy. In part 1 of this book, on the basis of an examination of voter behaviour and the inter-relations of the different parts of government in Great Britain and the US, I argue that this is not the right way in which to approach the making of economic policy. A much more sensible approach to the particular circumstances of the governmental decision-making unit, I contend, is the so-called 'satisficing' approach in which the decision maker applies tried and tested rules of thumb, searching for new rules if and only if the old ones let him down by leading to persistently unsatisfactory values of targets. A formal model is constructed from this approach in Part 2 and tested against British data separately for the years of 'Keynesian demand management' in 1946–73 and for the subsequent period, in which the prevailing rule of thumb changed. Part 3 extends the approach by examining what happens to the predictions and estimated policy effects of a forecasting model if government is seen as reacting automatically to economic circumstance; it also examines the specific question of the extent to which political factors are disturbing the stability of the economy.

The one really pleasant part of writing this book is to thank the people who kept me at it and, I hope, made it into a better end product. Edward Elgar of Wheatsheaf Books originally, many years ago, conceived the idea of putting my various ideas on economic policy-making into a book. The project started, faltered, lay dormant for a number of years, and was then revived on his own initiative. I hope that he now has something which is worthy of the care which he has put into nurturing it. My colleagues John Hudson, Rudolf Klein, Alan Lewis, Frank Longstreth and Helen Weinreich-Haste all contributed ideas, and it will give an indication of the kind of cross-fertilisation which is possible at Bath across the usual disciplinary garden hedges if I say that although this is basically an economics book, only one of these people is formally labelled as an economist. Judy Harbutt and Susan Powell typed a beautiful first and second draft of the book. James Alt, Peter Jackson, Ann Robinson and a friend who must remain anonymous read the entire first draft and provided trenchant comments and criticism; I would like to pay particular tribute to Ann as someone who has influenced my thinking over nearly ten years now. But although those criticisms enriched the book beyond measure, I have sometimes stuck out for my own original position, and I am solely to blame for any errors in this final version.

Paul Mosley, February 1983

Glossary

Authorities
The agencies responsible for instituting changes in the instruments (qv) of economic policy. The President, the Congress and the Federal Reserve in the USA, the Treasury and the Bank of England in the UK.

Closed economy
An economy in which international trade or the international movement of capital play an insignificant role.

Coefficient
A coefficient measures the extent to which one economic category – for example consumption – is related to another, say income. If when incomes rise by £100 million consumption rises by £95 million the coefficient of consumption on income is 0.95. Coefficients can be derived from available evidence using econometric techniques. Such coefficients are called *estimated coefficients.* Alternatively they can be derived more from prior beliefs about relationships than from available information. Coefficients obtained in this way are called *imposed coefficients* since they are imposed over the available evidence.

Correlation
Two economic magnitudes are said to be correlated if movements in one are related to movements in the other.

Crowding-out
Crowding-out occurs when a rise in public expenditure causes a fall in private expenditure.

Demand elasticity
The responsiveness of demand for a particular item to changes in its price or to changes in purchasers' incomes. The price elasticity of demand measures the responsiveness of demand to price changes. The income elasticity of demand measures the respon-

siveness of demand to changes in income. The *income elasticity of demand for money* measures the extent to which higher incomes raise the demand for financial assets to be held in the form of money.

Demand for money
The degree to which individuals and institutions wish to hold their assets in the form of money.

Direct controls
A general phrase to describe *quantitative* restrictions – that is, restrictions on the rate of increase at which wages or prices may rise, or on bank lending. One simple form of direct controls is for the authorities simply to tell commercial banks how much they are to be allowed to lend. The supplementary special deposits scheme (qv) was a form of direct control.

Disintermediation
Intermediation occurs when a financial institution issues liabilities of a kind preferred by lenders to the institution (for example, bank current account deposits) and invests a proportion of the funds received in higher-yielding earning assets of a form which borrowers prefer (for example, overdrafts). Disintermediation occurs when such processes are unwound.

Domestic credit expansion (DCE)
Domestic credit expansion is a measure of *domestically* generated credit; that is, excluding credit generated abroad. It has two main elements: (i) that part of the public sector borrowing requirement (qv) which is not offset by purchases of public sector debt by the UK private sector (excluding banks); and (ii) the increase in bank lending in sterling to the private sector.

Endogenous
Generated from within. When considering one part of the economy changes that occur and are caused by elements within that part are said to be endogenous. In the context of the UK economy as a whole any economic changes that spring from within the UK can be called endogenous changes. In the context of an economic model (see model) variables (qv) calculated by the model itself are said to be endogenous variables.

Exogenous
Generated from outside. Changes caused by factors outside of the sector of the economy under investigation are said to be

exogenous. When considering the UK economy as a whole a fall in the level of US activity will be seen as exerting an exogenous influence on the UK economy. In an economic model (qv) variables determined by the modeller rather than by the model are said to be exogenous variables.

Estimation
Calculating on the basis of statistical evidence the effect of variables (qv) on each other.

Fiscal policy
Government management of the economy by varying the size and content of taxation and public expenditure.

Indicator
An economic indicator provides information on the present or future state of the economy. Intermediate targets (qv) can also be indicators but indicators may in addition include economic magnitudes, such as the exchange rate, for which no target is set.

Instrument
An instrument of economic policy is a measure, under the control of government, which affects the achievement of a target variable (qv) by influencing behaviour in the economy. Examples of these include minimum lending rate, tax rates and public expenditure.

Intermediate target
An intermediate target (for example the rate of growth of the money supply) is selected because it is thought to provide a link between an instrument (qv) and a target variable (qv). Clearly, for an intermediate target to function efficiently it should be subject to government control and should bear some stable relationship to the target variable in question.

International competitiveness
The degree to which a country such as the UK can compete in international markets. One measure is an index comparing movements in the ratio of British to world unit labour costs (measured in say dollars). If the ratio increases over time the ability of British producers to compete declines.

Model
A model of the economy aims to abstract the basic features of an economy and represents them in a simplified form. Economic

models can be manipulated to see how moving one part of the model (that is, economy) affects the rest of the model. Any run on an econometric model showing the outturn resulting from particular assumptions for exogenous variables (qv) and policy instruments (qv) is called a *simulation.*

Money

There is no single universally accepted definition since money, in its various forms, has a variety of uses. One traditional characteristic of money is that it is a medium of exchange, used to transfer purchasing power. Notes and coin are therefore clearly part of any definition. The great majority of transactions that are not conducted in cash are settled by transferring claims on the banking system, so most definitions concentrate on liabilities of banks, although some wider measures have been proposed which include liabilities of other credit and deposit-taking institutions such as building societies. A number of definitions of money are used:

M1 A narrow definition consisting of notes and coin in circulation with the public plus sterling current accounts held by the private sector.

£M3 This comprises notes and coin in circulation with the public plus all sterling deposits held by UK residents in both the public and private sectors.

M3 Equal to £M3 plus all deposits held by UK residents in other currencies.

PSL (Private Sector Liquidity) 1 This comprises notes and coin in circulation with the public plus all sterling deposits held by UK residents in the private sector, except those with original maturities of over two years, plus other money market instruments and certificates of tax deposit.

PSL2 This by and large is PSL1 plus private sector deposits with savings institutions (excluding building societies).

Money supply

The stock of money, however defined, in existence.

Open economy

An economy in which international trade and international capital movements play an important role.

Parameter

A coefficient (qv) unchanged in a particular exercise examining the relationships between economic magnitudes.

Policy optimisation
A technique of simulating an economic model in which the policy instruments (qv) are varied so as best to meet some specified desired values of, and preferences between, the government's target variables.

Public sector borrowing requirement (PSBR)
The excess of public spending over public revenue.

Ready Reckoner
A summary of the impact on the economy – estimated from simulations (qv) on an economic model (qv) – of changes in policy instruments (qv), or in exogenous variables (qv) on the values of target variables (qv)

Real incomes
The quantity of goods and services which money can buy.

Real public sector borrowing requirement
The PSBR adjusted to allow for the fact that at a time of inflation the national debt is declining in real value.

Regression
An econometric technique used to estimate coefficients (qv).

Reserve assets
Banks currently are required to maintain reserve assets amounting to at least 10 per cent of their eligible liabilities. Reserve assets comprise (i) balances with the Bank of England (other than special and supplementary deposits); (ii) money at call; (iii) Treasury and certain local authority and commercial bills; (iv) British Government stocks and nationalised industries stocks guaranteed by the government with one year or less to maturity.

Simulation – see model.

Supplementary special deposits scheme (the 'Corset')
Under the scheme – originally introduced in December 1973 and ended in June 1980 – institutions transferred deposits to the Bank of England if the growth in the interest-bearing element of their eligible liabilities exceeded defined limits. These deposits did not earn interest.

Target (variable)
Ultimate objective of policy, thought to have a bearing on the public's welfare; for example, unemployment, price inflation, the rate of growth of personal disposable income.

Trade-off
If changes in one aspect of the economy bring about changes (usually in the opposite direction) in another there is said to be a trade-off between them, especially when both are objectives. An example would be a relation between inflation and unemployment whereby a reduction in unemployment was matched by an increase in the rate of inflation (the Phillips Curve).

Variable
Any aspect of the economy whose behaviour can be separately measured may be called a variable. Consumption, retail prices, the price of gold, the number of days lost in strikes, the level of milk production are all variables.

Velocity of circulation of money
The ratio of income to money. If national income rises but the money stock remains constant the velocity of circulation rises.

Part 1
COMPONENTS OF THE POLICY-MAKING PROCESS

1 Economic Theory and the Policy-Making Process

1.1 What this book is about

This book investigates whether it is possible to explain the macro-economic policy actions of governments in any systematic way. It is only relatively recently that this question has been asked. For a science frequently accused of pushing to excessive lengths the assumption that individual human beings are guided by self-interest, positive economics has until recently shown very little willingness to recognise that economic policy itself might be guided by the rational pursuit of self-interest by those in government, or any other rational principle. As a result, texts on 'economic policy' fall into two groups. On the one hand, there are *normative* texts which take as given a particular picture of how an economy works and then proceed to ask how an economy functioning in that manner could be made to work better, for example, with a lower level of unemployment, a more stable level of national income or a faster rate of growth.[1] On the other hand, there are *positive* texts which describe how policy *actually was* made in particular countries.[2] These books present a splendidly detailed narrative of policy-making but seldom step back from this narrative to ask whether policy was determined by any factor more systematic than a random and *ad hoc* response to crisis.

This book treads a middle path between these two groups of writings. Like the first group, it applies a formal theoretical approach; but like the second group it is concerned with positive rather than normative questions. The intention is to discuss whether economic policy in

Britain and the United States since the Second World War can be represented as some sort of systematic response to the state of the economy. The advantage of this approach is, first of all, that it enables the observer of the policy-making process to glimpse the wood as well as the trees – the overall pattern of macro-economic policy as well as the individual actions which it comprises. Secondly, however, as we demonstrate in Chapter 6 below, failure to incorporate the elementary insight that macro-economic policy responds in a systematic way to economic conditions may bias the forecasts for the economy that are made by policy-makers in business and in government. A better understanding of the policy-making process may therefore enable policy-makers themselves, who are dependent on such forecasts, to do their job more efficiently. The analysis is throughout confined to those instruments of policy which can be manipulated quantitatively: public expenditure, tax rates and interest rates. It does not consider instruments with a primarily international use such as exchange rates and import duties.

1.2 The 'Keynesian' tradition: policy as an exogenous variable

In orthodox macro-economics, government expenditure and the other instruments of policy are left exogenous, that is, they are left to be determined outside the system of relationships by which the macro-economy is explained.[3] Leif Johansen provides a typical statement of this tradition when he writes at the start of his textbook *Public Economics* that 'We regard the public sector as autonomous, i.e. we do not try to build any theory in explanation of the factual actions of the public authorities in various situations.'[4]

The question generally asked in such textbooks is not what the government *actually* does, therefore, but what it *ought* to do. For it is easily possible, once some statement about the objectives of government has been made, to infer what the values of government policy instruments ought to be. For example, suppose that the government has only one objective, a target level of money national income. Once this is specified, then the appropriate level of government expenditure can be specified as the amount of expenditure which will lead to the achievement of this national income target.[5]

In all of this effort to spell out what the government *should* do, the question of whether real-world governments *actually do* (or indeed can) follow optimal policies is simply sidestepped, as Johansen candidly admits. The relationships which conventional macro-economics sets out between the government's policy targets and its policy instruments[6] are simply *prescriptions* or *decision rules,* which a government can follow if it possesses the requisite information and powers, and wishes to optimise social welfare in the particular sense which is implicit in the set of targets chosen by the author of the decision rule. Will a real-world government actually wish to maximise social welfare, or behave as if this were its intention? As we shall see in section 1.4 below, certain writers have assumed that the answer to at least one of these questions is yes, and they have proceeded to construct predictive models of economic policy-making on this basis. More importantly, many other writers, both professional economists and laymen, have implicitly assumed that the government is trying to manipulate the economy 'in the public interest' in the sense that they ascribe all deviations from the economy's socially optimal path to governmental incompetence.

To take but two examples from very many, an influential paper on British fiscal policy during the 1960s and 1970s has claimed that:

> The record of demand management during the last twenty years has been *extremely poor.* Throughout this whole period fiscal policy has been operated in alternating directions to produce periods of strong demand expansion, followed by reversals of policy in crisis conditions. Thus in 1953/4, 1958/9, 1962/3 and most notoriously in 1971/2 demand-expansionary policies were introduced, each time in a more panicky atmosphere than the previous time. Then always, just two years later, the direction was reversed, demand-deflationary policies being initiated in 1955/6, 1960/1, 1964/5 and now again in 1973/4.

The strong reversals of policy indicate that the outcome of previous phases of policy was not acceptable and had to be corrected. The process in part has been the result of swings in the Government's choice of policy objectives. *But the story also suggests that some of the outcomes were not properly foreseen* – in particular that the conventional forecasting systems on which policy is based may underestimate the full effect of changes in policy [authors' italics].[7]

and an eminent American economist has insisted that

There is by now wide agreement that the Federal Reserve System pumped up the economy to an *unhealthy* degree in 1972.... I can do no more than speculate on the motives. But one does not need to understand motivation to recognise a *mistake*. The Fed *erred* in 1972 – and in a big way [author's italics].[8]

This approach treats post-war economic intervention in the Western capitalist countries as an inefficiently carried out exercise in control engineering, and ascribes their disappointing performance in stabilising their economies to 'technical mistakes'. On this view, more economic research, leading to a more exact knowledge of the economy's response to policy measures, is all that is needed to make it perform better.

The contention of this book is that this is a dangerously simple-minded view, since it criticises the agencies of economic policy for failing to do what, very possibly, they never set out to achieve. If, in fact, politicians desire above all to stay in power, or bureaucrats to keep the influence of their department as big as possible – which are scarcely original or unreasonable propositions – then analyses and prescriptions based on the assumption that the government acts so as to stabilise the economy 'in the public interest' are likely to fall wide of the mark. Our task in succeeding chapters will be to develop the implications of this statement. The task has in fact been begun, by two schools of thought with widely differing political presuppositions. Let us begin by considering their contributions.

1.3 Attempts to explain government economic policy, I: Kalecki

As early as 1943 the practice of treating economic policy as exogenous had been criticised by Kalecki, who took issue with Keynes' optimistic assumption that public expenditure could be used at will to counteract slumps in capitalist economies. His argument was that whereas Keynesian programmes of demand expansion would command universal political support during the slump, businessmen would urge a deliberate deflation of the economy on the government once full employment was approached in order to preclude the increase in the power of workers and organised trade unions that would otherwise result:

> Under a regime of permanent full employment, 'the sack' would cease to play its role as a disciplinary measure. The social position of the boss would be undermined and the self-assurance and class consciousness of the working class would grow. Strikes for wage increases and improvements in conditions of work would create political tension. It is true that profits would be higher under a regime of full employment than they are on the average under *laisser-faire;* and even the rise in wage rates resulting from the stronger bargaining power of the workers is less likely to reduce profits than to increase prices, and thus affects adversely only the rentier interests. Their class instinct (however) tells them that lasting full employment is unsound from their point of view and that unemployment is an integral part of the 'normal' capitalist system.[9]

This forecast, originally derived by Kalecki from Marxian analysis, was supported by him with reference to the experience of a number of Western democratic governments which had experimented with reflationary programmes in the late 1930s. In the United States, for example, New Deal expenditures had been sharply cut back in the second half of 1937, and in France the Prime Minister, Leon Blum, had fallen from office in 1938 after his refusal to restrain an inflationary boom, following on a public works programme which he had sponsored, led to an investment strike by big business.[10] But Kalecki emphasised that his prediction only applied to democratic political systems. 'One of the important functions of fascism, as typified by the Nazi system', Kalecki noted, 'was to remove the capitalist objections to full employment.'[11]

Kalecki's piece has stimulated remarkably few attempts at empirical verification or incorporation into models of policy-making. Perhaps in the past it has seemed so self-evidently true to the one ideological camp, and so self-evidently false to the other, as to stimulate nobody. But the present recession has brought Kalecki's thesis back into the mouths of people who may be unaware that they are quoting it.[12] We consider its applicability to the post-war world in Chapters 5 and 7 below.

1.4 Attempts to explain government economic policy, II: non-Marxian approaches

In the early 1960s the idea that government expenditure could reasonably be considered as an exogenous variable came to be challenged from an entirely different political quarter. Peacock and Wiseman (1962), investigating the reasons for the secular increase in the ratio of UK government expenditure to national income over the hundred years to 1960, noted that the increase was not a steady one, but rather seemed to be concentrated in short bursts, particularly during the two world wars. These bursts caused a once-for-all upward shift or 'displacement' of the government expenditure/national income ratio; Peacock and Wiseman suggested that this shift was due to the fact that in periods of war or other social upheaval the electorate's idea of a 'tolerable burden of taxation', which is fixed in normal times, would be shifted upwards.[13] Other writers since Peacock and Wiseman have suggested that there are deep-rooted pressures in the social system to which government is forced to accommodate by increasing the share of government expenditure in national income; these include O'Connor (1973), King (1975) and Hirsch (1976).[14] But all of these writings are essentially speculative in the sense that having supplied plausible hypotheses on the cause of the secular rise in the ratio of state expenditures to national income, they then make no serious attempt at a test of those hypotheses.

When attempts to test predictive models of economic policy were finally made in the 1970s, they forfeited much of the richness of Kalecki's and for that matter of Peacock and Wiseman's approach. In the interests of developing testable models, the long-period forces which they examined were banished from the analysis and the complicated business of

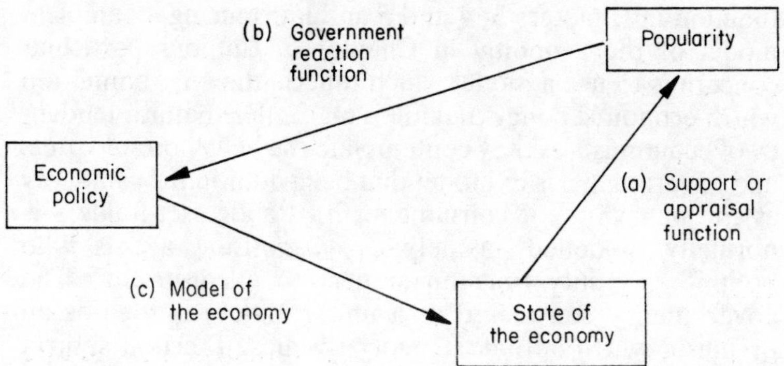

Figure 1.1 The interdependence of economics and politics: conventional representation

the making of economic policy was reduced to three simple relationships:

(a) The *support* or *appraisal* function. Conventionally, one of the elements in the government's welfare function, if not the only one, is the government's probability of re-election. An estimate of this probability, at a particular moment of time, can be provided by the government's lead on the opinion polls. This in turn is influenced by the state of the economy. The support function measures this relationship between government popularity and the state of the economy.

(b) The *reaction function.* Economic policy is manipulated so as to optimise, or at least improve, the government's welfare.

(c) A *model of the economy,* which explains the effects of the policy measures undertaken under (b) on the macro-economy.

This three-equation model (Figure 1.1) exists, now, in a considerable variety of shapes and sizes.

1.5 General line of approach taken by this book

In this book we make our way around this roundabout, considering the support function in Chapter 2, the reaction function in Chapters 3, 4 and 5 and introducing a complete model of the economy in Chapter 6. But our particular concern is to use a model which reflects the environment in which economic policy-making is made. The natural tendency of economists as they contemplate the behaviour of voters and governments is to model that behaviour in the same way as the behaviour of consumers, firms and asset-holders is normally modelled, namely as *maximising* agents who optimise a utility function subject to a constraint. 'The government' (considered as a unitary body) is seen as an organism which optimises a social welfare function subject to a constraint represented by the behaviour of the economy,[15] and 'the voter' as an individual who maximises an individual utility function in a state of perfect information.[16]

But there are several good reasons for thinking that, even if traditional maximising theory is right for firms and consumers, it is wrong for voters and above all for governments. In the first place, governments state quite explicitly that they do not maximise anything at all. A recent UK government report on the process of macro-economic policy making in Britain and the United States made it clear that optimal control methods were not used in either country,[17] and indeed could not be unless ministers or the President, as the case might be, became willing to spell out their 'utility function' in the shape of their answers to a set of hypothetical questions concerning their preferences between different states of the economy. This they have good political reasons for not doing. A politician who spells out the relative weight he attaches (for example) to getting unemployment and inflation down gives the public a free rod with which to beat his back should he subsequently need to act in a way inconsistent with those stated preferences.[18]

Secondly, governments are not under 'competitive pressure' in the same sense that a business firm normally is. It may be true that in some industries the competitive process will gradually weed out all those firms whose policies are not consistent with the objectives of profit or growth maximisation, so that actual observed behaviour amongst the business community is forced to approximate to a 'maximising' model.[19] But this Darwinian analogy is very difficult to apply to government. 'Competition', in democracies, only manifests itself in the shape of regular elections every few years, and in the mid-term the governing party can, given a reasonable majority, pursue what economic policy it wishes without fear of losing power. The concept of 'failure' is, in any case, much more nebulous for an economic policy-maker than for the management of a firm who can be judged by the profit level which they achieve. (Has government failed if unemployment goes above 10 per cent? There is no clear answer.) It is therefore not possible to identify any environmental forces which compel governments to optimise any objective function.

Finally, the very nature of the environment in which economic policy-making takes place imposes limits on the way in which it can be done. It is unfortunately necessary at this point to engage in semantic discourse, since the subject of policy-making has over many years developed a vivid language of mechanical metaphor which easily misleads the casual observer. Governments *manage, control* or *steer* the economy, to quote the title of Samuel Brittan's famous account (Brittan, 1971) of the post-war Treasury, by manipulating the *instruments* of economic policy: tax revenue, public spending, interest rates, incomes policy. Chancellors of the Exchequer in their annual budgets either increase effective demand by *opening the accelerator*, reduce it and impose a *touch on the brakes*, or keep it unaltered with the phrase 'steady as she goes'.[20] This sort of metaphor is misleading twice over. As a recent Chancellor of the Exchequer has acknowledged, the effect of instruments of policy on the targets is unpredictable:

> It is not possible to manage an economy the way that you can hope to manage a business, or even a house... (An important) reason why management is perhaps the wrong word when you are talking about the economy is that the government has no direct control over the actors in the economic process. It can't make people work if they don't want to, it can't make people invest if they don't want to, and it can't make them manage their affairs better if they don't want to and haven't the ability to do so. You are always coming up against the fact that you don't really control your raw material at all, you can only hope to influence it in a general way.[21]

But, worse than this, *none* of the instruments mentioned above really is an instrument in the sense that a government can forecast with certainty what its value is going to be over a given year. A given change in tax rates does not lead to a predictable change in tax yield because the tax base cannot be forecast with certainty;[22] public expenditure cannot be forecast with certainty either since many of its categories, such as unemployment benefits, themselves depend on the level of future economic activity which is uncertain;[23] interest rates cannot be forecast with certainty because they depend on the growth of the demand and supply of loans, which themselves depend partly on the behaviour of private banks; an incomes policy norm can be breached by covert increases in non-wage benefits. In a democracy it is indeed difficult to make these instruments 'bite harder', since that involves restriction on the freedom of institutions conventionally thought autonomous, and the alternative is to move a stage back from trying to manipulate these powerful instruments which are ultimately uncontrollable to manipulating less powerful instruments which are more controllable. The trade-off implied here is discussed formally in Appendix II. The critical point for our present purposes is that 'expected utility maximisation' may be an inappropriate procedure in face of these two levels of uncertainty. So great is the likelihood that things may turn out differently from the Treasury's 'central forecast', and that a policy based on this central forecast may make things worse rather than better,[24] that even *trying* to maximise the government's expected utility *ex ante* may not be a sensible procedure to adopt. It may be more sensible, rather, simply to react *ex post* by means of a simple rule of thumb when things can clearly be seen to have gone wrong.[25]

For these reasons we reject, in the case of governments, the conventional behavioural hypothesis of maximisation subject to constraint. Rather we shall be concerned to examine the hypothesis that governments behave as *satisficing* organisations. This means that unlike the 'rational economic man' of orthodox neo-classical economic theory, they do not *optimise* a utility function by scanning all the options that are open to them and choosing the best available, but rather proceed by maintaining unchanged behaviour patterns and decision rules *unless and until the existing situation becomes unbearable.*[26] At this point they engage in 'search behaviour' in order to seek out strategies (new decision rules) that will restore their utility once again to an acceptable level. This involves them in scanning a *limited* number of policy options. Once they have found a satisfactory one, search behaviour once again stops and the new behaviour pattern continues until such time as the situation becomes intolerable once again.[27] Governments, on this view, may not know what they want, but they know what they don't want.

The voter, of course, operates in a different institutional environment, but the arguments we have presented above against applying 'maximising' theory and in favour of applying 'satisficing' theory to governments apply to him and her also. Voters, like governments, are not exposed to competitive pressures forcing them to behave in a maximising manner. Also, the critical swing voters who determine the outcomes of elections are, it seems, very ignorant of the nature of the options in front of them: they are the least exposed to the media and the least well able to perceive the existence of conflicts between the various objectives of economic and social policy.[28] In such a state of ignorance the only kind of judgement they will be able to form about a government's economic policy is whether it has delivered them results which are 'good enough', from their subjective point of view, or 'not good enough'.

Here also, therefore, assumptions of satisficing or 'bounded rationality'[29] seem to be a good point of departure. But that is all that they are. The real test is whether they can explain what actually happened. We consider this in the next four chapters.

Notes

1 Examples of this literature are Tinbergen (1952), Allen (1967) and Theil (1956, 1958, 1968) who takes a real-world economy – the United States in the 1930s depression – and proceeds to demonstrate

how Keynesian policies could have increased its income and employment levels.

2 Examples of this literature are Dow (1964), Cohen (1971), Brittan (1971) and Blackaby (1979) for the UK, Blinder (1979) for the US, and Kirschen (ed.) (1971) for a sample of European countries.

3 Consider for example the simplest macro-economic model,

$Y \equiv C + I + G$ (1) national income Y is, by definition, made up of private consumption C, private investment I and government expenditure G

$C = a + bY$ (2) private consumption is a linear function of income

$I = I_0$ (3) private investment is autonomous

$G = G_0$ (4) government expenditure also is autonomous

The statement that government expenditure is left *autonomous* or *exogenous* means that it is left to be decided, presumably at the government's bidding, outside the system that is being explained.

4 Johansen (1965), p. 6.

5 The equilibrium level of money national income when government expenditure is zero, by substitution of equations (2), (3) and (4) from footnote 3 into (1), is:

$$\bar{Y} = \frac{a + I_0}{1 - b} \qquad (5)$$

This equilibrium income $\bar{Y}$ will not necessarily be the government's target level of national income, which we may call Y^*. However, if there is any discrepancy between the two, 'optimal' government expenditure can be prescribed as the amount of expenditure which will get rid of the gap between actual and target levels. This will be

$$G^* = (1 - b)\left[Y^* - \frac{a + I_0}{1 - b}\right] \qquad (6)$$

or, otherwise put, the gap between equilibrium and target levels of national income divided by the government expenditure multiplier.

6 An example of such relationships is the formula (6) in note 5 above.

7 Cripps, Godley and Fetherston, in evidence to United Kingdom (1974).

8 Blinder (1979), pp. 184–7.

9 Kalecki (1943), p. 326.

10 For the details of this episode, see Kalecki (1938).

11 Kalecki (1943), p. 326. For a fascinating extension of this line of argument, which contends also that in the long run full employment, free collective bargaining, stable prices and a democratic political system are incompatible, see the pamphlet by Jay (1976).

12 Consider for example the following allegation by Tony Benn, at the time Shadow Secretary of State for Industry:

Mr Benn yesterday accused the Government of seeking to create a major depression in order to increase the profit margins of industry. He also claimed that rearmament would be the solution eventually sought to the problems of unemployment.

In a remarkable speech to about 3,000 students and trade unionists in Manchester, Mr Benn claimed that the Government was attacking trade unions, cutting public expenditure, destroying the Welfare State, and deliberately creating unemployment, all to aid its friends in business . . . The policies were evidence of he failure of capitalism and the result would be as in the 1930s. 'If you go to Jarrow, Clydeside, the North West or Ebbw Vale, you will find that what brought full employment back was rearmament and war. It is no accident that this Government, faced with unemployment, is trying to whip up cold war so that people will accept that rearmament is part of the answer.

'What brought Hitler to power was 6 million unemployed. We will not accept that capitalism will solve its crisis by the extreme unemployment which was to lead to so many deaths in the Second World War.' (quoted in *Financial Times,* 19 February 1980)

13 Peacock and Wiseman (1967), p.viii. Peacock and Wiseman's study began as an investigation of the hypothesis put forward by the nineteenth century German writer, Adolph Wagner, which was that a secular increase in the ratio of government expenditure to national income was inevitable in every society as the bureaucracy and the economy became more complex (Peacock and Wiseman (1967), pp. 18ff).

14 There is a concise summary of writing on the long-run forces underlying public expenditure in the essay by Klein (1976).

15 See for example Wood (1967), Fisher (1968, 1970), Pissarides (1972), Friedlaender (1973), Friedman (1978).

16 See Hibbs and Vassilatos in Hibbs and Fassbender (1981).

17 United Kingdom (1978), pp. 82 and 83.

18 The United Kingdom *Report on Policy Optimisation* comments:

As we have been told in evidence by politicians and civil servants who have worked closely with ministers, Chancellors would not commit themselves on hypothetical questions. It is easy to see why. If the Chancellor's criterion function became known, as it easily might, his actions could be anticipated, and argument about appropriateness of the criterion, in the Cabinet, in Parliament, and in the country at large, could inhibit its use without replacing it by anything equally decisive. (United Kingdom (1978), pp. 60–1).

19 See the essay by Alchian (1950).

20 James Callaghan (UK Chancellor of the Exchequer), *Hansard,* 11 April 1967, col. 1010.

21 Healey (1981), pp. 1 and 3.
22 See Allan (1965), and for further development, Appendix II below.
23 The US government classifies federal expenditures according to whether they are or are not 'relatively uncontrollable'. On this criterion, the percentage of the budget which counted as 'relatively uncontrollable' had grown from 59 per cent in 1967 to 76 per cent in 1981. Reischauer (1981), p. 9.
24 For a theoretical demonstration of this point see the essay by Brainard (1967).
25 This is described as 'adaptive' rather than 'omniscient' search by Cyert and March (1963), p. 99.
26 What is 'bearable' at any given time itself depends on past experience: acceptable-level goals are revised upwards or downwards over time as performance exceeds or falls short of aspiration.
27 A formal statement of 'statisficing' theory is given at Appendix I below.
28 Butler and Stokes (1971), Table 10.6, p. 225.
29 The phrase is from Simon (1972).

2 What the Electorate Wants: Voters' Perception and Evaluation of the Economy

'All political history' declared Harold Wilson in 1968 after four years' experience as prime minister of Great Britain, 'shows that the standing of a Government and its ability to hold the confidence of the electorate at a General Election depend on the success of its economic policy'.[1] Unless this statement is false – and it does come from the only British prime minister this century to win four general elections – we should therefore expect there to be some systematic relationship in all western democracies, at least, between some measurable indicators of the state of the economy and the popularity of the governing party, which that governing party can use as a guide when framing its pre-election economic policy. Can such a relationship – a 'support function', as we have called it above – be found, what variables does it involve and what is its theoretical basis? These are the questions which this chapter tries to answer. The analysis is, at this stage, largely confined to Great Britain.

2.1 Existing empirical results

A large number of studies have now been carried out which take the lead of the governing party on the opinion polls (or, in some cases, the votes actually won by the governing party

TABLE 2.1 USA, Great Britain and other countries: response of governing party's popularity to economic variables

*Investigator**	*Time period investigated*	*Dependent variable*	*Response of dependent variable to a 1 per cent increase in:*			*Other independent variables in regression*
			Real per capita GNP	*Consumer price index*	*Unemployment rate*	
United States of America						
Kramer, 1971	1896–1964	Presidential popularity	. .	–	. .	
Lepper, 1974	1896–1964	As above	+	–	. .	
Stigler, 1973	1900–70	As above	NA	NA	. .	
Mueller, 1970	1945–69	As above	NA	NA	–3.18	Dummy variables for individual Presidents
Arcelus and Meltzer, 1975	1896–1970	Congressional vote of Democratic Party	. .	–0.52(1)	. .	See note (1)
Goodman and Kramer, 1975	1896–1970	As above	+	–	. .	
Bloom and Price, 1975	1896–1970	Congressional vote	+0.75(2)	NA	NA	
Tufte, 1978	1946–76	As above	+	NA	NA	
Great Britain						
Goodhart and Bhansali, 1970	1947–68	Governing party's popularity (Gallup Poll)	NA	–0.12	–0.86(3)	
			NA	–0.026	–1.25(4)	See note (5)
Mosley, 1978	1953–75	Governing party's popularity lead over principal opposition party	NA	. .	–0.011	
			NA	. .	–0.013(7)	See note (6)
Frey and Schneider, 1978b	1959–74	As above	+0.81	–0.61	–6.01	Dummy variable for Conservative and Labour governments

Borooah and Van der Ploeg, 1982	1953–77	Governing party's popularity lead over opposition	+0.006	−0.016	. .	See note (9)
Pissarides, 1980	1953–77	As above	+0.26	−0.57	. .	See note (8)
France						
Lafay, 1981	1961–77	Governing party's popularity	+2.82(11)	−6.39	−0.22	See note (10)
West Germany						
Peretz, 1981	1955–76	As above	NA	. .	−0.00065	See note (12)

*See Bibliography, pp. 245–52 for details

Symbols: . . not statistically significant

Notes

(1) Arcelus and Meltzer use each major political party's vote as the dependent variable, regardless of whether or not it is the governing party, and then model incumbency by means of a dummy variable. The results reported are those for the Democratic party; the vote for the Republican party in Congress elections was not significantly correlated with any economic variable.
(2) This result only applies in the case of falling real income. Bloom and Price found that the effect of real income changes on party popularity was asymmetric, with incumbent parties being penalised for declines in real income but not rewarded for increases.
(3) Average of unemployment rate lagged six, five and four months.
(4) Unemployment lagged six months.
(5) Time since last election and time to next election.
(6) Time since last election and time to nearest election.
(7) In this regression unemployment is measured as deviations from a linear time trend and lagged six months.
(8) In addition to the three economic variables for which regression coefficients are quoted Pissarides considers the following independent variables (brackets denote an insignificant regression coefficient at the 99% level): last month's value of the governing party's lead, (dummies for each successive administration), time since last election, time to next election, the pound/dollar exchange rate.
(9) Borooah and van der Ploeg express all independent variables in first difference terms. Additional variables considered are changes in exchange rate and tax rates.
(10) Dummy variables for individual prime ministers. Report is contained in Hibbs and Fassbender (1981).
(11) Index of real wages.
(12) Change in industrial production, lagged popularity, and SPD dummy. Report is containd in Hibbs and Fassbender (1981).

at elections) as dependent variable and then try to find out which economic variables are correlated with it. However, as Table 2.1 illustrates, these studies are very far from speaking with one voice. In the United States, three commentators (Tufte, Goodman and Kramer, and Lepper) find that real income per capita is a significant positive influence on popularity, two (Kramer and Arcelus and Meltzer) find that it is an insignificant influence, and one (Bloom and Price) finds that the relationship is asymmetric, with governments suffering the penalty of declining popularity in times of falling real income but not being rewarded by increasing popularity when income is rising. Price inflation is generally a negative influence on popularity, and unemployment, with one exception, is an insignificant influence.

In Britain, there is diversity of a different sort: the three investigators who have studied the effect of real income changes find that they have a positive influence on popularity, but three out of five investigators find that unemployment is a significant negative influence (against five out of six in America who found that it was an insignificant influence) and the picture on inflation is muddy, with four investigators out of five reporting a significant negative influence, and one (the present author) reporting insignificant results. Worse than this, the relationship between popularity and economic variables appears to be an unstable one: my own findings for 1953–75 (Mosley 1978) suggest that although, *over the entire period*, inflation has an insignificant influence on popularity, the practice of cutting up the period into discrete slices of time yields a gradually increasing salience of inflation over time, and underlying this a tendency for the electorate's aversion to unemployment to become stronger in time of 'unemployment crisis' (that is, above-trend unemployment) and for its aversion to inflation to become stronger in times of 'inflation crisis' (that is, above-trend inflation). There is, in short, a lot to explain.

And, as yet, there is very little theory to explain it. Most of the literature summarised above, our own contribution included, works with the following threadbare theoretical framework: 'people dislike increases in the national unemployment rate (and penalise the government for it accordingly); they also dislike increases in the national inflation rate (and penalise the government for it accordingly); finally, they like increases in per capita GDP (and reward the government for it accordingly)'. This is not even internally consistent. For even if we assume that people are entirely selfish (that is, concerned only with their own economic welfare), confine the discussion to 'floating voters' (that is, those who do not identify with any particular party), and assume finally that they are entirely myopic – that is, they penalise the government for *all* declines in their economic welfare, even if they result from events manifestly outside the government's control – we still have no answer to the question 'why should changes in the inflation rate and in unemployment affect a voter's behaviour *independently* of their effect on his real income? We may be able to get an answer to this question by postulating *either* altruism *or* inaccurate perception of their economic welfare on the part of voters; but if that is the explanation of observed patterns of voting which the writers listed in Table 2.1 have in mind, they are certainly keeping their cards very close to their chest. The truth is that all we have so far in this research field is measurement without theory, or, more precisely, measurement underlain by more than one theory. I therefore propose to start by putting forward *two* theories of voter response to the economy which are transparently naive but which are at least, I claim, psychologically plausible and internally consistent. I call these 'the rational self-interested voter' and 'the impulsive voter' respectively.

2.2 Two models of voter behaviour

(i) The rational self-interested voter

Let us begin by stating:

> Hypothesis I. The only economic variables by which voters are influenced in their voting behaviour is changes in their *own* perceived standard of living.

As a basis for this hypothesis, imagine all those voters

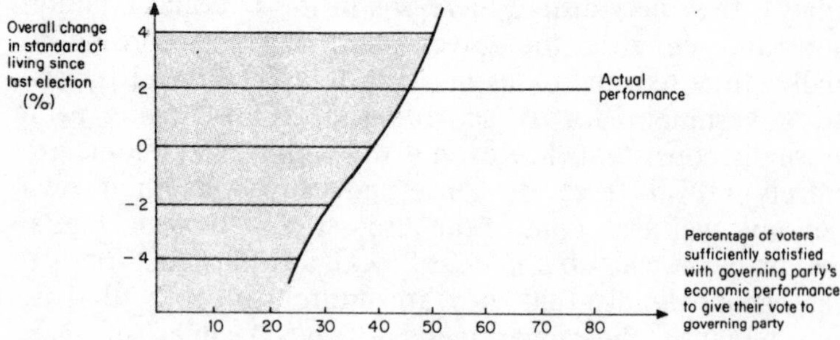

Figure 2.1 Evaluation of the economy; the 'selfish voter' view

whose vote is sensitive to the state of the economy[2] as being distributed along a continuum, represented by the horizontal axis in Figure 2.1.

Everyone is assumed to have his own personal yardstick for the movement in the standard of living over the electoral period: Figure 2.1 depicts a hypothetical frequency distribution of these 'yardsticks'. If the actual movement in the standard of living over this period, as perceived by an individual voter, exceeds or matches up to this yardstick the voter votes for the government; if it does not he votes for an opposition party. In the hypothetical situation depicted in Figure 2.1, the standard of living has improved for everybody by 2 per cent, and this is good enough to secure just under 50 per cent of the vote for the governing party. This formulation of course leaves open the question of how voters measure their own standard of living. Do they, for example, consider the range of publicly provided goods and services to which they have access – the so-called 'social wage' – or do they merely consider their own post-tax income? Do they behave as if they had an accurate perception of the movement in their own standard of living, however defined? Questions such as this can only be resolved by empirical investigation, and our findings on these matters are presented in Section 2.3 below.

On this hypothesis, changes in unemployment and prices (and all other determinants of the standard of living such as the 'social wage') influence the vote only inasmuch as they themselves influence the standard of living of individuals; they have no *independent* influence. If we wish we can broaden this model by admitting long-run changes in party identification and other matters (for example, foreign policy issues and the personalities of individual candidates) into the picture, as depicted in Figure 2.2. But the point remains that, on the hypothesis of completely selfish voting, only personal standards of living can be admitted into support functions as an independent variable. Inflation and unemployment, in particular, will only affect popularity inasmuch as they affect personal disposable income.

If this hypothesis is correct, then *removing* unemployment and inflation from regression equations such as those depicted in Table 2.1 will not reduce their predictive power. The correct model to represent the mechanism depicted in Figure 2.2 will then be

$$\begin{aligned}\text{government popularity} = b_0 + b_1 &\text{ (perceived short-run change in standard of living)} \\ + b_2 &\text{ (shift parameters representing changes in party identification, personality of head of government, etc.)} \\ + u_p &\end{aligned}$$

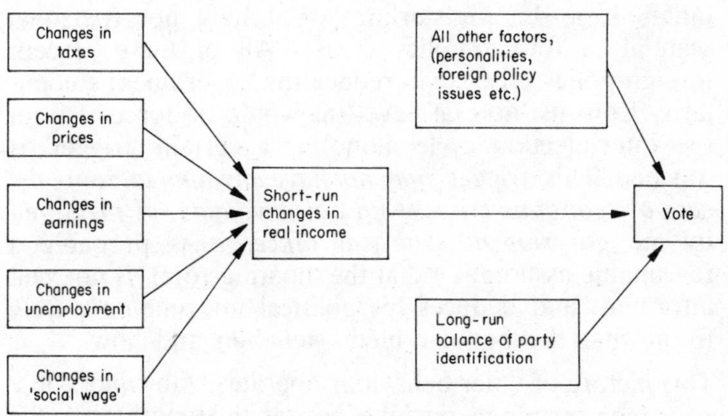

Figure 2.2 The 'selfish voter': a more complex view
Source: adapted from Bloom and Price (1975)

where b_0, b_1, b_2 are fixed numbers and u_p is a random error term reflecting the influence of 'other factors.' The expected arithmetic sign of the coefficient b_1 is *positive*.[3] If we wish to model the voter's reactions in the spirit of 'satisficing' theory, then the short-run change in the standard of living will be a discontinuous variable; only if it crosses a certain threshold (say, x per cent increase in a given year) will government popularity alter.

(ii) The 'naive and sentimental' or 'impulsive' voter

On another stylised view, voters do not award or withhold their vote to the government on the basis of any *objectively* measurable variables at all. Rather, the partisans vote for the party to which they have always owed their loyalty and the others ('floaters') drift between government, opposition and abstention (or voting for third parties) on the following basis:

> Hypothesis II. In the neighbourhood of elections there is a drift towards the government: in the mid-term there is a drift away, as the voter is aware that any decisions he makes will not influence the balance of power. Voting patterns deviate from this normal inter-election cycle if and only if there is a 'crisis'. The origin of this crisis may be economic (above-normal unemployment, increasing inflation, a run on sterling) or it may not (personal scandal, a foreign-policy crisis). All of these, except foreign-policy crises, will reduce the government's popularity from its 'normal' level (as would be forecast from the inter-election cycle alone) if a certain 'trigger' is touched. This 'trigger' *may not have anything to do, in the case of economic crises, with objective data, as measured by the government statistical office:* it is probably a reasonable assumption that the 'floating voter' is not well informed, and deduces his political information purely from what the popular media tell him and how.[4]

This picture of voter behaviour operates with what is in a sense a more primitive model of man than Hypothesis I: the voter no longer seeks through his vote to maximise, or improve, his per capita income; rather, he behaves as a purely reactive animal, withdrawing his vote from the government if and only if some 'crisis' jerks him into a sense of dissatisfaction. However – and for the moment we are, of course, reasoning purely on *a priori* grounds, without looking at the actual data – there are reasons for thinking Hypothesis II more psychologically plausible than Hypothesis I of completely self-interested voting. Firstly, it squares – as Hypothesis I does not – with the observed finding that many voters (especially 'floaters') are quite ignorant about what has happened to their economic welfare, or if they do profess to know, are often wrong. Secondly, it squares as Hypothesis I does not with the observed finding that when people vote they do not take account purely of their own or of their family's own welfare but also consider the welfare of others or more broadly the welfare of 'the nation'; naive they may be, but they do not lack 'sentiment' in the sense of concern with a broader reference group than their own households. Indeed, if we are to make any sense at all of the response of British government popularity to unemployment, we must either assume, following Hypothesis I, that the vote is correlated with changes in the personal disposable income of unemployed individuals and their dependents,[5] or else we must assume that, when peaks in unemployment cause government popularity to drop, this means, following Hypothesis II, that some people have withdrawn their vote from the government because they are alarmed by the sense of economic crisis which the rise in the unemployment figures produces.[6] This can be seen either as 'altruistic' or 'precautionary' voting, but the distinction is not important.[7] The important thing is that some shifts in the vote probably cannot be explained purely by changes in individual well-being, and Hypothesis II captures these shifts by ascribing them to 'crisis' headlines in the media which may make individuals worry either on their own or on other people's account.

Specifically, Hypothesis II can be modelled as:

government
popularity $= b_0 + b_1$ (time to nearest election)

$+b_2$ ('crisis dummies')
$+b_3$ (shift parameters reflecting change in party identification)

The 'crisis dummies' need to be very carefully specified since they lie at the heart of the voter's reaction process. One approach, following our earlier paper (Mosley, 1978) would be to assume that any movement of unemployment or prices above its trend level, at least, represents a 'crisis' and to represent the degree of 'crisis' by the distance that unemployment or inflation is above its trend level. A 'satisficing' response pattern can be incorporated into this formulation by assuming, as seems to be empirically accurate,[8] that voters' reactions are only triggered off by sharp changes in unemployment or inflation, that is, that falls in government popularity are only associated with changes in unemployment of inflation which exceed a certain 'threshold' level. On this formulation, the changes themselves become the dummy variables, and then if and only if they are big enough. But this still leaves unanswered the question of whether voters know what is happening to inflation and unemployment, and of what influence the media have on that impression. We can try and get around this difficulty by assuming that the degree to which an economic variable assumes 'crisis' proportions depends not only on its value as measured by the Government Statistical Service but also on the frequency with which it is mentioned in the popular newspapers and other media over and above some arbitrary 'threshold' level.

2.3 The models tested

We have so far, *for the individual voter*, the following models:

I 'Selfish voter': popularity←perceived short-run change in standard of living, shift parameters

II 'Impulsive voter': popularity←perceived unemployment, perceived inflation, other 'crisis indicators', shift parameters

The main 'shift parameters' that we shall want to consider are time since the last election and time to the nearest election. The first reflects the falling-away of support which always hits a government when the period of post-election euphoria is over, and the second reflects the cyclical pattern which the popularity of the government always undergoes in the mid-term between elections as electors become free to express a 'protest vote' without any risk that this will actually overturn the governing party. These patterns are clearly apparent in Figure 2.3 below.

For the economy as a whole it is possible to set up the two hypotheses as:

I 'Selfish voters' only: $V = b_0 + b_1 \left(\frac{Y}{L}\right) + b_2(\text{last}) + b_3\ (\text{nearest}) + u_\text{I}$

where V = lead of governing party over principal opposition party, as recorded by Gallup Poll;

$\frac{Y}{L}$ = personal disposable income per capita, as recorded by *Economic Trends Annual Supplement*, 1982 edition, table 45 and equivalent figures for earlier years;

last = time since last election in months;

nearest = time to nearest election in months;

u_I = random error term

b_0, b_1, b_2, b_3 = fixed parameters

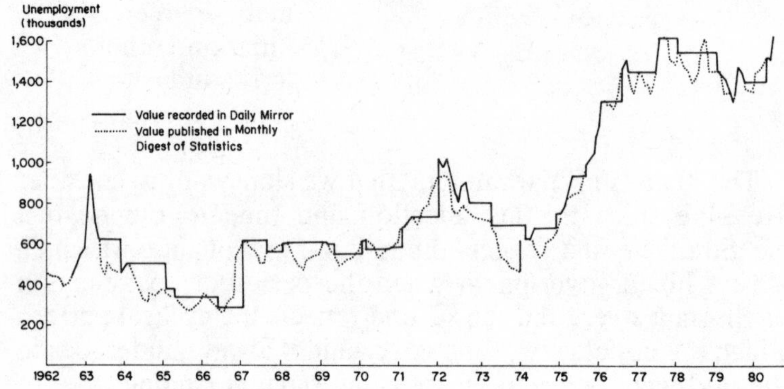

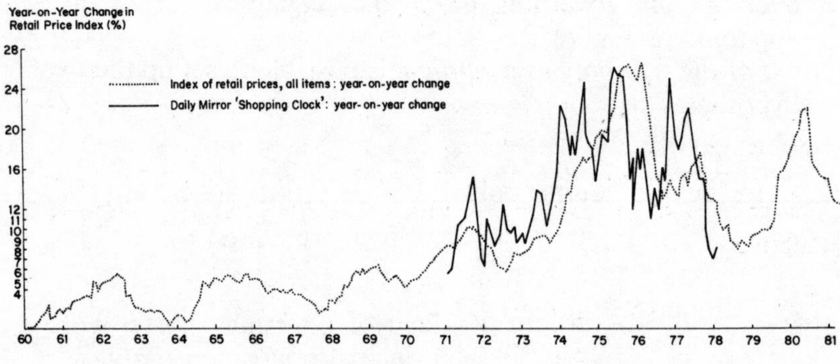

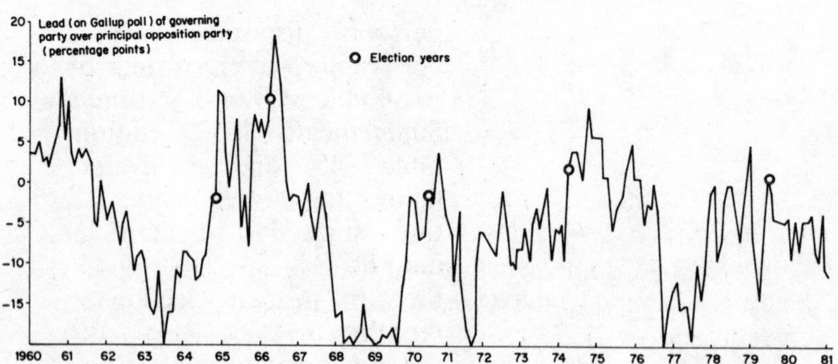

Figure 2.3 Great Britain: unemployment, inflation and government popularity, 1960–81

II 'Impulsive voters' only: $V = b_4 + b_5 U^* + b_6 P^* + b_7$ (last) $+ b_8$ (nearest) $+ u_{II}$

where U^* = deviation of unemployment (in thousands) from its trend, as measured by a seven-period moving average.[9]

P^* = deviation of rate of change of retail price index, all items, from its trend, as measured by a seven-period moving average.[9]

V, last, nearest are defined as in equation I above.

u_{II} = random error term.

b_4, b_5, b_6, b_7, b_8 = fixed parameters.

Since we are now talking about voters in the aggregate rather than individuals it may make sense to assume that some people are 'selfish' and some are 'impulsive' voters, and to represent voting behaviour in the aggregate by a composite model which combines features of models I and II above.

III Composite model:

$$V = b_9 + b_{10}\left(\frac{Y}{L}\right) + b_{11} U^* + b_{12} P^* + b_{13}(\text{last}) + b_{14}(\text{nearest}) + u_{III}$$

where V, $\frac{Y}{L}$, U^*, P^*, last, nearest are defined as in equations I and II above.

u_{III} = random error term

$b_9, b_{10}, b_{11}, b_{12}, b_{13}, b_{14}$ = fixed parameters.

In tables 2.2 and 2.3 we present the results of regression analysis designed to test these three hypotheses. The period of estimation is 1953:I to 1981:II, and there are thus 339 monthly observations.

The two tables suggest that *if the period 1953—81 is taken as a whole*, there is very little to choose between the

TABLE 2.2 Models of determination of government popularity: analysis by time period. Dependent variable: lead of governing party over principal opposition party, as measured by Gallup Poll

Time period	*Model*	*Regression coefficients on independent variables:*						r^2	*DW*
		Constant	*Real per capita disposable income (£)*	*Unemploy-ment, deviation from trend (000s)*	*Inflation, deviation from trend (%)*	*Time since last election (months)*	*Time to nearest election (months)*		
January 1953 to	I (rational	3.62	−0.21			−0.053	−0.58**	0.6656	1.1006
September 1959	self-interested)	(1.63)	(1.00)			(1.32)	(7.33)		
(Conservative)	II (impulsive)	3.19**		−0.019	0.078	−0.018	−0.46**	0.5379	0.7462
82 observations		(2.81)		(1.19)	(0.16)	(0.69)	(9.18)		
	III (composite)	3.22**	−0.27	−0.023	0.086	−0.035	−0.47**	0.5540	0.8289
		(2.86)	(1.65)	(1.47)	(0.18)	(1.24)	(9.39)		
October 1959 to	I	9.24**	0.043			−0.34**	−0.19**	0.6677	0.4952
September 1964		(3.76)	(0.15)			(8.44)	(2.63)		
(Conservative)	II	9.54**		−0.012	−0.076	−0.34**	−0.19**	0.6731	0.4885
60 observations		(5.96)		(0.96)	(0.55)	(10.20)	(2.88)		
	III	9.15**	0.058	−0.13	−0.11	−0.34**	−0.19**	0.6733	0.4919
		(3.65)	(0.20)	(0.96)	(0.079)	(8.32)	(2.55)		
October 1964 to	I	11.16**	0.68**			−0.34**	−0.97**	0.8189	1.3471
May 1970		(8.53)	(2.94)			(8.16)	(11.80)		
(Labour)	II	12.30**		−0.0049	−1.15	−0.32**	−1.01**	0.7956	1.1995
68 observations		(9.20)		(0.17)	(0.58)	(7.33)	(11.58)		
	III	11.14**	0.68**	−0.0041	0.14	−0.33**	−0.97**	0.8189	1.3461
		(8.35)	(2.82)	(−0.15)	(0.073)	(8.01)	(11.61)		

June 1970 to	I	−1.24	0.59*			−0.13*	−0.42	0.2493	2.1198
January 1974		(0.61)	(2.18)			(2.08)	(3.24)		
(Conservative)	II	−0.84		0.011	−1.81	−0.086	−0.31*	0.1744	1.9201
45 observations		(0.39)		(0.36)	(0.73)	(1.34)	(2.44)		
	III	−1.21	0.58	0.010	−0.47	0.13*	−0.42**	0.2521	2.1099
		(0.58)	(0.29)	(0.35)	(0.19)	(2.02)	(3.13)		
February 1974 to	I	3.84	−0.15			−0.064	−0.48	0.3069	0.9625
April 1979		(2.48)	(0.64)			(1.03)	(4.04)		
(Labour) *plus*	II	3.94**		0.00068	−1.24	−0.11**	−0.42**	0.3265	0.9984
May 1979 to		(2.64)		(0.95)	(1.65)	(2.55)	(4.94)		
March 1981	III	4.27**	−0.18	0.0016	−1.26*	−0.77	−0.48**	0.3310	1.0143
(Conservative)		(2.72)	(0.72)	(0.13)	(1.67)	(1.23)	(4.01)		
84 observations									
Whole period	I	4.72**	0.28**			−0.17**	−0.44**	0.3648	0.6738
339 observations		(5.07)	(2.54)			(7.35)	(8.91)		
	II	5.46**		−0.0044	−0.89*	−0.16**	−0.45**	0.3493	0.6557
		(6.60)		(0.48)	(1.67)	(7.15)	(10.22)		
	III	5.04**	0.19*	−0.0049	−0.78	−0.12**	−0.43**	0.3556	0.6582
		(5.88)	(1.79)	(0.53)	(1.47)	(7.39)	(9.54)		

Notes: Figures in brackets beneath coefficients are Student's t-statistics: **denotes significance at 1% level; *denotes significance at 5% level.

Sources: Real per capita disposable income: *Economic Trends Annual Supplement,* December 1981 issue, Table 1.4. Unemployment and inflation: *Monthly Digest of Statistics,* various issues. Unemployment is not seasonally adjusted; inflation is the year-on-year change in the index of retail prices, all items.

TABLE 2.3 Models of determination of government polularity: analysis by state of the economy. Dependent variable: lead of governing party over principal opposition party, as measured by Gallup Poll

Time period	*Model*	*Regression coefficients on independent variables:*						r^2	*DW*
		Constant	*Real per capita disposable income, 1975 prices (£)*	*Unemployment, deviation from trend (000s)*	*Inflation deviation from trend (%)*	*Time since last election (months)*	*Time to nearest election (months)*		
Whole period	I (rational	4.72**	−0.28**			−0.17**	−0.44**	0.3648	0.6738
339 observations	self-interested)	(5.07)	(2.54)			(7.35)	(8.91)		
	II (impulsive)	5.46**		−0.0044	−0.89*	−0.16**	−0.45**	0.3493	0.6557
		(6.60)		(0.48)	(1.67)	(7.15)	(10.22)		
	III (composite)	5.04**	0.19*	−0.0049	−0.78	−0.12**	−0.43**	0.3556	0.6587
		(5.88)	(1.79)	(0.53)	(1.47)	(7.39)	(9.54)		
'Unemployment	I	3.29**	−0.96			−0.069	−0.41	0.2884	0.9129
crisis years'		(2.92)	(0.54)			(1.71)	(5.64)		
(i.e. 1956–7,	II	3.27**		−0.00056	−0.90	−0.91**	−0.38**	0.2952	0.9314
1963, 1967,		(3.01)		(0.048)	(1.32)	(2.63)	(6.37)		
1971–2, 1975–81)	III	3.47**	−0.11	−0.00016	−0.92	−0.077	−0.41	0.2971	0.9432
		(3.06)	(0.63)	(0.013)	(1.36)	(1.87)	(5.61)		
'Inflation	I	4.52	−0.37			−0.091	−0.50**	0.4100	1.0839
crisis years'		(3.97)	(2.03)			(2.16)	(6.64)		
(i.e. 1955–7,	II	3.80**		0.0066	−0.62*	−0.13**	−0.41**	0.3963	1.0414
1965, 1971,		(3.52)		(0.57)	(2.10)	(3.16)	(6.38)		
1974–7, 1979–81)	III	4.71**	−0.39	0.0064	−0.73**	−0.98*	−0.50**	0.4209	1.1198
		(4.12)	(1.31)	(0.56)	(2.13)	(2.29)	(6.66)		
'Non-crisis	I	10.25**	0.49**			−0.28	−0.66	0.5149	0.5162
years' (i.e. 1953–4,		(7.05)	(3.43)			(8.93)	(9.74)		
1958–62, 1964,	II	11.07**		−0.0088	−1.21	−0.28**	−0.64**	0.4828	0.4789
1966, 1968–70,		(7.46)		(0.59)	(1.13)	(8.43)	(9.07)		
1973)	III	10.19**	0.48**	−0.01	−0.87	−0.28**	−0.66**	0.5191	0.5200
		(6.98)	(3.34)	(0.70)	(0.84)	(8.90)	(9.61)		

Notes: Figures in brackets beneath coefficients are Student's t-statistics: **denotes significance at 1% level; *denotes significance at 5% level.

different models; the 'rational self-interest', 'impulsive' and 'composite' models all explain about 35 per cent of the variance in government popularity. The 'rational self-interest' model, in which real per capita income is the only explanatory variable, is marginally the best of the three, and nothing is gained by adding in inflation and unemployment as additional explanatory variables over the entire period. But in certain sub-periods of the overall time-span the explanatory power of the 'rational self-interest' model is increased by adding in the inflation and unemployment terms.

Indeed, the 'support' function is not stable over time. In Table 2.2 the period under investigation is sliced up into successive periods of Conservative and Labour administration, and a casual look at the data will show that the shape of the relationship shifted around a great deal. A 1 per cent rise in unemployment is associated with an 0.023 per cent decrease in popularity in the composite model in 1953–59, but with a (statistically very insignificant) 0.0016 per cent *increase* in 1974–9. A 1 per cent increase in inflation is associated with an 0.086 per cent *increase* in popularity in 1953–9 but with an 0.47 per cent decrease in popularity in 1970–4 and a 1.26 per cent decrease in 1974–81. Indeed, one of the features of the period is that inflation, which had no significant or perceptible effect on popularity in the fifties and sixties, becomes more and more of an electoral liability as time goes by.

In addition to this trend, there is a cyclical oscillation to be observed. In Table 2.2 we divide the period under examination into three sub-periods, 'unemployment crisis periods', which we define as those periods when unemployment was above its trend for the period 1953–81, 'inflation crisis periods', that is, those periods when inflation was above its trend for the period, and 'non-crisis periods', which are years of neither unemployment nor inflation crisis.[10] If the 'impulsive' model is used, unemployment is *only* significant during periods of unemployment crisis early on in the period under examination, and inflation is *only* significant during periods of inflation crisis. In other words, it looks as if changes in popularity are by no means stably related to economic conditions, but have to be triggered off by abnormal movements in the economy. As Alt and Chrystal, examining these same data, conclude, 'the only incontrovertible result... is that in the popularity function the economic coefficients increase in magnitude and significance during periods of accelerating deterioration of these conditions'.[11] But, we might add, the extent to which they increase is highly unpredictable, and the support functions displayed here could not be adopted as a guide by a governing party wishing to manipulate the economy so as to maximise the level of its support. We return to this point later.

We can begin to make some sense of these results by considering the way in which the electorate receives information about economic affairs. On the one hand, they get information about their *own* economic welfare from their wage packets and weekly shopping bills; that is the channel of influence which is captured by the 'rational self-interested' model. But beyond this, they get information about the *overall state of the economy* from the media – radio, TV, newspapers – and this does not arrive on a regular once-a-week basis. It arrives in scattered doses which are usually correlated with sudden worsenings in the state of the economy: foreign exchange crises, peak levels of inflation, record levels of unemployment, indeed records of any sort. Since the targets of macro-economic policy are in general defined as things to be got away from rather than things to aim at, it follows that there is 'news value' in stories about the economy when and only when we are sailing towards the rocks. There is no news value associated with being in clear water, in part because nobody knows exactly what 'clear water' is. A slight improvement in industrial production or unemployment may be nice but it is not worth giving publicity to it because experts nearly always represent it as simply a small and delusory mitigation of the latest crisis, rather than an achievement in itself. From the point of view of the mass media, good news is (almost) no news.

These observations apply to all of the media but they can be vividly illustrated in relation to the popular press. As Figure 2.3 illustrates, the *Sun* and the *Daily Mirror* make information on unemployment available in an asymmetric manner: a good deal of information is offered when unemployment is getting worse, the subject occasionally gets on to the front pages when it hits a peak level, but very little information is forthcoming when unemployment is falling. In the case of inflation, almost *no* information is transmitted by the *Daily Mirror, Daily Express* or *Sun* throughout the 1960s, a decade in which inflation did not exceed 6 per cent, nor did radio or TV mention it at all frequently.[12] In 1971, when inflation rose into double figures for the first time since the war, a trigger was suddenly released. Mention of the monthly change in the retail price index began to creep on to the inside pages of the popular newspapers, dramatic headlines (see Figure 2.4) suddenly appeared, representing inflation as a threat to the stability of every family's daily life, and the *Daily Mirror* devised their own index of retail prices, the 'Shopping Clock', which was publicised on page 3 of every Saturday's issue from 1971 until 1978, when the rate of inflation fell into single figures again. At this point the index was withdrawn.[13] Only at times of economic crisis, it is clear, do the popular media pull back the curtains from the windows through which the mass electorate perceives trends in the economy. The state of affairs in the United States, with regard to inflation at any rate, appears to be broadly similar.[14]

The implications of all this for our analysis become clear if we make use of an ancient analogy. In this simple view of the world, firms sell their products for money in the economic market-place, and governments sell their policies for votes in the political market-place. The relationship reflecting the response of consumers of goods is known as a demand function, and the relationship reflecting the response of voters is known as a support function. The support functions we have examined can only 'work' in the economic sphere, however, to the extent that voters are given information about the economy. We have hypothesised that they will be motivated partly by changes in their own economic welfare (the 'rational self-interest' model) and partly by 'panics' arising from changes in the overall economy. Voters will have quite good and regular information concerning their

Daily Mirror

3d. Friday, January 25, 1963 No. 18,382

814,632

JOBLESS TOTAL SOARS

Glimmer of hope in the big freeze

A WARM ray of hope came to shivering Britain from the Meteorological Office last night.

Spokesmen there predicted a slight thaw "within the next few days."

A belt of warmer air was expected to reach the North during the night, the Midlands today and the South by the week-end.

The Freeze—Back Page.

Dartmoor runaway in ice peril

TWO Dartmoor prisoners escaped from a working party clearing a road blocked by snowdrifts yesterday—and fled into the white wilderness of the icy moor.

One of the men was later recaptured after warders had followed his footprints in the snow.

Last night prison officials described the escape plan as "crazy"—because there are still 15ft. snowdrifts on Dartmoor, and the two stood little chance of survival in the Arctic conditions unless they got shelter.

Helicopters

The men—William Crook and Roy Fox, both 34—were serving five-year sentences for housebreaking.

By BRIAN MORTON-SMITH

BRITAIN'S jobless men and women now total a staggering 814,632—a leap of nearly a quarter of a million since mid-December.

The Big Freeze is partly to blame. It has silenced the busy building sites, hit industries, kept the fishing fleets in harbour and turned farmlands into iron-hard wastes.

The total is the worst since the Arctic February of 1947, when 1,874,061 Britons were queuing for the dole.

'Worst since 1947' shock for MPs

Failure

Queues

Callaghan may stand as Leader

By WILLIAM CREIG

Pressure

INJURED—BUT SHE WINS

From PAT MENNEM, Monte Carlo, Thursday

Refused

Daily Mirror

BRITAIN'S BIGGEST DAILY SALE

3p Thursday, June 15, 1972 No. 21,283

SHOCK ISSUE

WHO WANTS THIS FOR A FAIR DAY'S PAY?

A dustbin full of money—but will it be worth more than wastepaper?

Please turn to Page 2

Figure 2.4 The first front-page appearance in the *Daily Mirror* since World War 2 of (a) unemployment, 25 January 1963; (b) inflation, 15 June 1972

own well-being, but as we have seen they are given proper information about the general economy only at times of crisis. The implication is that *'the impulsive model' which reflects the concern voters feel about the state of the general economy will only be operational when the economy is 'in crisis'*. This implication, as we have seen, broadly squares with our empirical findings: unemployment was only significant when it was above trend, and inflation has only been significant since it was proclaimed by the media as a cause for crisis in the early 1970s. What at first sight looks like an instability in the popularity function prompted by nothing except the capriciousness of voters turns out, on second sight, to be caused by variations in the intensity with which voters are exposed to information about developments in the economy. Indeed, if we take the composite Model III and replace *actual* levels by *perceived* levels, where the *perceived* level is interpreted either as the value currently published in the popular press or, if no value is published that month, the last value to have been put before the public, then the explanatory power of the model is greatly increased.[15] It is apparent that whereas the public's *self-interested and rational* response to changes in per capita disposable income operates in a fairly continuous and regular manner, its *impulsive* (and partly irrational?) response to unemployment and inflation 'crises' operates in a highly discontinuous manner, that is, only when these 'crises' are presented as such in the popular media. We develop the implications of this statement in our last section.

2.4 Conclusions

Two main conclusions emerge from the analysis so far. The first is that although voters in both the US and the UK may think the economy is 'the most important issue facing the government', the response of government popularity to the state of the economy is, in Britain at any rate, anything but steady and reliable. Over the entire period 1953–81 the level of real personal per capita disposable income is, as a rationalistic self-interested voting model might predict, the economic variable most closely associated with government popularity, but 'most closely associated' is not saying much. In certain periods, for example 1959–64 and 1974–9, the relationship between popularity and per capita disposable income is simply not significant once electoral cycle variations are taken into account, that is, a government could not have expected to reap any kind of electoral dividend from the kind of increase in disposable income that is under its control, such as a tax cut or an increase in transfer payments. When the model is elaborated to allow for 'impulse responses' of voters to unemployment and inflation, the popularity function becomes even less stable. Inflation and unemployment are only significant influences on popularity if they are above their 'crisis levels' (that is, significantly above their trend) and even this is only a necessary, not a sufficient, condition in the case of unemployment. Hence, even if we simplify for the moment and ignore the motives of bureaucrats in the Treasury and elsewhere, the governing party simply could not pick a politically optimal policy package which would maximise its popularity lead on the opinion polls, that is, chance of getting re-elected. A 5 per cent reduction in inflation would, if we use the data for the entire period 1953–81, lead *ceteris paribus* to a 3.9 per cent increase in government popularity; but if we use the figures for the most recent period 1974–81 it would lead to a 6.3 per cent increase, and if we use data for 1964–70 it would lead to a 0.7 per cent *cut*. A reduction in unemployment of half a million would lead to an increase in popularity of 2.5 per cent, an 0.8 per cent *cut* or a 2 per cent increase depending on which of these three periods is taken. The 'vote function' relating popularity, inflation and unemployment[16] is just too unstable to act as a menu for policy choice, even if a government's popularity level were important at times other than election time. Given the impossibility of controlling popularity even if that were desirable, governments may well decide to fall back on some much more simple rule of thumb such as 'give the economy some sort of boost just before election time so as to raise personal disposable income, but not so obvious a boost as to make the electioneering element obvious'. It can't do any harm, electorally speaking, and it *may* do the governing party some good.

A second conclusion is that since voters can only respond to what they know about, the manner in which economic information is presented to the public has an influence on the government's popularity as well as the state of the economy itself. It is therefore an additional tool of economic policy, to the extent that the government can control the press. In countries with a free press there are limits to this control, but through the glosses on the economic situation which their press releases convey (for example, 'this inflation is caused by outside forces', 'this unemployment is strictly temporary') and their friendships with Fleet Street editors, members of the government can influence the way that news about the economy is presented by the media and interpreted by the public. This procedure has analogies with that by which, according to Galbraith (1968), businessmen, instead of taking the wishes of consumers as sovereign, educate them to like – and buy – the products which they have already decided to make. An example of the process in action in Great Britain is provided by the *Sun* newspaper. Created in 1964 as the successor to the old, Labour-Party-supporting *Daily Herald*, it remained loyal to the Labour Party for approximately the next ten years, with a circulation of just over a million. In the early 1970s it mounted a determined, and successful, drive to increase its circulation and, as it did so, it moved to the right. It blamed the Labour Party for much of the inflation of 1975 and for the sterling crises of 1976; it attacked the high level of public expenditure and taxation of the time;[17] it urged its mainly working-class readership to vote Tory at the 1979 general election[18] and by doing so did a great deal to win it for the Conservative Party; having done so, it then *exculpated* them for much of the blame for the inflation which followed.[19] It is pointless now to trace just who took what initiatives in the development of the relationship between the *Sun* and the governing Conservative Party. The point is that now the relationship exists, the government possesses a means of influencing public opinion[20] on the economy which is perhaps as effective a way of influencing popularity as acting on the economy itself. Given that acting on the economy itself is a chancy business whose electoral rewards, as we have seen, are likely to be highly uncertain, the temptation for the governing party must be to let the Treasury (or equivalent agencies) run the economy except during the year or so before an election and to try and get the media to present as favourable an image as possible of the way this is being done during the interim. Just how the Treasury does run the economy 'in the interim' will be a major concern of our next three chapters.

Notes

1 Excerpt from speech to Parliamentary Labour Party, reported *Financial Times,* 8 March 1968. Hibbs and Vassilatos, in Hibbs and Fassbender (eds) (1981) p. 32, report that, from 1970 on, more than 70 per cent of the American voting public identified an economic issue as 'the most important problem' facing the country in every year.

2 We assume that the behaviour of all voters whose vote is *not* sensitive to the state of the economy will have a random 'white noise' effect on the response of popularity to the state of the economy.

3 There are, of course, possible problems of aggregation: that is, if a majority of people have experienced a fall in their standard of living but per capita GDP has risen (as may occur if income is very unequally distributed) then the sign of coefficient b_1 may be negative, that is, a fall in popularity may be associated with an increase in GDP even if Hypothesis I is true.

4 Butler and Stokes (1971), Table 10.6; Alt (1979).

5 This on its own is not a sufficient explanation: the observed correlation between unemployment and changes in per capita disposable income over the years 1953–81 was 0.0007. (Source: as for Tables 2.2 and 2.3.)

6 People who actually *become* (or cease to become) unemployed could not affect popularity much: even at present (1982) the unemployed are only one in ten of the adult working population and in most years since the war the proportion has been much less.

7 Collard (1978) pp. 4–5, discusses the motives people may have for behaviour instigated by considerations other than their own economic welfare.

8 Alt (1979), p. 95, emphasises that 'people do not perceive small changes in economic well-being, even when these do occur'.

9 Not the absolute value of unemployment or inflation, since we

believe that the voter evaluates these variables in relation to 'acceptable levels' which move up or down as performance exceeds or falls short of previous aspiration and are not absolute. In previous work (Mosley 1978) we modelled the 'acceptable level' by a least-square trend drawn over the entire period under analysis. But this was silly: a least-square line drawn in 1978 takes account of experience from 1955 through to 1979, whereas individuals judging economic performance in 1960 (say) only have experience from 1955 to 1960 to assess when judging the 'acceptable' level. See the criticism of my 1978 paper by Alt and Chrystal (1981, pp. 188–9). We therefore, for the purposes of this exercise, define the 'acceptable' level as the current value of a seven-period moving average.

10 1971, 1975–7 and 1979–81 are years of *both* 'unemployment crisis' and 'inflation crisis'.

11 Alt and Chrystal (1981), p. 191.

12 Behrend (1981) reports that her enquiries in the 1960s revealed widespread ignorance concerning the level and even the existence of inflation, but this ignorance was no longer apparent when the enquiries were repeated in the 1970s.

13 For detail on these matters, see my attempt to explain the presentation of the economy by the popular media in Mosley (1984).

14 Hibbs (1979) shows that in the United States in the early 1970s, particularly 1972–5, the proportion of people stating that they thought inflation a more serious problem than unemployment suddenly rose sharply. This almost certainly had a lot to do with President Ford's widely publicised campaign to 'WHIP INFLATION NOW' (Blinder, 1979) which also whipped up a number of irrational fears about inflation in the American public in the hope of moderating wage deals and price increases. Hibbs comments (p. 712) 'neither the income, wealth or tax effects of inflation appear large enough to explain widespread aversion to rising prices; less tangible subjective and psychological factors are probably more important than objective costs'.

15 Model III as tested against data for the entire period 1/1953–3/1981 reads, by transcription from Table 2.2,

$$\begin{array}{l}\text{Government}\\ \text{popularity}\\ \text{lead}\end{array} = \underset{(5.88)}{5.04^{**}} + \underset{(1.79)}{0.19^{*}}\begin{bmatrix}\text{real per}\\ \text{capita}\\ \text{disposable}\\ \text{income}\end{bmatrix} - \underset{(0.53)}{0.0049}\begin{bmatrix}\text{unemployment,}\\ \text{deviation}\\ \text{from trend}\end{bmatrix}$$

$$- \underset{(1.47)}{0.78^{*}}\begin{bmatrix}\text{inflation,}\\ \text{deviation}\\ \text{from trend}\end{bmatrix} - \underset{(7.39)}{0.17^{*}}\begin{bmatrix}\text{time since}\\ \text{last}\\ \text{election}\end{bmatrix} - \underset{(9.54)}{0.43^{**}}\begin{bmatrix}\text{time to}\\ \text{nearest}\\ \text{election}\end{bmatrix};$$

$$r^2 = 0.3556$$

If the unemployment figure from the Central Statistical office used in this regression is replaced by the most recent unemployment figure published by the *Daily Mirror*, and if the inflation figure from the Central Statistical Office used there is replaced by the most recent inflation figure published by the *Daily Mirror,* then the estimated equation over the same period becomes:

$$\begin{array}{l}\text{Government popularity lead} = \underset{(5.30)}{5.11^{**}} + \underset{(1.83)}{0.12^{*}}\begin{bmatrix}\text{real per}\\ \text{capita}\\ \text{disposable}\\ \text{income}\end{bmatrix} - \underset{(1.85)}{0.007^{*}}\begin{bmatrix}\text{unemployment,}\\ \text{deviation}\\ \text{from trend}\end{bmatrix}\\ \qquad - \underset{(3.99)}{0.89^{**}}\begin{bmatrix}\text{inflation,}\\ \text{deviation}\\ \text{from trend}\end{bmatrix} - \underset{(7.11)}{0.18^{**}}\begin{bmatrix}\text{time since}\\ \text{last}\\ \text{election}\end{bmatrix} - \underset{(9.53)}{0.53^{**}}\begin{bmatrix}\text{time to}\\ \text{nearest}\\ \text{election}\end{bmatrix};\\ r^2 = 0.4757\end{array}$$

The proportion of the variance in the government popularity lead that can be ascribed to economic and cycle variables increases, in other words, from about 36 per cent to about 47 per cent if 'perceived' rather than actual values of the economic variables are used.

16 Goodhart and Bhansali (1970) estimate what we have described above as the 'impulsive model':

$$\text{popularity} = b_0 + b_1\ [\text{unemployment}] + b_2\ [\text{inflation}] + \text{election-cycle terms}$$

They then represent the estimated model, which for 1968 is:

$$\text{popularity} = 12.73 - 0.026\ [\text{unemployment lagged 6 months}] - 1.21\ [\text{inflation}] + \text{election-cycle terms}$$

as a 'vote function', that is, the relationship which states what the value of the Gallup popularity index will be for each given state of the economy. Graphically, the vote function looks like this:

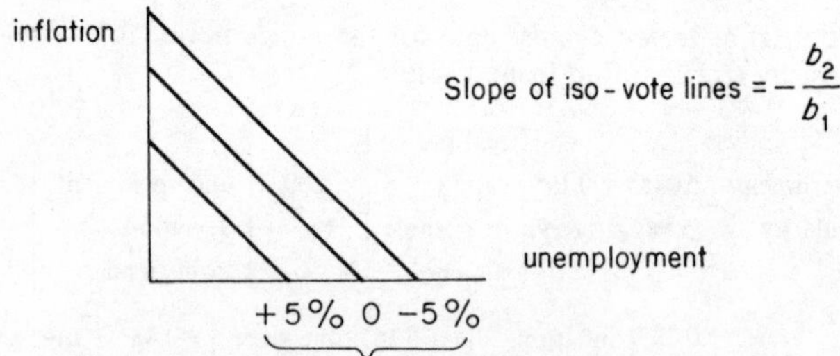

Value of Gallup popularity index corresponding to all states of the economy on the line indicated

If a short-term Phillips curve is added the vote function can be interpreted as a governing party's objective function which must be maximised subject to this constraint:

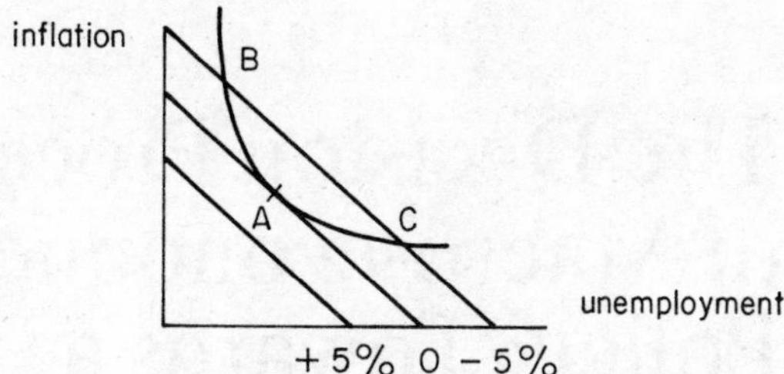

Point A is an optimum point, in terms of popularity, for the governing party; if one takes a satisficing approach, then points B and C could be interpreted as 'minimum tolerance levels' which trigger off economic policy action of some sort from the government.

17 *Sun,* 28 October 1976, front page.

18 *Sun,* 3 May 1979, front page.

19 For example, *Sun,* 2 April 1981, p. 2.

20 British opinion can be influenced both directly – for example, by representing current levels of unemployment as being the best that the government can do – and indirectly – for example, in the early summer of 1982, by drawing exclusive attention on the front page to the war in the Falkland Islands and giving no publicity at all to the bad economic news of the time.

3 The Decision Processes of Macro-economic Policy: Towards a Theoretical Approach

On the whole, running the economy is more like gardening than operating a computer. DENIS HEALEY, *UK Chancellor of the Exchequer 1974–9, quoted in Hennessy (1977)*

'Callaghan and Healey are skilfully and unscrupulously preparing the ground' Tony said, when finally we had some gossip of our own. 'By leaking the desire and intention, they're going to bounce Cabinet. If the Treasury is defeated (in its plan to impose large public expenditure cuts), there now really will be a frightful run on the pound because of the public mood and expectation that is being created in advance. And no alternative strategy has been carefully worked out.'

'I though the Cambridge School had one.'

'It requires even bigger cuts in public expenditure. There is very little informed public opinion. And for months I've not had time to think properly about economics and consult. God, I wish I didn't have to be away so much.' ANTHONY CROSLAND, *member of UK Cabinet, 1974–7, quoted in Crosland (1982), p. 342.*

1. United Kingdom: the structure

In Great Britain the legislature, in the shape of Parliament, has very limited power to initiate tax, public spending, money supply or interest rate changes.[1] Hence, political influences on macro-economic policy are confined to those which result from the governing party's pressures on members of Cabinet. The governing party will have a hard job decoding the wishes of the people regarding macro-economic policy: the opinion polls, as we have seen in the last chapter, send out signals which are delphic and also unstable from period to period. And in any case, there is no compelling reason for a governing party with a secure majority to pay any attention to them. We conclude that, except during the immediate run-up to an election, the executive machinery of government has considerable freedom of action in determining what macro-economic policy should be.

By 'the executive machinery of government' we mean, in Great Britain, agencies operating on two separate levels. On the upper level there is the Cabinet of selected government ministers, and the Treasury,[2] who between them determine what the broad thrust of macro-economic policy will be in any given time period. On the lower level are those agencies which manipulate the levers of economic policy with which we are here concerned. The Inland Revenue obtains money from the public through taxes, the Bank of England borrows and prints money on behalf of the government and the spending ministries – education, health, transport, overseas aid and so on – spend it.

It is, however, too simple to see these three 'second-level' agencies simply as bodies which carry out the Treasury's instructions. Each of them, in fact, has a different sort of bargaining relationship with the Treasury.

The *Bank of England* (founded in 1694 but only brought under state ownership in 1946) is, among other functions,[3] the government's banker; when the government runs a deficit, the Bank borrows on its behalf. The size of this deficit, or public sector borrowing requirement (PSBR) is generally an important element in the growth of the money supply, since not all of it can be borrowed from non-bank sources.[4] The key decision which the Bank has to take within the constraint already imposed by the size of the PSBR is what level of interest rates to aim at (which means abandoning control over the money supply) or alternatively what level of monetary growth to aim at (which means abandoning control over interest rates). In the 1950s and 1960s, broadly, the Bank followed the first strategy, and since the early 1970s it has followed the second. But it has recently done so within the limits of a medium-term financial strategy, laid down against its wishes by the Treasury, which still further circumscribes its freedom of action.[5] In principle the Bank, in the words of one of its most independently-minded governors, has accepted the role of 'a good wife: to nag, but in the last analysis to obey';[6] however this has not prevented bruising clashes between the Bank and Treasury ministers, either because the Bank was suspected of not allowing the money supply to rise enough to accommodate the needs of businessmen (as in March 1966)[7] or because it went to the opposite extreme, as in the summer of 1980, and allowed money supply to grow between June and August by more than twice the maximum permissible under the medium-term financial strategy.[8] The Bank has a tendency to regard as targets of monetary policy variables such as the exchange rate and the stability of interest rates, which Treasury ministers would think of either as instruments or as variables which should be left to the free play of the market, and this difference of approach can lead to clashes too. In principle, it may be 'the Bank who advises, but the Government who decides';[9] but an adviser's power can become considerable at times of financial crisis, such as the autumn of 1976, when the adviser is the only reliable interpreter of what measures of domestic economic policy Britain's overseas creditors are insisting on in return for short-term credit. The fact that Bank of England staff have a completely independent career structure from civil servants increases their independence of posture.

The *spending ministries* (Defence, Education, Health, Social Security, Transport, Environment and so on) indicate to the Treasury every summer how much money they would like to spend in the following financial year. They ask for as much as they think they can get away with,[10] but what they think they can get away with is limited by both visible and invisible constraints. In full public view are the figures in the Public Expenditure White Paper, which lays down each March targets for each major branch of public spending five years in advance;[11] less blatant is the constraint imposed on civil servants in the spending ministry by their desire to stay on good terms with the Treasury.[12] Unlike Bank of England employees, civil servants in spending ministries have a common career structure with those in the Treasury and the headship of both the Home Civil Service and the Government Economic Service is located within the Treasury. The implication of this is that they will think twice before doing something of which the Treasury might disapprove, such as put in a spending bid which can be exposed as irresponsible or extravagant. Ministers in spending ministries may try to exert an upward pressure on what their civil servants ask for, but they can seldom make much headway except during the later years of an election cycle.[13] For these reasons, spending ministries do not by any means have a free hand when they bargain with the Treasury every autumn – not even as free a hand as the Bank of England, which at least has one policy instrument under its control. At the macro-economic level the Treasury has, in particular, the advantage of being able to 'divide and rule': it negotiates piece-wise with each ministry concerning that ministry's spending, and keeps within its own walls the central 'Budget judgement' concerning what *overall* levels of expenditure should be for the coming year.[14]

The *Inland Revenue*, finally, in conjunction with the Department of Customs and Excise, collects the taxes which the Treasury tells it to collect. Unlike the spending ministries it does not in any meaningful sense 'bargain' with the Treasury, but simply advises on the administrative feasibility and likely yield of prospective tax measures.[15] Like the spending ministries it is excluded from the 'Budget judgement'.

Macro-economic policy in Great Britain, we have argued, is made by a decision-making inner circle and an executive outer circle whose three members possess different degrees of bargaining power vis-à-vis the inner circle. In the next three sections we examine the formal processes of policy-making within the inner circle.

3.2 Macro-policy making in normal times: the Treasury 'policy cycle'

Figure 3.1 shows how functions have been divided within the Treasury before and after the reorganisation of 1975.

For our present purpose, which is to discuss how

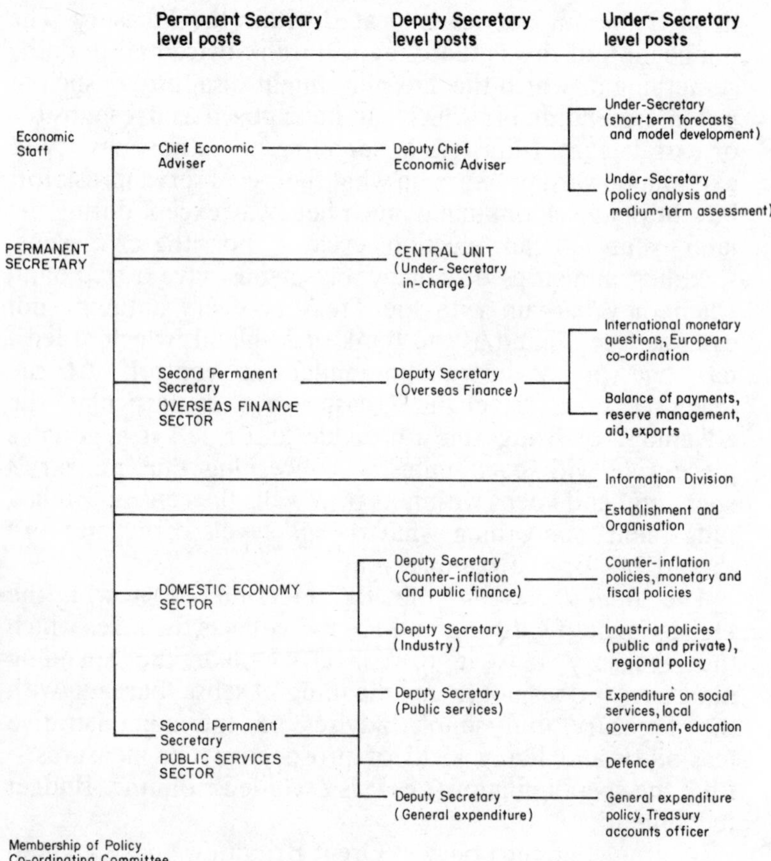

Figure 3.1 United Kingdom: organisation of HM Treasury (since 1975 management review)

instrument variables such as public expenditure totals, tax rates and interest rates are determined, certain parts of the Treasury which deal with establishments, information and certain sub-divisions of public expenditure are not relevant. The permutation of these instrument variables which Treasury officials offer to the Chancellor as policy options emerges from an interaction between the groups marked off in separate blocks in Figure 3.2: the economics staff, the Central Unit and the Policy Co-ordinating Committee. The

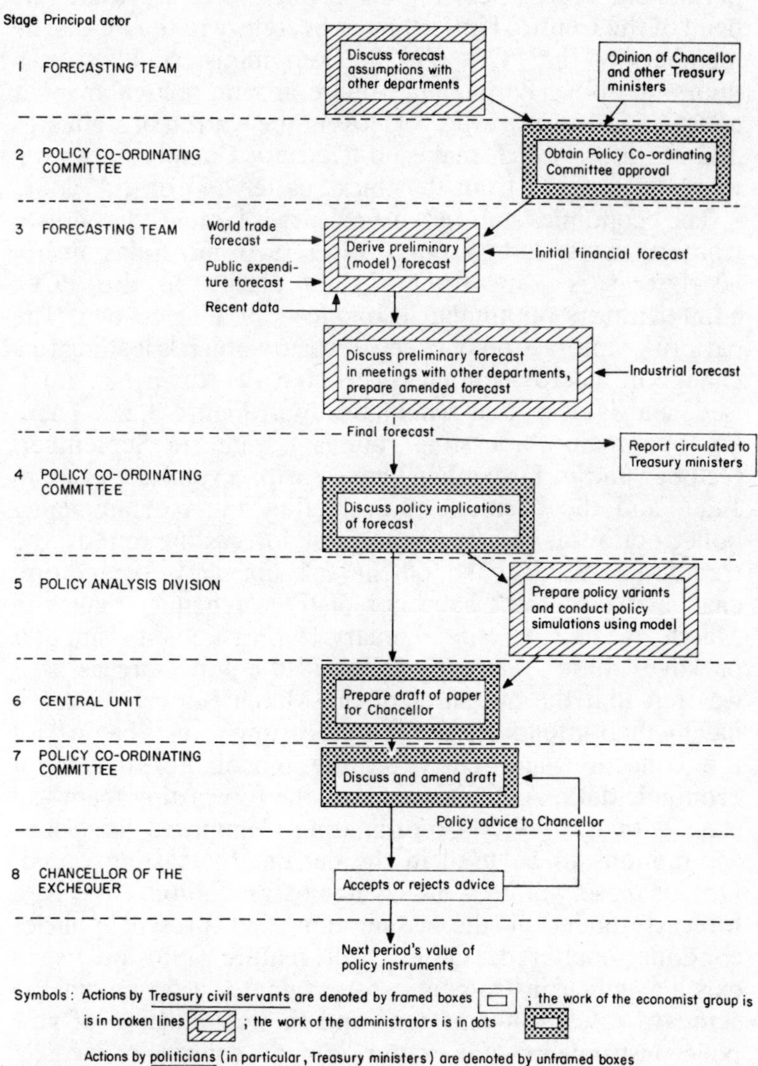
Stage Principal actor
1 FORECASTING TEAM
Discuss forecast assumptions with other departments
Opinion of Chancellor and other Treasury ministers
2 POLICY CO-ORDINATING COMMITTEE
Obtain Policy Co-ordinating Committee approval
3 FORECASTING TEAM
World trade forecast
Public expenditure forecast
Recent data
Derive preliminary (model) forecast
Initial financial forecast
Discuss preliminary forecast in meetings with other departments, prepare amended forecast
Industrial forecast
Final forecast
Report circulated to Treasury ministers
4 POLICY CO-ORDINATING COMMITTEE
Discuss policy implications of forecast
5 POLICY ANALYSIS DIVISION
Prepare policy variants and conduct policy simulations using model
6 CENTRAL UNIT
Prepare draft of paper for Chancellor
7 POLICY CO-ORDINATING COMMITTEE
Discuss and amend draft
Policy advice to Chancellor
8 CHANCELLOR OF THE EXCHEQUER
Accepts or rejects advice
Next period's value of policy instruments
Symbols : Actions by Treasury civil servants are denoted by framed boxes ; the work of the economist group is is in broken lines ; the work of the administrators is in dots
Actions by politicians (in particular, Treasury ministers) are denoted by unframed boxes

Figure 3.2 United Kingdom Treasury: simplified diagram of main activities in preparation of forecasts and policy advice

Policy Co-ordinating Committe (PCC) consists of the four permanent secretaries, the six deputy secretaries and the head of the Central Unit acting as Secretary to the PCC. The members of the PCC, plus the four ministers, all sit two floors up above Parliament Square around a circular inner courtyard. A visitor who gets lost in the warren of staircases and corridors which make up Treasury Chambers can tell when he is there from the thick scarlet lino on the floor.

The economics staff in the Treasury is large – it has grown from 10 in 1960, to around 50 in 1970 and today nearly 80 – but it is kept firmly in its place: on the PCC, administrators outnumber economists by nine to two. The pattern of interaction between Treasury officials leading to a change in macro-economic instruments is somewhat ritualised, and is described schematically in Figure 3.2.[16] There are two main forecasting rounds a year, in September/October and in December/January with a subsidiary one in June, and the business of evaluating and recommending policy options is closely tied to these forecasting rounds: the traditional 'Budget statement' of tax and expenditure changes which the Chancellor of the Exchequer makes in March is tied to the January forecast, and 'summer packages' have frequently followed the June forecast if it was felt that the measures of the March Budget were not having their intended effect.[17] Forecasting rounds begin with the collection and entry on the model[18] of the latest economic data. At the same time, the forecasting team will clear with the Policy Co-ordinating Committee the policy assumptions to be used in the current forecasting round. One of these will be a 'no-change extrapolation', that is, a forecast made on the assumption that present policies continue unaltered. Others will feature adjustments to existing policy instruments – for example, a 5p cut in the standard rate of income tax – and the introduction of new policy instruments – for example, import controls or incomes policies. The Chancellor can, at this stage, communicate to the Policy Co-ordinating Committee any policy changes whose implications he would like to see explored. Thereafter the forecasting round follows the sequence depicted in Figure 3.2. The forecasting team present their forecast of what will happen over the next year in the event of no change in policy (the 'central case'), which is made in conjunction with experts in other departments, in particular the Inland Revenue, the spending ministries and the Bank of England, who will sometimes tell the Treasury team to over-ride some of the relationships in the model in the light of up-to-date information.[19] The Policy Analysis Division of the economics staff, after receiving a preliminary draft of the forecast, then makes a projection of what would happen to the economy if policy were altered in specific ways. This is presented in the form of a set of 'ready reckoners', that is, forecasts of what would happen if *one policy instrument only* were changed by some handy conventional amount such as 1 per cent.[20] Three such 'ready reckoners', as published by the UK Treasury, are set out in Table 3.1.

These 'ready reckoners' can then be combined by the Policy Analysis Division into hypothetical policy packages which the Chancellor might wish to consider for use in his Budget, for example, '£1 per week on child benefit plus £2 billion increase in public investment'. Five such hypothetical policy packages are presented in Table 3.2; each of them was recommended to the Chancellor in advance of his 1982 Budget by a different British interest group. Their consequences are derived from the ready reckoners set out in Table 3.1. These consequences are the constraint on policy choice; they are spelled out in Table 3.2 and Figure 3.3. In practice, the Policy Analysis Division examine a good many more. The limits to the search process are set on the one hand by the capacity of the Treasury computer, and more importantly by the 'house view' of Treasury civil servants concerning the limits of what is politically feasible.[21] The set of policy options on whose consequences there exists an up-to-date forecast is the portion of the universe which is visible to the Chancellor at that time. He now has to choose, in conjunction with senior Treasury staff (stages 6–8 of the policy cycle in Figure 3.2) where he wants to be within it.

This is now done in January of every year at a country house in Kent, at a weekend house-party attended by all members of the Policy Co-ordinating Committee and all Treasury ministers. We shall be considering the decision

TABLE 3.1. Some Treasury 'ready reckoners': estimated policy effects in 1982.

Simulations	*Hypothetical policy change*	*Effect on target variables:*	*Inflation %*	*Unemployment '000s*	*Real personal disposable income % growth*	*PSBR (£ million) (% of nominal GDP in brackets)*
1	Increase in central government expenditure on goods and services of 0.5 per cent of GDP	after 1 year after 4 years	0.2 0.6	−75 −15	0.4 0.4	900 (0.3) 1400 (0.4)
2	Increase in income tax of 0.5 per cent of GDP	after 1 year after 4 years	zero −0.4	10 30	−0.7 −1.0	−1050 (−0.4) −1200 (−0.4)
3	1 per cent increase in rate of VAT	after 1 year after 4 years	1.0 1.1	−48 −101	−1.0 −1.4	1000 (0.4) 1250 (0.4)

Note: The table shows the effect, on the assumptions stated, of the change in policy given in the left-hand column on the target variables listed in the top row. Effects are measured in terms of deviations from the 'base run', that is, the value of the target variable which would materialise if policy were left unchanged.

Sources Rows 1 and 2: United Kingdom (1982) Tables 1 and 2, p. 150; Row 3: Mowl (1980), p. 51.

TABLE 3.2. United Kingdom: consequences of certain hypothetical policy actions proposed for 1982 budget.

Package recommended by:	*Proposal in respect of:*		*Calculated effect after one year (four years) on:*			*Derivation*
	Government revenue	*Government spending*	*Inflation (%)*	*Unemployment ('000s)*	*PSBR (£ million)*	
1. Chambers of Commerce		5% reduction	−0.8 (−2.4)	300 (60)	−3600 (−6400)	Table 3.1 simulation 1
2. Confederation of British Industry	2% off employers' National Insurance contributions	£250 m increase	0.1 (0.7)	−5 (−40)	1750 (2500)	Table 3.1 simulations 1 and 2, assuming effect of change in N.I. contributions same as change in income tax
3. Conservative Party 'left'	2% off employers' National Insurance contributions	2% increase in unemployment pay	0.2 (1.0)	−7 (−60)	2500 (2900)	Table 3.1 simulations 1 and 2
4. Trades Union Congress	2½% off rate of VAT	£2.1 billion increase in public investment; £1.7 billion increase in expenditure on training	3.0 (4.4)	−320 (−290)	4900 (7300)	Table 3.1 simulations 1 and 3
5. Labour Party	2½% off rate of VAT	£4.5 billion increase evenly divided between: capital projects, training, industrial subsidies, social benefits	3.1 (4.7)	−360 (−300)	5300 (8000)	Table 3.1 simulations 1 and 3

Source For contents of policy packages, *Sunday Times*, 14 February 1982; for their effects, see final column of this table.

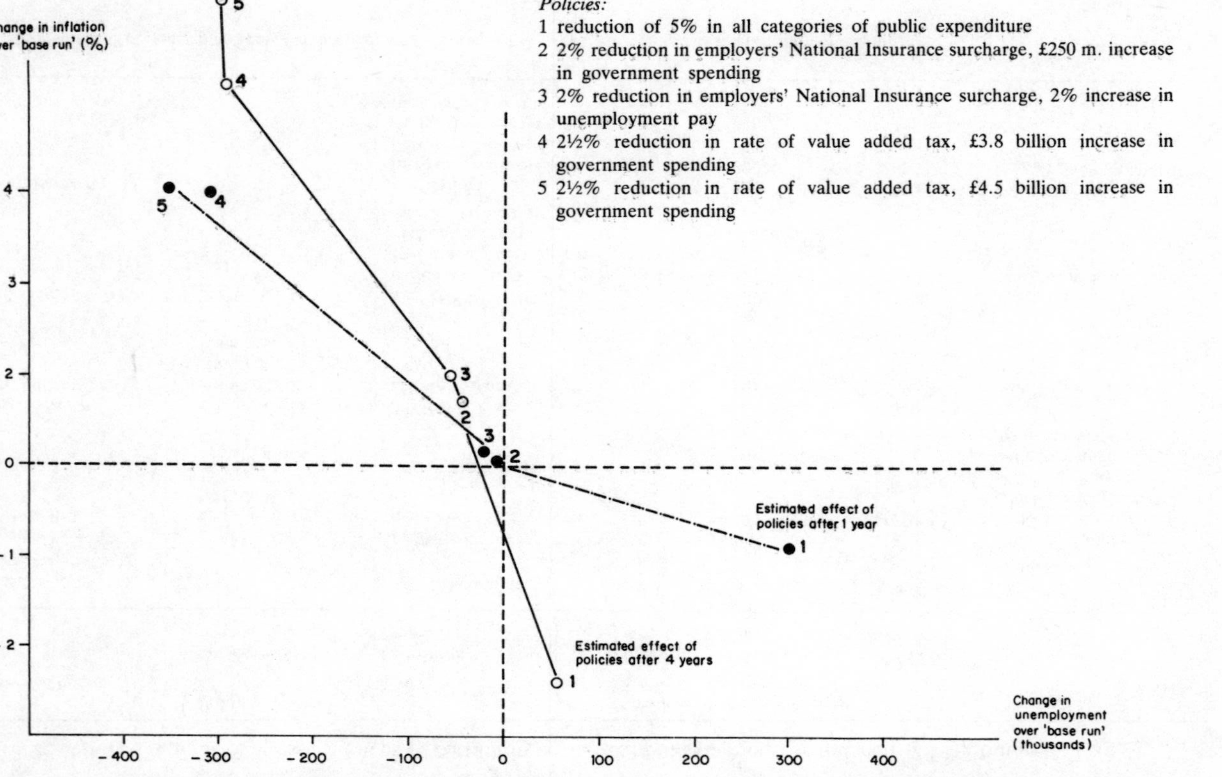

Figure 3.3 United Kingdom, Spring 1982: estimated consequences for unemployment and inflation of certain hypothetical policy options

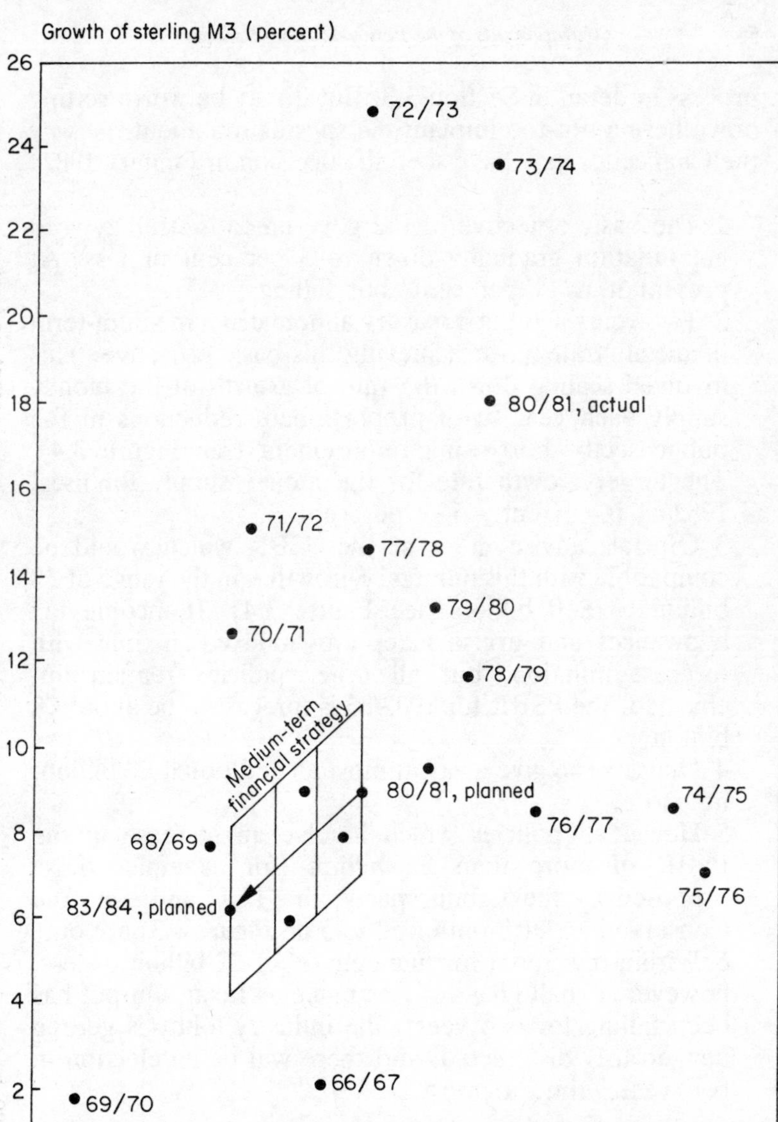

Figure 3.4 Monetary growth and the ratio of the public sector borrowing requirement to gross domestic product, financial years 1963–4 through 1983–4

Sources (a) United Kingdom 1981, Vol. II, p. 129; (b) *Economic Trends*, various issues.

process in detail in Section 3.3. But it may be worth setting down here a not-too-implausible speculation about the way the Chancellor may have seen the decision in January 1982.

1 The basic objective of the government's strategy is to get inflation gradually down to 5 per cent or less. At present it is 11 per cent, but falling.
2 Two years ago the Treasury announced a medium-term financial strategy for achieving this basic objective. This involved scaling down the rate of growth of the money supply each year, with proportionate reductions in the public sector borrowing requirement (see Figure 3.4). The target growth rate for the money supply for fiscal 1982/83 is currently 5–9 per cent.
3 Officials advise me that the PSBR which would be compatible with this monetary growth is in the range of £8 billion to £10 billion (see Figure 3.4). If income tax allowances and excise taxes are 'indexed' in line with forecast inflation, but all other policies remain unchanged, the PSBR for 1982/83 is forecast to be about £8 billion.
4 Hence I can give away at most an additional £2 billion; no more.
5 Hence all policies which involve an increase in the PSBR of more than £2 billion (for example, those proposed by the Labour party, the TUC and even the Conservative 'left': options 2 to 5 on Figure 3.3) are out.
6 Within my 'room for manoeuvre' of £2 billion or less, however, I shall give away as much as I can. Output has been falling for two years, the industry lobby is getting dangerously disaffected, and there will be an election in two years' time at most.

The amount eventually given away in the 1982 spring Budget was £2.3 billion, with a further concession in the autumn on the employers' national insurance surcharge. In addition the target range of growth of the money supply (sterling M_3) was allowed to slip upwards – from 5–9 per cent to 8–12 per cent in respect of the 1982/83 fiscal year.

3.3 Macro-policy making under stress: the 1976 sterling crisis

Such is the formal structure of short-term policy-making. Fairly frequently, however, policy and forecasting rounds cannot be allowed to run for their normal period of about six weeks, because of the need to take quick action in response to an emergency. A consideration of how the Treasury responded to the sterling crisis of summer 1976 will both fill out our abstract account of its procedures and show how those procedures themselves are modified under stress. The story is taken partly from the testimony of a politician – Joel Barnett, at the time Chief Secretary to the Treasury – and partly from the account of a civil servant – Sir Leo Pliatzky, at the time Second Permanent Secretary responsible for public expenditure.

The initial trigger is described by Pliatzky:

> During the early months of 1976 the exchange rate for sterling had been fairly stable at around $2.05 to the pound. By July there had been a depreciation of sterling of 12 per cent against the dollar . . . The holders of sterling began to rush to sell their holdings and move into other currencies. Although there were rational grounds for concern about Britain's underlying industrial performance and the longer-term outlook for controlling inflation, there was also a certain irrationality, with which it was difficult to cope, about the psychology of the break in confidence and in particular the belief that had got into currency that our North Sea oil had now all been mortgaged. However, whatever the rationality or otherwise of the run on sterling, it was a fact and it had somehow to be staunched.[22]

Initially the Bank of England, on its own initiative, sought to staunch the flow by borrowing from other central banks, but this did not stop sterling falling. 'Further measures to restore confidence therefore had to be considered', as Pliatzky puts it, and there was little argument within the Treasury about the choice of instrument:

> Public expenditure cuts, going beyond the last White Paper cuts and starting earlier, were the front runners, since it was the size of our expenditure programmes and of the borrowing to finance them which, in the eyes of the financial world, were at the heart of our problem.[23]

There was more discussion about the amount by which this instrument could be changed. But the Chancellor, Denis Healey, made it clear to the Treasury that there were political limits to the amount of deflation which could be considered, which were set by the need to carry the Cabinet and the trade unions. Once this statement had been made, the Treasury 'house view' quickly converged towards unanimity.

There was a conflict between what was required from the point of view of restoring financial confidence and what was considered feasible and negotiable in Cabinet, and there were fairly strong differences of view on the question of feasibility. A possible package of £1 billion at 1976 survey prices was the starting point for discussion. This was the minimum which might have any hope of making the required impression, but there could be no assurance that it would do the trick. One maverick point of view was that there would be no point in a £1 billion package and that we should either raise it to £2 billion or do nothing at all on the expenditure front and find other ways of financing ourselves out of trouble. But one look at a £2 billion package[24] was enough to rule this one out of consideration. Though £1 billion might be the minimum from one point of view, it looked like the maximum from the point of view of acceptability to the Cabinet – especially as the Chancellor proposed at the same time to find room for further micro measures to help industry and employment (which might) make the package a little less unacceptable vis-à-vis the trade union leaders on whose support he counted on the incomes policy front.[25]

£1 billion it was; but still the fall of sterling continued. The IMF was asked for a standby credit of £4 billion, but asked for further reductions in public expenditure of £3 billion in 1977–8 and £4 billion in 1978–9 as a condition of making such a loan. But, according to Pliatzky, 'It was never on the cards that Treasury Ministers would put such proposals to Cabinet, let alone succeed in getting approval for them.'[26]

Hence the Treasury's policy analysts were left with the job of searching for alternative changes in policy instruments which might satisfy the IMF:

One severe limitation on the room for manoeuvre was the virtual untouchability of social security, by far the largest single programme. So far from being reduced, the main benefits would go on rising in line with prices or, in the case of pensions, in line with earnings, unless new legislation could be passed; but the political judgement was that, not only would Cabinet turn this course down, but even if they went along with it the Government's supporters in the House would not stand for it.

There was initially a greater disposition to suspend the inflation-proofing of civil service pensions, until it was appreciated that this too would require legislation, and that the indexation scheme applied not merely to top civil servants but to large numbers of local government and health service workers on pretty low pensions, along with the armed forces, the policy, judges and Members of Parliament.

The current expenditure of the local authorities was another large area which we had to leave untouched, as we had done in July, for the practical reason that there was no way of ensuring that cuts in this expenditure would take place. In previous exercises we had too often seen spending ministries offer up reductions in programmes such as education on the basis that those would be effected through paper cuts in the current expenditure of local authorities on these programmes rather than through reductions in expenditure within the control of Ministers themselves. But the more items that were ruled out for political or practical reasons, the more we faced the possibility that a crude across-the-board moratorium on capital projects would have to feature prominently in any package. The forecasters were involved in a number of these meetings, when they presented successive updatings of the short-term forecasts and variants which simulated the effects on the economy of possible fiscal and monetary measures. The Chancellor showed a consuming interest in the line-by-line details of their computer print-outs.

When eventually he put proposals to Cabinet on which it was believed that a settlement could be reached with the Fund, it was common knowledge that resistance came not only from Tony Benn and other supporters of the alternative strategy of import controls but from others also, especially Tony Crosland, who held that there was no economic case for cutting expenditure while unemployment was high.

Throughout all this the Prime Minister, by all accounts, held his hand in Cabinet until, at the end of a running debate spread over several meetings, he came out in support of the Chancellor. It may well be that he had intended to do so all along from the time that the Chancellor had put his proposals forward, but the fact remained that until then Denis Healey had had to bear the heat of the battle. Cabinet as a whole now accepted the Prime Minister's judgement or at least swallowed their objections.[27]

The package eventually agreed was, in the short term, a £1 billion cut in public expenditure in 1977/78, £1½ billion in 1978/79, the sale of £500 m. of government-owned shares in the British Petroleum Company, an end to the regional employment premium, and a six-month postponement of all new starts in a wide range of public works projects. In the longer term, a set of targets for the growth of the money supply over the next six years was announced.[28]

At first glance, the assent of Cabinet to the Treasury's

deflationary proposals might have appeared a hair's breadth decision. In fact, as Anthony Crosland himself related to his wife in the quotation at the head of this chapter, it was nothing of the kind. Any attempt to oppose the Treasury's proposals to deal with the crisis, which had been leaked in advance, would have perpetuated the very crisis which the proposals were meant to deal with. As Crosland goes on to relate, the Cabinet is seldom a match for the Treasury if the Chancellor has the Prime Minister's support:

> As usual...the Chancellor has a built-in majority: PM squared beforehand, the ex-chancellors parading their wounds, and eight people – as always, the Lord Chancellor, Lord Privy Seal, Wales, Agriculture, etc. – too timid to resist talk of the pound and international confidence etc. etc.[29]

The *magnitude* of the public spending cuts for 1977/78 and 1978/79 had, therefore, now been settled. But their *apportionment* now had to be negotiated slice by slice in Cabinet by Joel Barnett, the Chief Secretary to the Treasury. The process, as Barnett himself relates, had very little to do with economic rationality:

> On Thursday 11 November...Cabinet at last agreed the Expenditure White Paper. It was a not untypical example of how such decisions are made. I got £180 million out of the £200 million for which I had asked, when I would have been quite happy to settle for £100 million. On defence, I had asked for £10 million, and was helped enormously by Fred Mulley, the Secretary of State. Fred spoke at such great length that the Prime Minister left the Cabinet room for some time – I assume for the toilet – and was still speaking when he returned. Jim then put pressure on Fred and I got £30 million, rather more than I expected. The other interesting case was overseas aid. Until then, there had been no cut. I reluctantly suggested £35 million, which led to a struggle, with Tony Crosland seeking to keep this one programme free from cuts, but we eventually agreed on £20 million. It turned out that John Morris, Secretary of State for Wales, was the luckiest Minister in that we did not reach his programme until late in the proceedings. I asked for £30 million, but because we were already so near our target, Jim asked John for an offer. He said £5 million and to his astonishment had it promptly accepted. I had no doubt that he was ready to be pushed to £20 million. I later had one last try, suggesting that we made no cut in overseas aid and substitute a further £5 million cut from Wales, but the Prime Minister pushed it aside – it was nearly lunchtime.[30]

3.4 Modelling economic policy-making in the UK

In the light of these descriptions of policy-making in normal times and under stress we can now focus on two questions: who makes macro-economic policy, and how?

The question of whether it is Treasury civil servants or government ministers who hold the ultimate power in economic policy-making is ultimately as difficult to resolve, as the question of whether it is producers or consumers who decide how many motor-cars shall be produced. Treasury civil servants, as we have seen, go to enormous lengths to find out what the Chancellor and the Cabinet will and will not 'buy' before even making a formal policy proposal. But at the same time, they waste no opportunity of instructing Treasury ministers in their proper role,[31] which is to raise money to finance government spending, and to say no to proposals which cannot be financed without breaching other policy objectives. Should a Treasury minister for any reason resist such instructions, there is a variety of techniques which civil servants can use. As Joel Barnett relates:

> Quite apart from the time it takes to get an understanding of the way the machine works, the sheer weight of work gives one little time to sit back and just think about the way the job should be done.
>
> I hope I am not doing officials an injustice, but I think they prefer it that way. When you are very busy, the temptation to take the easy way is very strong. You know that life will be much smoother if you simply agree with a long and complex recommendation, especially when disagreement could well involve more meetings in an already over-long day. Life was not made easier for me by officials putting up long briefs which required, or so it was said, a decision 'immediately'. It did not take long to learn that decisions required 'today' could normally wait a week or more.
>
> Another tactic deployed by officials is delay. This may occur when officials find themselves unhappy with a decision being contemplated by a Minister, or more frequently a ministerial request for further information that seems likely to lead to a decision with which they strongly disagree. In such cases they may well decide the best approach is to 'play it long'. The Minister, bogged down with so many other concerns, may forget it long enough for the particular issue to die, or the Minister himself may 'die', in the ministerial sense, by moving on to another post.
>
> Another area where officials were quite brilliant was in the different ways they had of fudging figures, particularly on expenditure decisions. The prevailing belief among them was that our poor industrial and economic performance meant we must restrain the growth of public

expenditure. Consequently all their considerable efforts in presenting the figures would be geared to that end . . . It was a case of changing this and that assumption and abracadabra – the Public Sector Borrowing Requirement (PSBR) is about the figure you first thought of. I thought I had done a fair amount of juggling with figures as an accountant, but when it came to the kind of sophisticated 'massaging' and 'fudging' I learned as Chief Secretary, I realised I had been a babe in arms by comparison.[32]

Over and above their difficulties in interpreting figures. Treasury Ministers face problems in questioning the forecasting procedures by which those figures are generated.[33] Mr Healey, as we have seen, did his best to probe the forecasts of the Treasury model team 'line by line'.[34] But on another occasion in early 1979, anxious to engineer the normal pre-election boom, he

recognised that we would need to increase VAT and other indirect taxes if we were to make the popular income tax cuts, but they were naturally very worried about the inflationary consequences. All this was probably one more reason for the Chancellor to give a final hammering to the Treasury forecasters. Their borrowing requirement figures were much higher than those of outside forecasters, and Denis just did not believe them. Denis was just about as thuggish as he could be, throwing question after question about the assumptions they had taken in arriving at their PSBR, but the forecasters stood up to it well. Indeed, at the end, still unhappy about what he considered over-pessimistic assumptions, the Chancellor could not prove them wrong, and in the engaging manner he frequently assumed at the end of a tough session, he said, 'I retire bruised, battered, b. . . . d, and bewildered.' He had to accept that his optimism might be misplaced but, as he equally fairly put it, given the margin of error, he could have come up with a similar figure on the back of an envelope.[35]

Quite apart from all these factors which discourage Treasury ministers from picking a fight with their civil servants, there is the fact that except in the run-up to an election they will have little motive to do so. As we saw in the last chapter,[36] the response of electoral popularity to the state of the economy is so unstable that even if a chancellor could always win a fight within the Treasury there is no guarantee that it would make the government any more popular. And in any case, as long as the governing party has a reasonable-sized majority in Parliament, the chancellor and prime minister have little reason to manipulate the economy in pursuit of short-term popularity, except in the vicinity of an election.

There are therefore a variety of influences at work tending to build consensus within the Treasury, to the point where it is scarcely worth trying to identify the separate influence of ministers and officials on the decision-making process. An appearance of unanimity is always maintained. As a senior Treasury official has said, 'There is an absolutely binding convention, which has never been breached, that argument (namely, in the PCC) is free up to the time the Chancellor makes up his mind. Then all the energy goes into securing what the Chancellor wants.'[37] But the Chancellor, as we have seen, is more likely to 'know what he wants', independently of the standard Treasury view, during the run-up to an election. And Treasury civil servants, anticipating this, are more likely to lean in his direction without his even having to ask. There are thus two distinct phases to the intra-Treasury consensus in each election cycle: in the first three years or so the officials pull the Treasury ministers along but after that the institution tends to assume what a former Treasury official has called a 'defensive and apologetic' posture as the ministers make it more clear what measures they cannot expect the Cabinet to wear.

Let us now move to our second question: how is macro-economic policy made? From all that has been said it will be clear that the process of policy choice, even outside times of economic crisis, at no point approximates to the model of 'rational economic man' offered by neo-classical economic theory. In that model the chooser optimises an objective function, or ranking of possible states of the world, subject to a constraint; it has been applied to macro-economic policy making by a number of authors, for example Fisher (1968, 1970), Pissarides (1972), Friedlaender (1973). But in the UK Treasury there is *no objective function*. Or rather, there is an objective function with two values: 'this is good enough' and 'this is not good enough'. At stage 4 of the forecasting round, the PCC have to decide whether the forecast path for the economy if existing policies are left unaltered leads to a good enough outcome to warrant those policies being continued. If the answer is 'yes', the Chancellor is recommended to stick with existing policies; if the answer is 'no', and the application of prevailing rules of thumb does not yield obvious prescriptions for what should be done, search behaviour begins. The Policy Analysis Division is asked to investigate the consequences of certain alternative policies, many of which will have been suggested to it by Treasury ministers. This it does by producing a set of 'ready reckoners' which can be assembled into packages such as those displayed in Table 3.2 and Figure 3.3, corresponding to a set of hypothetical changes in policy. These ready reckoners between them give the Treasury and its ministers a view of part of the constraint, that is, the set of alternative states of the world which is feasible if certain policy instruments are deployed. The search goes on until a package of measures is discovered which the Chancellor declares 'satisfactory'; in normal times the criterion of 'satisfactoriness' will be the predicted consequences for the public sector borrowing requirement, and in an emergency it will be simply the end of the emergency. Initially the instruments considered are those which are fairly easy to manipulate; if all simulations with these instruments yield unsatisfactory results, the cycle begins again, with instruments which are costlier to use and less certain in their effect. The account of the 1976 sterling crisis set out above describes two phases of the cycle; in the first, quite quick agreement was reached on a £1 billion cut in public expenditure; but this failed to stop the sterling exchange rate falling, which led in turn not only to an intensified use of the existing instrument (that is, cuts in public expenditure) but also to suggestions for the use of other instruments, for example, import controls and changes in interest rates. Under the stress of the need for a quick decision the search:

(a) embraced at the first stage only one instrument and two options (a £1 billion cut in public expenditure, or a £2 billion cut);
(b) when extended, concentrated on *speed and certainty of effect*, above all. Hence social security cuts and de-indexing of pensions were quickly rejected as policy

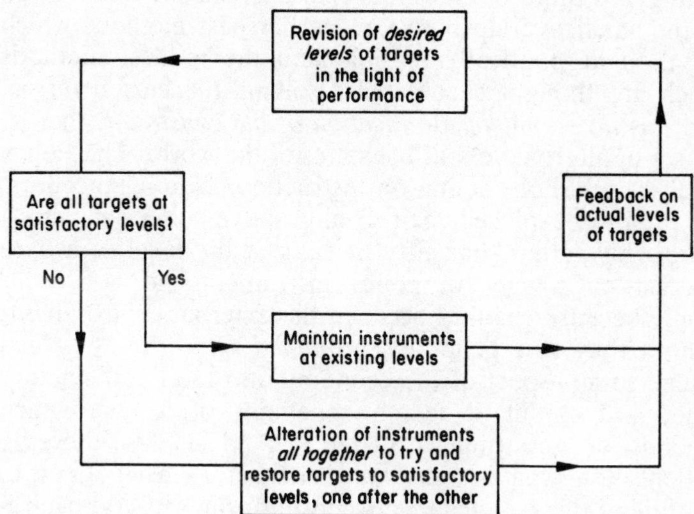

Figure 3.5 Macro-policy making: circular flow chart

tools, because even if feasible they would require new legislation, and local authority expenditure cuts were out because there was no certainty that they would take effect;
(c) was confined to a few people only; even the Cabinet were only brought in when deciding how cuts were to be allocated, not when deciding what the size of the overall cut should be.

The overall policy-making sequence can be summarised by Figure 3.5.

This is the very essence of what we have previously described as a satisficing process.[38] There is *no objective function*, in the shape of a consistent set of preferences between alternative states of the world – indeed, as we have seen, it could be described as politically irrational for Treasury ministers to have one[39]; there is only a one-off decision about whether things are good enough or not good enough. What is 'good enough' in normal times is determined by the requirements of the medium-term financial strategy; in times of crisis it is characteristically determined by the small overlap between the harshest methods which are thought politically feasible and the mildest methods which are thought capable of resolving the current crisis. There is *no complete specification of the constraint*, that is, the set of alternative feasible states of the world. The Policy Analysis Division, acting on instructions from chancellors, will prefer to explore five or six alternative policy packages[40] thoroughly rather than fifty or sixty at the level of a bare forecast.[41] Changes in policy instruments do not occur simply because changes occur in the external environment; rather, they are generally *prompted by 'crises'*[42] which plunge some aspect of the economy into the unsatisfactory zone, and stimulate search behaviour of a type which depends on the time available.[43] And finally, there is evidence that what is considered 'satisfactory' itself adapts to continuing discrepancies between performance and aspiration. In the 1950s an unemployment rate of half a million was enough to stimulate reflation whereas today (1983) anything below two and a half million would be considered a real achievement. The unemployment target was replaced, in 1980, by a medium-term financial strategy setting target ranges for the money supply in each financial year, but this was itself relaxed in both 1981 and 1982.

3.5 The economic policy-making structure in the USA

The structure of macro-economic policy-making in the United States of America differs in two fundamental and two minor respects from the British system described above. The central bank is genuinely independent rather than quasi-deferential; the legislature exercises genuine power in the scrutiny and control of public expenditure and taxation measures; top civil service jobs are all presidential appointees so that the innermost policy-making circle is more effectively politicised than in Britain; and the business of economic forecasting on which rival policies are based is far more decentralised and competitive. The latter two constitute divergences from the British system of relatively minor importance and will be considered only in passing, but the first two influence the way in which the policy-making system works and are discussed here. Both reflect the application in the economic sphere of the doctrine of 'separation of powers' within the process of government.

The Federal Reserve System

The Federal Reserve Act, passed by Congress in 1913, created as America's central bank a Federal Reserve System consisting of a presidentially appointed Board of Governors in Washington and twelve regional Federal Reserve Banks, each with its own board of directors made up of private citizens. Each of the twelve Federal Reserve Banks has its own minimum lending rate ('Federal Funds rate') at which member banks can borrow money, but minimum reserve requirements are set by the Board of Governors and the most important tool of monetary policy, namely open-market operations, is managed by the Federal Open Market Committee, a body consisting of the seven members of the Board of Governors and five of the twelve presidents of the regional Federal Reserve Banks.

The original 1913 act included a number of features designed to provide a degree of independence from political pressures, and the Banking Acts of 1933 and 1935 reinforced that independence.[44] But until the 1960s the Federal Reserve never acted in such a way as to provoke open political controversy. The reasons were twofold: the cautious economic philosophy of the Eisenhower years[45] precluded the large government deficits which would have required the Federal Reserve to let interest rates rise to penal levels if it wanted 'sound money'; and the operating strategies of open market operations at that time acted to damp cyclical fluctuations in interest rates, thereby 'accommodating' market forces and preserving a low profile for monetary policy among the many factors influencing the course of economic events.

In the 1960s the Federal Reserve became a much more overt actor in the policy-making game. Expansionist policies were followed throughout the Kennedy years,[46] and the Johnson administration threw an increase in Vietnam war expenditure on top of a continuing boom. When in December 1965 the Federal Reserve showed its reluctance to continue financing the resulting deficit by money creation and raised its discount rate, President Johnson clashed with its chairman publicly.[47] Nine years later, in the second half of 1974, the Federal Reserve savagely cut the growth rate of money supply and thereby exacerbated the world-wide recession, attracting severe governmental criticism once again.[48] And in the early years of the Reagan administration the Federal Reserve openly used its independence to 'bounce' the administration onto a path of financial rectitude in a way that would have been inconceivable in Great Britain. As Brittan described the strategy:

> The Fed has been deliberately erring on the tight side in its monetary policy because of alarm at the prospects for the Budget deficit. It has wanted to demonstrate that it will not bail out Congress and the Administration from the effects of their fiscal irresponsibility. It has not merely used tight money to offset fiscal laxity, but to more than offset it. In other words, it has produced a monetary-fiscal mix different from what it really considered optimal as an incentive to all politicians to mend their ways. One British observer has likened it to a game of 'chicken' in which the Fed threatens to drive off the cliff unless the politicians step back first.[49]

The Open Market Committee (whose deliberations are published after thirty-five days, placing them in far more of a goldfish bowl than the Bank of England) does not plan its strategy according to an explicit optimising model.[50] It does not use a precisely specified objective function to express its preferences in relation to the targets of economic policy, nor does it rely on a precise model of the macro-economic system or a model of the relevant financial linkages.[51] Rather, it satisfices with respect to an *instrument*, namely the monetary aggregates M_1, M_2 and M_3 for which tolerance limits are announced each year in advance. If money supply is running above the top of the target growth range, as M_1 did in the early months of 1982, the federal discount rate (analogous to minimum lending rate) is raised so as to restrict the demand for cash – sometimes, it seems from the quotation above, by more than is really necessary, to make the signal doubly clear. If money supply is growing below the bottom of the target range, federal discount rate may be cut,[52] although at a time of overriding inflationary crisis such a response is less automatic. This is the simplest form of 'satisficing': the search procedure, although by no means reduced to a reflex response, is limited to a scan of a few discrete quantitative changes in one major instrument.

The budgetary process

The US budgetary process has been perceptively described by many commentators[53] and we summarise only the bare bones of the system here. The essence of the matter is that Congress, unlike the UK Parliament, can and frequently does throw out or revise the administration's draft budget. Hence, decision-making on the level of taxation and federal expenditure has two stages. In the first, the Council of Economic Advisers, the Office of Management and Budget and the Treasury jointly help the President prepare his draft budget. In the second, Congress decides how this draft should be modified.

Of the three bodies advising the President, the Treasury runs the tax system, foreign economic policy, relations with the IMF, and manages the government's debt. The Office of Management and Budget is responsible to the President for the overall planning and control of federal expenditure: it imposes 'budget marks' or agency planning ceilings on the various spending departments during the summer, before they come back with detailed budget proposals in the autumn. Between them, these two bodies exercise the functions performed in Britain by the Inland Revenue and the Overseas Finance and Public Services sectors of the Treasury. But the Council of Economic Advisers, the *primus inter pares* of the three, is unique. Its three members are economics experts, predominantly university professors, who work full-time at the President's pleasure. Unlike the Treasury's Policy Analysis Division and the German Council of Macro-Economic Experts (*Sachverstaendigenrat* or SR) their function is not only to analyse the consequences of alternative policy proposals, but also to initiate new proposals in empathy with the President's wishes.[54] As Arthur Okun, Chairman of the Council of Economic Advisers under the Johnson administration, relates:

> No CEA member has ever claimed to be the spokesman for a purely professional view . . . To be effective, the adviser must operate with sensitivity and understanding of the President's values and aims. He must know the President's tastes, just as a good wife has to know how her husband takes his coffee. Thus, after Kennedy pledged to 'start this country moving again', his economists convinced him that a 4 per cent interim target for unemployment was an appropriate translation of that goal . . . When President Johnson set forth the vision of the Great Society, his economists shaped the strategies in the war against poverty to . . . (emphasise) the long-term benefits to the entire nation from investment in human resources. When President Nixon counselled the nation to lower its voice, his economists followed, in their pronouncements, with a stress on moderation and gradualism.[55]

Fundamentally, the President defines what is the 'satisficing' level of a particular economic target, and the CEA advises him, after appropriate search procedures, on the appropriate budgetary policies for its (re-)attainment. The President lays down a marker such as Truman's 'keep that GNP up to $200 billion',[56] or Kennedy's '94% employment is a grade of A-. Why incur the political cost of getting a straight A?'[57] and the CEA tells him how to keep the target in question within the acceptable zone. That advice implies instructions to the OMB and Treasury in framing their budgetary guidelines, and those agencies, in these matters, always respect the CEA's primacy.

The administration's budget now has to be presented to Congress. This process, even after appropriate attempts by the President to trim the budget of the items which he knew Congress 'would not wear'[58] involved, in the 1960s, vast and unpredictable delays: in implementing the three major tax bills of the 1960s, Congress delayed 18, 13 and 18 months.[59] The lag in effect of government stabilisation policy thus contained an unpredictable element.[60] In 1974 the system of congressional control was reformed by the imposition of a fixed time limit on the scrutiny of the budget; it must now be submitted by the President on 18 January or the 15th day after the Congress meets, and the process of Congressional scrutiny must be concluded by 25 September, that is, a week before the fiscal year begins. At the same time, two new integrative budget committees, one in the House of Representatives and one in the Senate, were set up to impose fixed overall spending limits as a framework for the deliberations of all the many specialised committees.[61] Finally, a new information agency – the Congressional Budget Office – was set up 'to provide the Congress with detailed budget information and studies of the budget impact of alternative policies'.[62] It is, in essence, a Policy Analysis Division at Congress's disposal; it 'does not make recommendations on policy matters but provides Congress with options and alternatives for its consideration'.[63] Although these reforms add predictability to the process by which Congress imposes its second guess on macro-economic policy, they do not reduce its power to do so. Even though between 1976 and 1980 the same Party controlled the Presidency and both Houses of Congress, and even though Budget Committees vote along party lines, they have regularly voted different levels of spending from those requested by the Administration. Table 3.3 shows the order of magnitude by which Congress alters the figures from the executive's proposals.

These decisions are based on the appraisal of a large amount of information, which has of course been increased by the creation of the Congressional Budget Office.[64] But much of the information has the effect not so much of widening Congress's view of the range of economic options which is available (the 'constraint' in the jargon used on page 51 above) but rather of exposing the range of disagreement which exists, for example between the different forecasting schools. In addition, there is also the suspicion in Congressmen's minds that all the forecasts may

TABLE 3.3. United States: successive versions of budget for fiscal year 1981 ($ billions)

	Original Carter proposal	*Congress 1st Concurrent resolution (June)*	*Senate (August)*	*House (November)*
Revenues	600	613.8	615.1	616.7
Outlay	615.8	613.6	633.0	631.7
Balance	−15.8	0.2	−17.9	−25

Source Robinson (1981), p. 16.

be wrong; for Congressional agencies, in spite of their independence from the executive, are highly dependent on the executive as a source of data,[65] and it is tempting for a deflationist President to 'talk up' the inflation forecast, for example, in order to try and impose unpopular policies, much as in Britain a deflationist Treasury may use pessimistic forecasts to put the squeeze on a chancellor who wishes to stimulate the economy. The critical limit on their capacity for rational action is not lack of information but lack of ability to evaluate numerous mutually conflicting pieces of information in the time required. In such a situation the tendency is for Congress to seek out an approach which is robust in face of this uncertainty. This may be savage cuts in a particular area; or, if no particular area commands consensus, then an across-the-board cut (in the event of a Republican-dominated Congress) or an across-the-board increase (in the case of a Democratic-dominated Congress) in the deficit will enable Congressmen to gain credit for purposive action without taking the responsibility for causing damage in specific areas.[66]

What is involved, therefore, in the making of American fiscal policy is a *two-stage* satisficing process. Two agencies, neither of them with any clear objective function, each make proposals for changes in taxes and spending in response to their own conception of whether the state of the economy is satisfactory or not, but the form of their reaction is constrained in each case, as we have seen, by expectations of the other party's likely behaviour.

We can illustrate the major points of this section further by a brief description of the American budgetary process as it operated in fiscal 1983. The major stages in the process were these:

18 January 1982: President Reagan submits his budget, providing for a 1983 budget deficit of $99 billion, by comparison with about $60 billion in each of 1980 and 1981.[67] This is more expansionary than the previous two budgets even allowing for the automatic increase in the deficit with rising unemployment.. But unemployment has risen by over half a million in each of the months October to December 1981, and inflation is down from 13.5 per cent in

1980 to 8.9 per cent now,[68] and the central Administration forecasts that it will fall to 6.5 per cent by the end of the year.[69]

15 April 1982: Budget Committees report first concurrent resolution on the budget to their Houses. By now it is clear that not only is unemployment continuing to rise faster than expected (it is already over 10 million, by comparison with 6½ million at the beginning of 1980), but inflation is falling faster than expected, and is now forecast to fall to 5.5 per cent by the end of the year.[70] At the same time, owing to the tightness of the monetary policy being adopted concurrently by the Federal Reserve, interest rates are at record levels. In the light of this information, Congress recommends a slightly higher 1983 deficit ($104 billion) than that suggested by the President.

July 1982: inflation is already down to just over 6 per cent – that is, below the beginning-of-year forecast – even though all three monetary aggregates (see Figure 3.6) are running above the top of their target ranges.[71] In response to this dramatic fall in the velocity of circulation of money the Federal Reserve chairman, in evidence before the House Budget Committee, admits that he is willing to see some over-shooting above the top end of the money growth target range for M_1 of 2½ to 5½ per cent in the latter half of 1982. Consistently with this policy, discount rate is reduced by half a point to 11½ per cent; in the subsequent six weeks, it is reduced four more times, to 10 per cent. This behaviour by the policy authorities can be seen as in response to a discrepancy between monetarist theory and reality – in particular, to a greater-than-expected success in bringing inflation under control even though all measures of money have grown faster than expected.[72]

19 August 1982: House of Representatives passes President Reagan's tax bill,[73] allowing for increases in tax revenue of $98 billion over three years; most involve the closing of loopholes rather than increases in existing tax rates. This is an uncomfortable measure for a president who is doctrinally opposed to tax increases, and has frequently said so in public. He justifies it by reference to the failure of the measures he has so far taken to prevent the budget

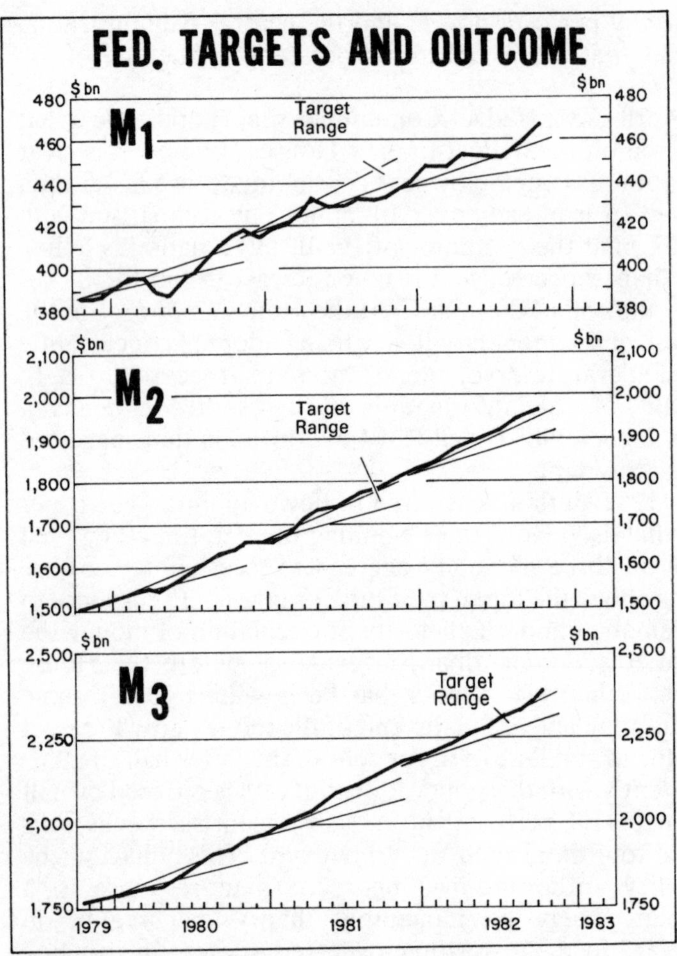

Figure 3.6 US money supply: outcome compared with Federal Reserve targets, 1979–82

deficit rising. He still forecasts a deficit of about $100 billion in fiscal 1983 falling to $70 billion by 1985; but not everyone agrees with him. The Congressional Budget Office is forecasting a deficit $150 billion for 1983, and Congress itself forecasts that, even after the President's measures have been passed, the deficit will be nearer $200 billion.[74]

September–October 1982. Market interest rates fall rapidly, under continued encouragement from the Federal Reserve. These continued movements are interpreted by some as a response to the *external* stimulus of overseas debt crises in Mexico, Brazil and elsewhere; by others more cynically as a response to political pressure from the Reagan administration ahead of the November elections.

November 1982. Congressional elections show substantial Democratic gains.

20 January 1983. Inflation rate for calendar 1982 is announced as 3.9 per cent, well below the lowest advance predictions.[75]

1 February 1983. President Reagan presents his 1984 budget. This forecasts that the budget deficit for fiscal 1983 will in fact turn out as $225 billion, or more than double the level originally forecast. A Federal spending freeze, cutbacks on defence spending plans, and 'standby taxes' to raise $40 billion to $50 billion a year for three years from October 1985 if the deficit is larger than anticipated, are brought in with the intention of cutting the Federal budget deficit down to just over $100 billion in current prices by 1988.

What is clear throughout this process is that all three policy authorities – the Administration, (a majority of) Congress and the Federal Reserve – achieved a consensus around July/August that the level of economic activity was unsatisfactorily depressed and took steps to raise it. This was entirely inconsistent with the policy of minimising inflation proclaimed by the Administration itself. But it is consistent with the 'satisficing' idea of an instinctive reaction of policy instruments by the authorities as soon as the tripwire of an 'unacceptable' level of unemployment – that is, 10 million – was crossed.

3.6 An explanatory model

In subsequent chapters we analyse in some detail the fiscal and monetary policy actions of the UK and US governments over the period 1945 to 1982. As a general explanatory framework for that analysis we need, in the light of the discussion of this chapter, a model with the following features:

(1) manipulation of instruments not governed by any objective function, but rather a response to whether the state of the economy is 'satisfactory' or not;
(2) manipulation of instruments according to standard rules of thumb if targets stray outside the satisfactory zone;
(3) search behaviour if the rules of thumb in (2) do not have the desired result, governed by the principles in paragraph 4 of Appendix I below;
(4) determination of 'satisfactory' levels of targets (and occasional replacement of one target by another) as a result of conflict between actors in the policy-making process;
(5) sensitivity of 'acceptable' levels of targets to discrepancy between actual attainment and performance;
(6) reflation of personal disposable income, regardless of the state of the economy, in an election year.

As a first stab at such an explanatory model we propose the following:

Equation 3.1
If x_i is any instrument, y_i is any target, and y^*_i is its desired value, then at time t:

$$\Delta x_i(t) = \alpha + \beta_1(y_i - y^*_i)_{(t-k)} + \beta_2 E$$

when $y_i < y^*_i$ (i.e. y has not reached its satisfactory level)

$$= 0 \text{ at other times (i.e. } y_i > y^*_i)$$

where: k = empirically determined lag
E = dummy for election year

Equation 3.2

$$y^*_i(t) = \text{moving average of } y_i \text{ at time } t$$

This model represents policy as a sort of Pavlovian reflex mechanism; when the economy strays into 'danger' red lights begin to flash and instruments are automatically manipulated as a response to the 'danger'. The model reasonably comfortably explains what one may call the routine parts of policy-making, namely (1) (2) (5) and (6) above. What it cannot do is analyse the search process by which *new* instruments were brought in at times of major crisis, or explain why the targets at which economic policy aimed sometimes changed. In the two chapters which follow we shall argue that these two non-routine processes, in the period since 1945, were strongly related to one another. When the Keynesian rules of thumb, which had successfully dealt with the *minor* crises of the 1950s and 1960s, failed to cope with the *major* crisis presented by simultaneous increases in inflation, unemployment and balance of payments deficit in the early 1970s, both governments were forced to embark on a search which ended by replacing one set of macro-economic targets and instruments with a new set.

Notes

1 See Robinson (1981), p. 5.

2 This central economic ministry is described by the recent *Report on Policy Optimisation* (United Kingdom, 1978, p. 20) as being empowered 'to manage the economy of the United Kingdom so as to achieve the economic objectives laid down by Ministry and approved by Parliament and to advise the Chancellor on all aspects of economic policy' but so old is it that its functions are not defined by law. As a result, Brittan writes (1971, p. 67) 'its powers and responsibilities have always been the subject of confusion and argument'.

3 It also acts as banker to the clearing banks, and administers the government's foreign exchange reserves on behalf of the Treasury.

4 In some recent years the figures have been as follows:

	1974	*1975*	*1976*	*1977*	*1978*	*1979*	*1980*	*1981*
Nominal public sector borrowing requirement (£bn)	6.4	10.5	9.1	6.0	8.3	12.6	12.3	10.2
Percentage growth of sterling M_3 (January to December)	16.4	8.8	8.2	7.8	14.7	12.5	16.4	16.0

Source: Bank of England Quarterly Bulletin, September 1982, Table 11.3.

In the early 1970s the PSBR and the money supply (Sterling M_3) showed a tendency to rise together, which led to a fixation with the PSBR in the context of monetary policy. But see further note 32 in Chapter 5.

5 The Bank's objection was to target ranges of money supply growth laid down more than one year in advance, not to money supply targets as such. The medium-term financial strategy, originally published in 1980, set out a series of target ranges for growth in 'Sterling M_3' (one definition of the money supply) which declined gradually from 9–13 per cent in the financial years 1976/77 to 4–8 per cent in the financial years 1982/83.

6 Montagu Norman, Governor of the Bank of England, 1920–44.

7 This episode is described in Blackaby (1979) p. 32, and also in Crossman (1979), p. 177.

8 This episode is thoroughly investigated by the House of Commons Treasury and Civil Service Committee in United Kingdom (1981), Vol. 2, pp. 167–296.

9 Denzil Davies, Treasury Minister in 1974–9 Labour government; cited in David Marsh, 'The Bank advises, but . . .' *Financial Times,* 6 May 1982.

10 The thesis that bureaucrats who spend money are motivated by the same growth objectives as managers of business corporations has been eloquently put by Niskanen (1973); the rebuttals contained in that volume are unconvincing. This is not to say that senior civil servants have *no* objectives but to spend as much as possible, and ingenious schemes have been put forward to give their motivation a twist such as the one in the TV programme *Yes Minister* (screened on 5 March 1981) in which a Treasury chief secretary offered to arrange a rapid knighthood for any spending permanent secretary who could cut the expenditures of his ministry in the coming year by 1 per cent. But they have not yet to our knowledge been implemented.

11 For the various attempts at medium-term planning of public expenditure in Britain since 1961 see Pliatzky (1982), pp. 33, 47, 139.

12 The relationships of mutual trust and obligation which exist between civil servants in the Treasury and in spending ministries are well described by Heclo and Wildavsky (1971) Chapter 2.

13 In particular spending ministries' bids were stamped on very hard by the Treasury during the first year of the last UK election cycle (see Malcolm Dean, 'Who's afraid of Mrs T', *Guardian,* 19 September 1979); but are currently (autumn 1982) being treated with a little more indulgence.

14 It is alleged that in 1980 'an attempt was made, under the leadership of Mr James Prior, to force a breach in the condition which permits Treasury ministers to retain virtually exclusive control over the "budget judgement" . . . . that revolt proved to be unsuccessful, and this year's budget (namely, 1981) was prepared under precisely the same exclusive conditions which have kept even the Cabinet in

ignorance of budgetary policy for decades.' Front page, *Guardian,* March 13, 1981.

15 See Robinson and Sandford (1983) for more detail of this relationship.

16 For more detail on Treasury policy-making procedures see Young (1983).

17 For example, in 1961, 1965, 1966, 1968, 1975. There was also an 'autumn package' in 1982.

18 A model is a collection of mathematical formulae which defines the relationships between such quantities as the levels of employment, income, taxes, government expenditure, interest rates, prices etc. Such a model is necessary in order to forecast the effect which a change a given *instrument* of economic policy (for example, the rate of VAT) will have on the *targets* of policy (for example, unemployment, prices, the exchange rate). The model used by the Treasury is represented in a schematic form as Figure 6.4.

19 For example, the initial forecast of industrial production will be made on the basis of an equation featuring demand, profitability, the exchange rate, and so forth as explanatory variables; but if there is say, a major strike in the steel industry, this will upset any forecast made purely on the basis of these variables. The radio broadcast by Young (1983), shortly to be published, is particularly useful on the discretionary over-riding of model relationships. The role of the model for economic policy-makers may be likened to the role of a compass for explorers. In general it provides a useful guide, but sometimes the user will know that is unreliable (as when a compass is used on magnetic rock) and on such occasions intuitive judgement must be substituted for mechanical aids.

20 This 'ready reckoner' measures the ratio $\Delta Y/\Delta X$ over a specified period where ΔX = arbitrary change in instrument and ΔY = resulting change in target of policy.

21 This 'house view' is formed formally by consultations at stage 1 of the forecast/policy cycle (see Figure 3.2) and informally by constant discussion between Treasury ministers and senior civil servants. The *Committee on Policy Optimisation,* put the matter in this way:

> It has been put to us that, in the recent past, no options seriously recommended by respected outside observers have gone unanalysed in the Treasury. At times, some options, such as a strict rule for the growth of the money supply, have not attracted much attention because most of the economists in the Treasury have regarded them as not being of major importance. At other times (*e.g. the present P.M.*), no doubt a formal incomes policy, with rigid control of the wage packet by government regulation, has not attracted much effort from the simulators, because it was judged politically impractical to persuade Ministers of any virtues which such a policy might have.

But, subject to these inevitable constraints upon the intellectual opinion of the Government's advisers, it is said that all 'known' policy instruments have been in the minds of the simulators in composing their analyses. (United Kingdom 1978, p. 20).

22 Pliatzky (1982), p. 148.
23 Pliatzky (1982), p. 149.
24 On the basis of a Policy Analysis Division simulation.
25 Pliatzky (1982), p. 149.
26 Pliatzky (1982), p. 153.
27 Pliatzky (1982), pp. 155 and 156.
28 See Figure 3.4 above, and Table 5.2 below.
29 Crosland (1982), p. 307.
30 Barnett (1982), p. 103.
31 This process of 'socialisation' of Treasury ministers is well described by Heclo and Wildavsky (1974), especially Chapter 4.
32 Barnett (1982), pp. 21–2.
33 It is common for ministers to believe that Treasury forecasts are over-pessimistic, and to argue that Treasury forecasters should use more optimistic forecasts for exogenous variables such as oil prices and the growth of world trade. See the testimony by Britton in Young (1983).
34 Barnett (1982), pp. 21–2.
35 Barnett (1982), p. 182.
36 p. 33–34 above.
37 Quoted in Hennessy (1977).
38 Chapter 1 above, pp. 12–13.
39 See p. 10 above.
40 By 'explore' we mean

(i) consider the sensitivity of the forecast to alternative assumptions. The Treasury central forecast may be wrong, and there is no shortage of macro-economic modelling teams outside the Treasury offering forecasts based on alternative assumptions about exogenous variables (such as world oil prices) and alternative specifications of the structure of the economy.

(ii) Consider how each policy 'package' might if necessary be defended in Cabinet: one defensible package to meet every crisis is what the chancellor really needs, rather than nine or ten which cannot be agreed in Cabinet.

The implications of this are that, contrary to the statement of the Committee on Policy Optimisation (note 21 above) policy-makers do not explore the entire (technically) feasible zone. As a former chief economic adviser to the Treasury put it:

What economists have to say may be neglected because its bearing on policy is obscure, contested, ambiguous or insufficiently precise; because economists' conclusions are not adapted to the needs of the policy makers: or because, for that or any other reason, they simply fail to gain a hearing. Policy makers, as a rule, are slightly deaf: there is too much noise. (Sir Alec Cairncross, in Cairncross (1982), p. 5.)

41 The problem is not shortage of computing time: the current version of the Treasury model needs only five minutes of computer time to solve for eight quarters with given values of the exogenous variables, and a further five minutes for each further examination of a single instrument change (giving twelve hypothetical changes per hour). What restricts choice is *not* 'lack of information' (as is suggested by many defences of 'satisficing' theory); rather, it is lack of resources for evaluating information, and in particular the matters mentioned by Sir Alec Cairncross in the previous footnote.

42 This (plus the uncertain effect of policy measures) are presumably Denis Healey's reasons for saying that economic policy-making is 'more like gardening than operating a computer' (cf. quotation at head of this chapter).

43 Most of our illustrative material has been drawn from the Treasury, but it is clear that the Bank of England adopt fundamentally the same procedure of choosing from a small set of simulations. See United Kingdom (1981), Vol. II, p. 59, where the Bank of England explain their reluctance to conduct optimal control experiments.

44 In particular, the Secretary of the Treasury was removed as an *ex officio* member of the Board of Governors.

45 These policies were never actively opposed by Congress, even under the Democratic majorities of the later 1950s.

46 For details of these, see Okun (1970), Chapter 2, and Chapter 4 below.

47 'My view and the view of the Secretary of Treasury and the Council of Economic Advisers is that the decision on interest rates should be a coordinated policy decision in January, when the nature and impact of the administration's budgetary and Vietnam decisions are known.' *Public Papers of the Presidents of the United States: Lyndon B. Johnson,* 1965 (1966), Vol. 2, p. 1137.

48 For discussion of this episode see Pierce (1979), Poole (1979) and Blinder (1979), pp. 185–194. Some of the criticism was to lead to slight restrictions on the freedom of manoeuvre of the Federal Reserve system, for example in 1975 the House and Senate committees responsible for oversight of monetary policy succeeded in having Congress pass Concurrent Resolution 133 requiring the chairman of the Federal Reserve Board to testify quarterly and report on the state of the economy and in particular the Federal Reserve's goals with respect to the growth in the money supply.

49 S. Brittan, 'New Signals from the Fed' *Financial Times,* 15 July 1982.

50 Friedman (1978), p. 29, ascribes this to 'the importance of information which the Open Market Committee can only incorporate in judgemental methods, given the current state of economic science'.

51 Friedman (1978) comments: 'the FRB–MIT econometric model is available, but the committee typically does not accept its implications at face value' (p. 30).

52 At the July 1982 meeting of the Open Market Committee the federal funds rate was lowered by half a point to 11.5 per cent and a decision was made to raise monetary growth from 3 to 5 per cent in the July–September period.

53 See Schick (1975), Congressional Budget Office (1976) and Robinson (1981).

54 Still less does the CEA engage in public criticism of the administration, as the SR commonly does. For a vivid comparison of the functions of the CEA and the SR in the sixties, see the essay by Wallich (1968).

55 Okun (1970), pp. 24, 25 and 27. For a valuable discussion on this issue, see Herbert Stein, James Tobin, Henry Wallich, 'How political must the Council of Economic Advisers be?' *Challenge* (March–April, 1974), 28–42.

56 Wallich (1968), p. 363.

57 Wallich (1968), p. 363.

58 Okun relates that:

> President Johnson stated publicly in 1968 that he had not proposed a general tax increase (in 1966) because 'it was evident that it would be impossible to get a tax increase in 1966.' He elaborated on this in a speech to the Business Council in December 1968: 'We knew we needed action on taxes in 1966. Many of you in this room will remember what happened when, in the month of March 1966, I asked how much support you would give me. Not a hand went up. And I was told that I could get but four votes in the Tax Committee of the Congress out of 25'. Quoted in Okun (1970), p. 71. The British reader will react: it couldn't happen here.

59 Tufte (1978), p. 139.

60 An econometric simulation (by Portney, 1975) concluded that two of the delays were costly and one was, by sheer good luck, beneficial in stabilisation terms.

61 For details of the membership of these committees see Robinson (1981) pp. 18–20.

62 US Congress, (1976) p. 1.

63 US. Congress (1976), p. 1.

64 In making a recommendation for Fiscal Year 1983, the House Budget Chairman provided, as background, estimates for 1982 and 1983 of: Gross National Product; Personal Income; Consumer Price Index; and unemployment as calculated by various different sources. The data sources used in 1982 were (a) the Administration (as in the President's Budget) (b) the Congressional Budget Office and (c) the House Budget Committee's own estimates produced by the Committee's economic staff. Next, alternative forecasts for the same

variables for several years ahead were presented from (a) the House Budget Committee (b) the Congressional Budget Office (c) the Administration (d) Data Resources Ltd. (e) Chase Econometrics (f) Wharton (g) UCLA and (h) University of Michigan. Further details were obtained from witnesses testifying before the Committee including the Chairman of the Council of Economic Advisers, the Director of the Office of Management and Budget, the Director of the Congressional Budget Office, and outside academics and financial experts. In the light of all this background material the Committee Chairman must make his own forecasts, based on a distillation of the various alternative estimates, for five years ahead and then make his recommendation. What the Chairman recommends has first to be accepted by the Committee – this is when party votes occur – and then by the House. (This is an updating of the description in Robinson (1981), pp. 25–6).

65 As one Congressional staff member said in interview: 'We are dependent on the Administration for raw material. There is only one source of unemployment figures – the Department of Labour.' Quoted in Robinson (1981), pp. 29–30.

66 This so-called 'meat-axe' strategy is discussed in Wildavsky (1964), pp. 142–9.

67 *Economic Report of the President and Annual Report of the Council of Economic Advisers* (1982), p. 98.

68 *Economic Report of the President and Annual Report of the Council of Economic Advisers* (1982), p. 6.

69 *Economic Report of the President and Annual Report of the Council of Economic Advisers* (1982), p. 8.

70 Congressional Budget Office, reported in *Financial Times,* 17 April 1982.

71 M_1: 2½ to 5½ per cent. M_2: 6 to 9 per cent. M_3: 6½ to 7½ per cent.

72 See Figures 3.6 and 3.7. The proposition applies even if monetary growth and inflation are averaged over a longer period. Over the three years to end 1982 the rate of growth of M_2 (average of the two previous years' figures) *rose* from 8.4 to 11.5 per cent; the rate of growth of the consumer price index *fell* from 8.9 to 7 per cent. These opposite tendencies pertain even if monetary growth is lagged two years.

73 This measure was opposed by 89 Republicans, who felt unable to support any kind of tax increase, but supported by nearly all mainstream Democrats.

74 *Financial Times,* 23 August 1982.

75 *Financial Times,* 22 January 1983.

Part 2
TESTED MODELS OF POLICY-MAKING

4 Years of Innocence: the Experiment with 'Fine Tuning' 1945–73

In 1965 President Johnson was making a controversial statement when he said: 'I do not believe recessions are inevitable.' That statement is no longer controversial. Recessions are now considered to be fundamentally preventable, like airplane crashes and unlike hurricanes.
ARTHUR M. OKUN, *The Political Economy of Prosperity* (1970), p. 33.

4.1 An outline history of the period

Shortly after the Second World War legislation was passed which made the governments of Britain and America legally responsible for the management of the economy by Keynesian principles. The United States Employment Act of 1946 declared that it was

the continuing policy and responsibility of the Federal Government to use all practical means ... with the assistance and co-operation of industry, agriculture, labour and State and local governments ... to promote maximum employment, production, and purchasing power.

The meaning of the last three goals was left unresolved when the Act was passed in 1946 and has remained open ever since.[1] In Britain, the *Employment Policy White Paper* bound the government to the equally nebulous goal of 'maintaining a high and stable level of employment after the war'.[2] This policy declaration, like its American equivalent, emphasised that in a democratic state the government could not be expected to achieve this objective on its own. Indeed, it went further, and spelled out the results which might follow if employers and workers did not collaborate with it:

If we are to operate with success a policy for maintaining a high and stable level of employment, it will be essential that employers and workers should exercise moderation in wage matters. The principle does mean ...that increases in the general level of wage rates must be related to increased productivity due to increased efficiency and effort...The stability of these two elements (namely, wages and prices) is a condition vital to the success of employment policy; and that condition can be realised only by the joint efforts of the Government, employers and organised labour...

It would be a disaster if the intention of the Government to maintain total expenditure (and thereby full employment) were interpreted as exonerating the citizen from the duty of fending for himself and resulted in a weakening of personal enterprise. For if an expansion of total expenditure were applied to any unemployment of a type due, not to absence of jobs, but to failure of workers to move to places and occupations where they were needed, the policy of the Government would be frustrated and a dangerous rise in prices might follow.[3]

It was, indeed, this caveat rather than the primary objective of reaching full employment which dominated policy making for seven years or so after the war. Budgets, in both countries, continued to follow the wartime principle of 'closing the inflationary gap', that is, reducing aggregate demand in each year by as much as was expected to be necessary to keep the rate of price rise down to a manageable level.[4] In pursuing this objective both governments were assisted by a number of direct controls on prices, rents and individual purchases. Moreover, when the world's first postwar recession developed, in the United States in 1949, there was little discretionary fiscal action of any sort. 'It is essential to sound fiscal policy to have a *budget surplus* now' declared President Truman in his annual economic report; 'this is our most effective weapon against inflation'.[5] When in 1951 inflationary pressure reappeared throughout the world as a result of the Korean war, this predominantly defensive view of macro-economic policy was strengthened, and large increases in tax rates were implemented in both countries.[6] Throughout this period monetary policy remained accommodating: the Federal Reserve and the Bank of England confined their open-market operations to augmenting the quantity of money by as much as might be necessary to keep interest rates stable. Central bank lending rates did not rise above 2 per cent before 1952.[7]

It is in 1953–4 that we see for the first time a budgetary policy that can properly be described as Keynesian. This is the more surprising because both Britain and the United States had recently passed under the control of conservative administrations, many of whose legislators were profoundly sceptical of the principle that deficit financing was the appropriate response to recession.[8] But when the British economy passed into mild recession in 1952–3, followed by the American in 1954, the political logic in favour of an expansionary budget was irresistible. Winston Churchill in 1951, and Eisenhower in 1952, had been elected into power promising to end the austerity associated with post-war control.[9] Both remembered the catastrophic depression of 1920–1 after the post-First World War boom had run its course, and neither could afford to be seen presiding over a depression of living standards to levels lower than those achieved by those whom they had ousted from office.[10] The consequence, which must be accounted a pioneering step in the history of economic policy-making, was the British budget of 1953 (which reduced purchase tax by a sixth, removed sixpence from the basic rate of income tax and restored 'initial' allowances on the purchase of industrial equipment by businessmen)[11] and the American budget of 1954, which cut the rate of personal and corporate income tax.[12]

For the rest of the 1950s economic policy in both countries now followed the pattern popularly known as 'stop-go'. If the growth in the economy which resulted from a budgetary stimulus of this sort sucked in imports at a faster rate than exports were growing, as occurred in Britain in 1956/57 and in both countries in 1960, there ensued a 'balance of payments crisis': any persistent balance of payments deficit meant an outflow of gold and foreign currency reserves, which in the last analysis, within the regime of fixed exchange rates which prevailed at that time, could only be stopped by devaluing the currency or deflating the economy. Since governments themselves represented any devaluation of the currency as a national humiliation, their only escape route was to deflate, as was done in the years mentioned.[13] But this in due course led to levels of unemployment which, especially in a general or presidential election year (such as 1959 in Great Britain, or 1962 in the United States), could not be reconciled with the government's legal obligation to ensure 'high and stable' or 'maximum' levels of employment. The inevitable consequence was the large discretionary reflations which occurred in those years.

Many people perceived that it was unsatisfactory to go around in circles in this way, but their diagnosis was almost always that the cycle occurred because governments intervened *too clumsily and too late,* rather than because they intervened at all. Dow's judgement on British macroeconomic policy of the fifties, made in 1964, was that

> The rapid expansion of demand and output in the years 1952–5, and that in 1958 too, were both due, directly and indirectly, to the influence of policy...This was not the intended effect; in each phase, it must be supposed, policy went further than intended, as in turn did the correction of these effects. Had tax changes been more gradual, and credit regulations less variable, demand and output would probably have grown much more steadily.[14]

whereas Okun's description of American policy during the same period was that:

> the use of the federal budget for stabilisation followed a fire-fighting strategy. Deliberate stimulus or restraint through budget deficits was applied only when the alarm sounded. At other times the orthodox rule of balancing the budget seemed to dominate. The basic strategy was to stick with orthodox principles unless the fire alarm of recession tolled loud and clear.[15]

The clear implication of such judgements was that policy should in future respond more quickly, and if possible automatically, to the threat of crisis, rather than reacting violently to it once it had materialised. The early 1960s saw the introduction in both Britain and the United States of America of 'regulators' designed to give the Chancellor of the Exchequer in the one case, and the President in the other, power to act quickly in anticipation of economic crisis. The former was given power to vary all the main indirect taxes up or down by up to 10 per cent at any time, and to impose a payroll tax on employers of up to four shillings per employee per week.[16] The US President passed a bill in 1962 which gave him authority to grant temporary income tax reductions and increases in capital expenditures as a 'defence-in-depth against future recessions'.[17]

In Britain this attempt to escape from the stop-go cycle had little success. The combined influence of discretionary and automatic stabilisers was unable to prevent the recession of 1962/63 or the more serious slump of 1970/71. Nor was it able to prevent balance-of-payments crises developing in 1964, 1966 and 1973 in response to the very measures which it had instituted to ease those slumps. Budgetary policy remained, as in the 1950s, a matter of responding *ex post*, when it was thought necessary, either to a balance of payments crisis by taking money out of the economy, or to an excessive level of unemployment by putting money into it. Monetary policy remained, as in the 1950s, a matter of not obstructing the intended effect of budgetary policy. If the tendency of budgetary policy was to reduce demand, the Bank of England stepped in to prevent any tendency for interest rates to fall by energetic sales of government debt and often other measures as well, such as instructions to banks to restrain their lending, a tightening of hire purchase controls and so forth. Expansionary budgets such as that of 1971 were accompanied by central bank purchases of government debt and removal of direct controls to prevent interest rates rising. The British government in the 1960s was in effect operating through a number of policy instruments on only one intermediate variable – the level of aggregate demand – and hoping by this means to influence several final targets: the balance of payments if that was in crisis, unemployment if that was in trouble, and growth if neither of them was. It got away with this strategy because, until 1974, no two of its ultimate targets were ever in crisis at the same time.[18]

In the United States the administration was far more successful in preventing recession during the 1960s. Its strategy was quite explicit – to use the federal budget of each year to push up demand towards the level of output which would be consistent with a national unemployment level of 4 per cent – this being the Council of Economic Advisers' interpretation of the phrase 'maximum employment' in the Employment Act.[19] This involved them in tax-cutting measures, as in 1964–5, when output was already rising quite fast, and only mild deflationary measures, as in 1968, in face of quite serious balance of payments deficits. From time to time, as in 1966, the Federal Reserve let the level of interest rates rise in opposition to the trend of fiscal policy and in opposition to the President's own wishes:[20] a form of public disagreement over policy that never occurred in Britain. But this did not stop output from rising almost continuously throughout the decade.[21] The prevailing climate of opinion amongst economic policy advisers in the US at the end of the 1970s was optimistic and self-congratulatory,[22] as the quotation at the head of this chapter illustrates. It was felt that macro-economics had become a science which could be applied with some precision to control economic welfare. The trend of inflation during the 1960s was, throughout the world, upwards at an accelerating rate, but although this evoked concern it did not cause policy-makers to deflate the economy unless its consequences manifested themselves – as for example they did in Britain in 1966 – in a balance-of-payments deficit. Rather, it was hoped to restrain inflation by means of some sort of voluntary incomes policy. In the United States, the Council of Economic Advisers established 'guideposts' in 1962 – that is, target figures for the rate of increase of money wages in each economic sector that 'would be consistent with general price stability and an efficient allocation of resources'.[23] The guideposts were voluntary. As late as 1971 the Council was insisting that mandatory wage-price controls were 'undesirable, unnecessary and probably unworkable'[24] but the following August the government was implementing them, in the shape of a legal limit of 5½ per cent on wage increases. In Britain, there were brief statutory freezes on wages and prices in 1961, 1966 and 1972; the first two were additional 'shock elements' in a deflationary package, and the third was an attempt, unsuccessful as it turned out, to prevent a planned government expansion of demand from spilling over into inflation and thence into balance of payments deficit. The second of these periods of statutory restraint was surrounded by a much longer period of voluntary restraint from October 1965 to January 1970, during which wage claims were vetted by a committee of the Trades Union Congress. The intention of all these episodes of incomes policy was to 'try and move the Phillips curve inward',[25] that is, to try and reduce the rate of inflation corresponding to a given state of excess demand in the labour market. These attempts to achieve 'stability of wages and prices...through the joint efforts of government employers and organised labour',[26] which the 1944 White Paper had identified as a precondition for the viability of a Keynesian high-employment strategy, were however regarded with impatience by most representatives of both employers and organised labour, and subsequent econometric studies were to demonstrate that what little progress incomes policies had made towards restraining inflation during the time that they were in force, was generally undone when the controls came off.[27]

4.2 The model to be tested

It will be apparent from this discussion that there was some variation during the period 1945–73 in the emphasis placed on different targets and instruments of policy. It would, however, be a reasonable generalisation that the conduct of economic policy between those years was governed by the following ground-rules.

(1) It was government's responsibility to keep the economy as close as practicable to full employment. This could be done by discretionary fiscal injections of aggregate demand into the system whenever unemployment became unacceptably high.

(2) Temporary balance of payments deficits could be ignored, but in the event of a *sustained* balance of payments deficit, or sustained inflation (whichever appeared first),[28] it would however be necessary to send this process into reverse, and reduce aggregate demand.

(3) The role of monetary policy was to accommodate such discretionary adjustments, in the sense of working

for an increase in interest rates when fiscal policy was deflationary and working for a cut when fiscal policy was aiming to stimulate employment.

(4) A voluntary incomes policy was government's best hope of restraining the general level of inflation and causing such deflationary action as was necessary to fall relatively more on prices and relatively less on jobs.

For reasons exhaustively discussed in Chapters 1 and 3, we interpret the attempts of governments to satisfy these ground-rules as a particular case of *satisficing behaviour*. Specifically, we shall test the hypothesis that the behaviour of the policy authorities in relation to specific instruments can be modelled by means of the following relationship, first set out at the end of the previous chapter. If x_i is any instrument, k is an empirically determined lag, y_i is any target, and y^*_i is its desired value, then

$$\left.\begin{array}{l}\Delta x_{i(t)} = \alpha + \beta\,(y_i - y^*_i)_{t-k} \text{ when } y_i > y^*_i{}^{29} \\ \quad\text{(i.e. } y_i \text{ has not been brought down} \\ \quad\text{to its satisfactory level)}^{30}\end{array}\right\} \quad \textit{Equation 3.1}$$

$$\Delta x_i = 0 \text{ at other times (i.e. } y_i < y^*_i)$$

$$y^*_{i(t)} = \text{moving average of } y_i \text{ at time } t. \qquad \textit{Equation 3.2}$$

Our task now is to identify the targets and instruments in relation to which this hypothesis should be tested. The assumption with which we shall work is that in Britain, the major targets of policy were unemployment and the balance of payments. The evidence for this statement is contained partly in the preceding discussion and partly in Figure 4.1. This diagram shows movements in the major variables which might possibly be targets for macro-economic policy – balance of payments, unemployment, changes in reserves, growth of gross national product and inflation[31] – and on it are superimposed the major 'deflationary' and 'reflationary' changes in policy instruments, as derived from Table 4.2. The major reflationary changes in policy – 1952, 1958, 1962 and 1971 – all occurred when unemployment had just risen to a postwar record level; they are also correlated with troughs in the growth rate of GNP, but not so closely. The major deflationary changes in policy – in 1951, 1956, 1965 and 1968 – are lagged on troughs in the balance of payments; they are also correlated with movements in reserves[32] and in the rate of retail price inflation,[33] but not so closely. We therefore conclude that the major targets at which policy was aimed in Great Britain during this period were unemployment and the balance of payments.

In the United States of America the response pattern was slightly different. The reflations of 1949, 1953, 1962 and 1971 are more closely related to unemployment than to any other variable, but the reflation of 1966–7 cannot be interpreted in terms of short-term stabilisation policy.[34] The deflations of 1948, 1951, 1958, 1966 and 1969 are more clearly related to recent rises in price inflation than any other variable, but that of 1958/59, untypically, seems to be a response to a balance of payments deficit.[35] Other balance of payments deficits, however, notably that of 1972, were simply overridden and accompanied by reflationary policy. It seems most reasonable to interpret US macro-economic policy, to the extent that it is a short-term response, as being a response to unemployment and the rate of price inflation.

The main instrument variables which we shall consider are fiscal policy, monetary policy, and in the next section, direct controls on the growth of wages and prices. Monetary policy is straightforward; we represent this by means of the central bank's discount rate in both Britain and the US. Budgetary policy is more of a problem. In Britain we have statistics of both public investment – which was to some degree, though a limited one,[36] used as an instrument throughout the postwar period – and the expected yield in a 'full year' of each budget's tax changes.[37] In the United States the latter figure is not available, and we choose instead to represent the impact of fiscal policy by means of the 'full employment budget surplus', that is, the level the budget surplus for a given year would assume at a standardised high level of economic activity. This concept has been criticised as a measure of fiscal stance[38] – also, of course, it is a measure of out-turn rather than of intention, since the executive cannot forecast the level of the budget deficit with accuracy.[39] However, it is probably the best measure we have.

The final thing which we need to resolve before proceeding

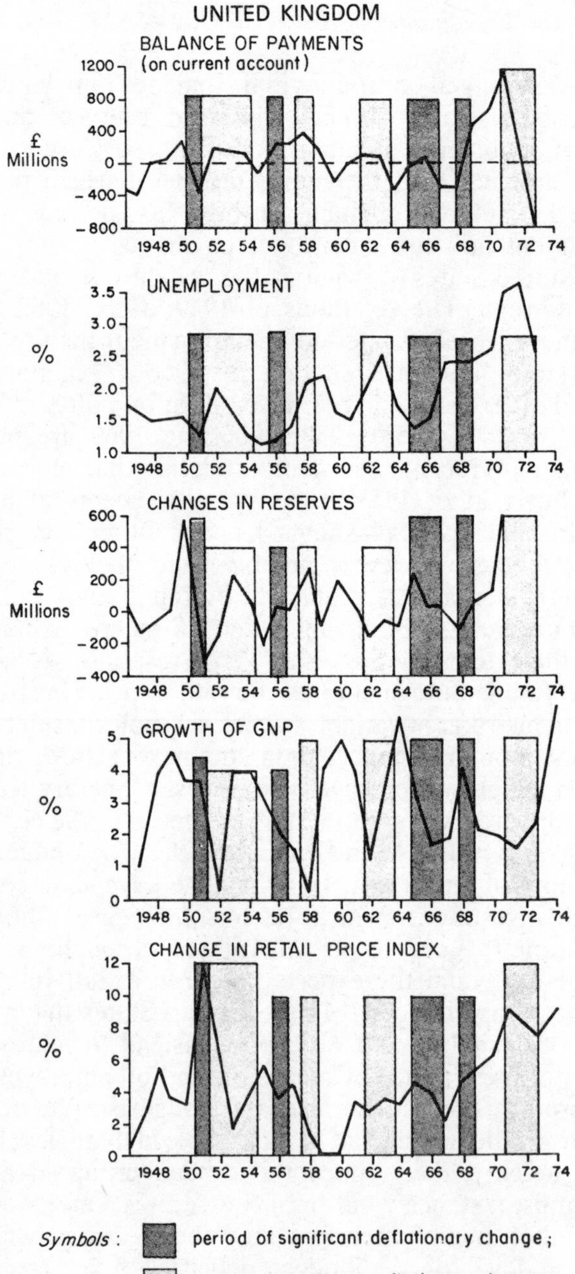

Figure 4.1 United States and Great Britain, 1948–73. Movements of possible targets of economic policy, with significant changes in policy instruments superimposed. For definition of 'significant' see Table 4.2 below.

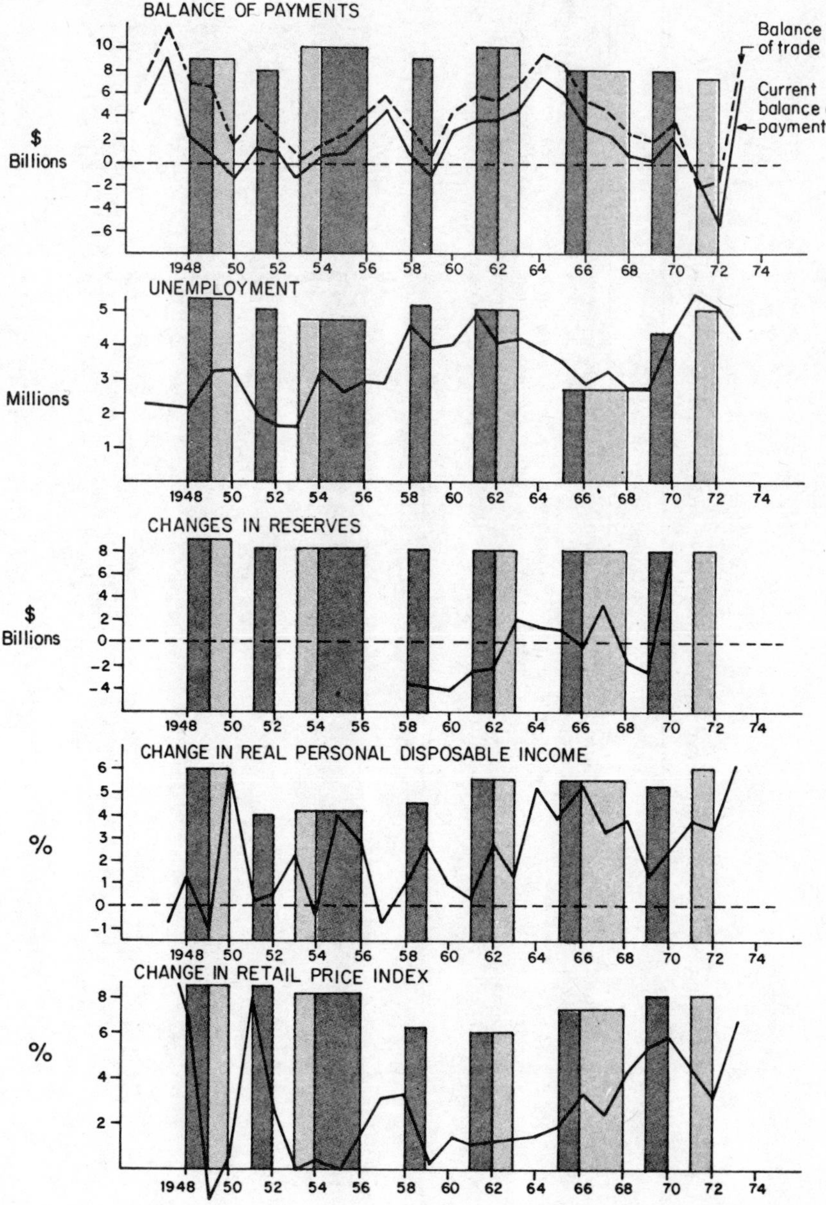

UNITED STATES OF AMERICA
BALANCE OF PAYMENTS
Balance of trade
Current balance of payments
$ Billions
UNEMPLOYMENT
Millions
CHANGES IN RESERVES
$ Billions
CHANGE IN REAL PERSONAL DISPOSABLE INCOME
%
CHANGE IN RETAIL PRICE INDEX
%

TABLE 4.1. Movements in possible targets of economic policy, 1946–73 (as measured at the time)

	United Kingdom						United States of America				
	Unemployment[1] (percentage)	*Change in reserves of gold and foreign currencies*	*Growth rate of: GDP*	*Growth rate of: Real personal disposable income*	*Current balance of payments (£m)*	*Change in retail price index[3] (%)*	*Unemployment (thousands)*	*Change in reserves of gold and foreign currencies*	*Growth rate of real per capita personal disposable income (%)[2]*	*Current balance of payments ($billion)*	*Change in consumer price index[3] (%)*
1946	1.8	54			−300	0.2	2272		..	7.8	..
1947	1.6	−154	1		−450	2.4	2141		4.9	11.6	14.3
1948	1.5	−55	3.5		—	5.9	2063		1.5	6.5	7.7
1949	1.5	−3	4.5		50	3.3	3088		−1.2	6.2	−1.4
1950	1.5	575	3.5		300	3.0	3941		5.8	1.9	0.9
1951	1.2	−344	3.5		−425	11.8	1878		0.1	3.8	8.2
1952	2.0	−175	..		170	6.7	1672		0.5	2.3	3.1
1953	1.6	240	4		151	1.4	1522		2.4	0.5	0
1954	1.3	87	4		121	3.4	3230		−0.3	1.9	0.3
1955	1.1	−229	3		−157	5.9	2653		4.1	2.1	−0.3
1956	1.2	42	2	3.2	209	3.3	2995		2.9	4.1	1.5
1957	1.4	13	1.5	—	216	4.4	2934		−0.8	5.9	3.3
1958	2.1	284	—	1.2	345	1.5	4681	−3529	0.8	2.3	3.4
1959	2.2	−119	4	5.4	153	—	3812	−3743	2.9	0.3	0.2
1960	1.6	177	5	4.8	−258	—	4017	−3881	1.1	4.1	1.5

1961	1.5	31	3.8	3.2	−1	3.4	4805	−2370	0.3	5.6	1.1
1962	2.0	−183	1.2	−0.5	115	2.7	4009	−2186	3.0	5.1	1.2
1963	2.5	−53	3.5	4.0	113	3.6	4147	2011	1.3	5.9	1.2
1964	1.7	−122	5.7	3.1	−382	3.1	3867	1564	5.3	8.5	1.4
1965	1.4	246	3.3	1.8	−49	4.7	3443	1289	3.9	7.1	1.8
1966	1.5	34	1.7	1.7	84	4.0	2864	−266	5.4	5.1	3.3
1967	2.4	16	1.8	0.9	−315	2.5	2982	3418	3.2	5.1	2.3
1968	2.4	−114	4.1	0.9	−271	4.8	2806	−1641	3.7	2.4	4.1
1969	2.4	44	2.1	0.9	443	5.4	2841	−2708	1.4	1.9	5.3
1970	2.6	125	2.0	3.7	681	6.3	4143	9839	2.5	3.5	5.8
1971	3.6	1348	1.5	1.3	1040	9.3	5001	29765	3.9	−2.7	4.3
1972	3.7	−936	2.3	8.5	162	7.1	4042	10297	3.4	−1.6	3.3
1973	2.6	3755	6.9	6.6	−1088	9.2	4302	5744	6.2	9.8	6.3

Notes:

1 Unemployment is not seasonally adjusted.

2 The measure given is the percentage change in average personal disposable income per head for a given year over the average level for the previous year in 1975 prices (UK) and 1958 prices (US).

3 The price index given is General index of retail prices, all items (UK) and consumers' price index (US).

Sources All United Kingdom statistics are taken from *current* issues of *Economic Trends* and all the United States statistics are taken from *current* issues of *Economic Report of the President and Annual Report of the Council of Economic Advisers*. Note that the figures displayed here are not the best estimates of the target variables available at the present time (winter 1983–4) but the best estimates available at the time when policies were made to respond to the values of these target variables. For a discussion of variation over time in governmental estimates of the variables displayed here, see Appendix V below.

TABLE 4.2. United Kingdom and United States: Main Acts of Economic Policy, 1946–73

	United Kingdom: Fiscal		United Kingdom: Monetary						United States of America: Fiscal		United States of America: Monetary	United States of America: Other	
	Budget change in taxes (£m)	Change in public invest-ment (£m)	Bank rate %	Change in hire purchase controls	Other	Incomes Policy*	Changes in external policy	Stance of policy (see notes below)	Full-employment budget surplus ($ billion) Level	Change	Federal discount rate (%)		Stance of policy (see notes below)
1946	−525*	. .	2						4.2		1		
1947	(50 Apr) (200 Oct)	. .	2			On			1.6	−2.6*	1		
1948	50	. .	2						8.3	6.7*	1 – 1½*		–
1949	−100	105*	2		'severe restraint'		Devalu-ation		−1.7	−10*	1½ – 1¾		+
1950	–	56	2						−0.5	1.2	1¾ – 1½		–
1951	375*	31	2 – 2½*		R			–	2.2	2.7*	1½ – 1¾		–
1952	−75	74	2½ – 4*	On				+	−1.6	−1.8	1¾		
1953	−400*	137*	4 – 3½*					+	−6.2	−4.6*	1¾		+
1954	–	6	3½ – 3*	Off				+	−1.1	5.1*	1¾ – 2		–
1955	(−150 Apr) (100 Oct)	−52	3 = 4½*	On	R				−0.7	0.4	1¾ – 1½		–
1956	–	6	4½ – 5½*	Tightened		On			5.5	6.2*	1½ – 2½*		–
1957	−125	54	5½ – 7*					–	6.6	1.1	2½ – 3		–
1958	−100	−29	7 – 4*	Off	R			+	8.9	2.3	3 – 3½ – 3		
1959	−350*	89	4						−2.7	−11.2*	3 – 4*		
1960	75	16	4 – 6	On					10.2	12.9*	4 – 3*		
1961	58 (budget) 196 (reg.)	116*	5 – 6	Loosened		Freeze July 61-Mar 62			13.1	2.9*	3		–
1962	10 (Apr) −130 (Oct)*	29	6 – 4½*					+	6.6	−6.5*	3		+
1963	−406*	71	4½ – 4*	Loosened				+	7.4	0.9	3 – 3½		
1964	101 (Apr)* 215 (Nov)	215*	4 – 7*						4.4	−3.0*	3½ – 4*		

1965	346*	73	7 – 6*	Tightened	On			–	3.4	1.0	4 – 4½*	"guideposts" introduced for wage increases in particular sectors	
1966	298 (budget)* 175 (reg.)	138*	6 – 7*	Tightened	R	Freeze July 66-Mar 67		–	– 4.0	– 7.4*	4½		+
1967	–12	266	7 – 5½ – 8*	Loosened then tightened			Devaluation (Nov)		– 9.0	– 5*	4		+
1968	923 (budget)* 250 (reg.)	25	8 – 7*	Tightened	R				– 28.1	– 19.1*	4⅔ – 5½*		
1969	249*	86	7 – 8*						0.8	27.3*	5½ – 6*		–
1970	– 202 (Mar)* – 440 (Oct)	150*	8 – 7*					+	1.9	1.1	6 – 5½*		*
1971	– 701 (Mar)* – 235 (Jul)	206*	7 – 6	Off	Removal of bank lending restrictions		Pound floated	+	– 7.1	– 8.2	4¾ – 5 – 4⅔	Mandatory limits introduced on pay increases	+
1972	– 1819*	164	6 – 9*		On				– 8	– 0.9	4½		
1973	– 462*	931*	9 – 7½ – 13						– 12.2	– 4.2	5½ – 7½*		

Notes:
Quantifiable changes in economic policy are starred * if they are 'significant'. This is an arbitrary term meaning: a change in central bank discount rate of ½% or more in a year (in both UK and US); a change in the full-employment budget surplus of $2 billion or more (in US); a budget change in taxes of £100 million or more (in UK); and a change in public investment of £100 million or more (in UK). If one or more instruments of policy are 'significantly' altered in a reflationary direction in a given year, the symbol + is entered under 'Stance of policy' (N.B. in U.K. budget tax changes and public investment changes count as *one* instrument between them) *provided that* no other instrument is at the same time altered in the opposite direction. If one or more instruments of policy are significantly altered in a deflationary direction, the symbol – is entered under 'Stance of policy' again provided that no other instrument is significantly altered in the opposite direction.

Sources: United Kingdom
Budget change in taxes : United Kingdom, *Financial Statement and Budget Report,* annual.
: The figure given in column 1 is the expected yield in a "full year" of tax changes as given by the Chancellor of the Exchequer in this *Report.*

All other data : From successive annual issues of the *National Institute Economic Review.*

United States of America : From successive annual issues of the *Economic Report of the President and Annual Report of the Council of Economic Advisers.*

to an empirical test is what meaning to attach to the concept of '"satisfactory" values of target variables' (y^*, in the notation of equation 3.1). This would be easy if governments were in the habit of spelling out in public what was a 'satisfactory' level of unemployment, inflation or the balance of payments. But the British government never did this during the period under examination, and the US President relatively seldom.[40] In the absence of words, we need to look to governments' actions. The one thing that they unequivocally demonstrate is that the levels of unemployment and balance of payments to which government responded in terms of 'significant' policy action increased steadily over time after the postwar period of disinflation was over (see Table 4.3(a) and (b)).

We interpret this as meaning that in both countries, the government's idea of what constituted 'satisfactory' economic performance gradually slipped as the economy's performance slipped. This is consistent with the basic 'satisficing' principle that aspiration levels adjust progressively over

TABLE 4.3(a) Postwar recessions: level to which unemployment rose before 'significant' reflationary action began

Great Britain	1953	1959	1963	1971
	1.6%	2.2%	2.5%	3.6%
United States	1953	1962	1966	1971
	1.9%	5.2%	3.0%	6.5%

Source Figure 4.1

TABLE 4.3(b) Postwar booms: level to which target variable rose before 'significant' deflationary action began

Great Britain: Balance of payments deficit in previous year (£·million)

1951	1956	1965	1974
−425	−157	−382	−1088

United States: inflation rate

1951	1954	1958	1961	1965	1969
8.2%	0.3%	3.4%	1.1%	1.8%	5.3%

Source Figure 4.1.

time to discrepancies between achievement and aspiration.[41] In this spirit we model the 'satisfactory' level of a target variable in any quarter as the average value of that target over the previous three years, or twelve quarters.[42] If the target variable rides above its 'satisfactory' value for only one or two quarters, we shall assume that the authorities treat the problem as temporary and take no discretionary action.[43] But if the target variable remains above its 'satisfactory' level for three quarters or more, we shall interpret this as provoking a 'crisis' in the policy authorities' minds. According to our theory, such 'crises' will stimulate macro-economic policy action of the appropriate kind for as long as the target variable remains above its satisfactory level. At other times, when there is 'no crisis', the theory will predict no macro-economic action of any sort. In other words we shall expect, if the theory is correct, to see a statistically significant relationship between targets and instruments when the targets are at 'unsatisfactory' levels and no significant response of targets to instruments when the targets are at 'satisfactory' levels.

What we actually observe is set out in Tables 4.4 and 4.5. These tables concern themselves only with those instruments which are continuously variable, namely budget tax changes, public investment, and interest rates; controls such as hire purchase restrictions and incomes policy, which can only be imposed in 'on-off' fashion, are discussed in Section 4.3 below.

In Great Britain we find that in five out of six cases the response of instruments to targets is significant and of the expected sign during 'crisis periods' as defined above, and not during 'non-crisis periods', consistently with the predictions of satisficing theory. Bank rate and budget tax changes[44] always behave as expected, although in the latter case they exhibit a *lagged* response to balance of payments crises, and the statistical relationship between budgetary changes and the current value of the balance of payments is insignificant and perverse.[45] Public investment changes behave as expected in response to the balance of payments, but 'perversely' in response to unemployment: it appears that more discretionary increases in public investment were

TABLE 4.4(a) Great Britain: empirical results for 'satisficing' equation (3.1), 1946–73

(1). Independent variable: unemployment percentage, measured U – U*,+

Equation no.	*Dependent variable*	*Period*	*Constant*	*Regression coefficient*	*Correlation coefficient*	*Student's T statistic for regression coefficient*
	Budget tax changes (£m)					
1.1		Whole period	– 24	– 0.39	0.33	3.71**
1.2		Crisis periods§	– 27	– 0.39	0.33	3.06**
1.3		Non-crisis periods§	– 22	– 0.42	0.15	0.87
	Public investment changes (£m)					
1.4		Whole period	24	– 0.026	0.07	0.76
1.5		Crisis periods§	19	0.05	0.16	0.95
1.6		Non-crisis periods§	13	– 0.18	0.25	2.27*
	Bank rate (%)					
1.7		Whole period	0.094	– 0.0011	0.25	2.71**
1.8		Crisis periods§	– 0.16	– 0.026	0.32	3.01**
1.9		Non-crisis periods§	0.03	– 0.036	0.05	0.28

Notes

* Significant at 5% level.

** Significant at 1% level.

+ U = actual value of unemployment at any time;
U* = desired value of unemployment at any time, interpreted as the average value of unemployment over the previous twelve quarters; see p. 103.

§ Crisis periods = the quarters 1952 I to 1953 I; 1958 I to 1959 II; 1962 I to 1963 IV; 1967 I to 1969 I; 1971 I to 1972 IV, that is, those for which unemployment was – and remained for three quarters or more – greater than its desired value. 34 observations.
Non-crisis periods = all other quarters during the period 1946 I to 1973 IV. 78 observations.

Sources See Tables 4.1 and 4.2.

TABLE 4.4(b) Great Britain: empirical results for 'satisficing' equation (3.1), 1946–73

(2). Indepedent variable: balance of payments, measured B – B*, +

Equation no.	*Dependent variable*	*Period*	*Constant*	*Regression coefficient*	*Correlation coefficient*	*Student's T statistic for regression coefficient*
	Budget tax changes (£m) (4 quarter lag)					
1.10		Whole period	– 23	– 0.12	0.06	0.59
1.11		Crisis periods§	– 36	– 0.41	0.25	2.22*
1.12		Non-crisis periods§	– 13	– 0.35	0.11	0.65
	Public investment changes (£m)					
1.13		Whole period	23	– 0.13	0.51	6.26**
1.14		Crisis periods§	– 9	– 0.29	0.72	6.08**
1.15		Non-crisis periods§	14	0.07	0.36	2.46*
	Change in bank rate (%)					
1.16		Whole period	0.072	– 0.002	0.57	7.32**
1.17		Crisis periods§	– 0.0043	– 0.003	0.61	4.43**
1.18		Non-crisis periods§	– 0.61	– 0.00043	0.01	0.095

Notes

* Significant at 5% level.

** Significant at 1% level.

+ B = actual value of the current balance of payments at any time; B* = desired value of the balance of payments at that time, interpreted as the average value of unemployment over the previous twelve quarters; see p. 103.

§ Crisis periods = the quarters 1947 I to 1947 IV; 1951 I to 1951 IV; 1955 I to 1955 IV; 1960 I to 1960 IV; 1964 I to 1965 I; 1966 I to 1966 III; 1967 II to 1968 II; 1972 I to 1973 IV; that is, those for which the balance of payments was – and remained for three quarters or more – less than its desired value. 36 observations. Non-crisis periods = all other quarters during the period 1946 I to 1973 IV. 76 observations.

Sources See Tables 4.1 and 4.2.

TABLE 4.5(a) United States: empirical results for 'satisficing' equation (3.1), 1946–73

(1) Independent variable: unemployment percentage, measured U – U⁺

Equation no.	*Dependent variable*	*Period*	*Constant*	*Regression coefficient*	*Correlation coefficient*	*Student's T statistic for regression coefficient*
	Change in full employment budget surplus ($ billion)					
1.19		Whole period	−0.21	0.0008	0.04	0.41
1.20		Crisis periods§	0.20	−0.0011	0.24	2.22*
1.21		Non-crisis periods§	0.31	−0.0044	0.17	1.03
	Change in federal discount rate (%)					
1.22		Whole period	0.075	−0.00091	0.28	3.08**
1.23		Crisis periods§	0.17	−0.00017	0.41	2.64**
1.24		Non-crisis periods§	0.12	−0.00037	0.06	0.50

Notes

* Significant at 5% level. ** Significant at 1% level.

\+ U = actual value of unemployment at any time; U* = desired value of unemployment at that time, as measured by the average value of unemployment over the preceding twelve quarters; see p. 103.

§ Crisis periods = the quarters 1947 I to 1950 II; 1954 I to 1955 II; 1958 I to 1959 IV; 1960 II to 1961 III; 1970 II to 1972 IV; that is, those periods for which unemployment was greater than its 'desired value'. 39 observations. Non-crisis periods = all other quarters during the period 1946 I to 1973 IV. 73 observations.

Sources See Tables 4.1 and 4.2.

TABLE 4.5(b) United States: empirical results for 'satisficing' equation, (3.1), 1946–73

(2) Independent variable: inflation rate, measured $\dot{p} - \dot{p}^*$.⁺

Equation no.	*Dependent variable*	*Period*	*Constant*	*Regression coefficient*	*Correlation coefficient*	*Student's T statistic for regression coefficient*
	Change in full employment budget surplus ($ billion)					
1.25		Whole period	−0.24	0.096	0.19	2.02*
1.26		Crisis periods§	1.01	−0.06	0.10	0.49
1.27		Non-crisis periods§	−0.41	0.019	0.68	0.79
	Change in federal discount rate (%)					
1.28		Whole period	0.059	−0.0029	0.038	−0.41
1.29		Crisis periods§	0.15	−0.018	0.17	−0.86
1.30		Non-crisis periods§	0.056	0.00038	0.002	0.035

Notes

* Significant at 5% level. ** Significant at 1% level.

\+ $\dot{p}$ = actual value of annual increase in consumer prices at any time; $\dot{p}^*$ = 'desired' value of annual increase in consumer prices at that time, as measured by the average value of consumer price inflation as measured over the preceding twelve quarters; see p. 103.

§ Crisis periods = the quarters 1946 I to 1947 IV; 1951 I to 1951 IV; 1956 I to 1958 II; 1969 II to 1970 I; 1973 I to 1973 IV; that is, those periods for which unemployment was greater than its 'desired value'. 27 observations. Non-crisis periods = all other quarters during the period 1946 I to 1973 IV. 85 observations.

Sources Tables 4.1 and 4.2.

made in 'non-crisis periods', that is, times when unemployment was low in relation to recent experience, than when it was high. The data suggest that public investment was used asymmetrically in Britain as a stabilisation tool; it was often cut, or rather postponed, in times of balance of payments crisis but seldom stimulated, following the Keynesian model,[46] as a deliberate measure to relieve unemployment.

For the United States the theory explains the data reasonably well in relation to unemployment, but thoroughly badly in relation to inflation. The quarterly change in the full-employment budget surplus, poor though that is as an indicator of the administration's *intentions,*[47] and the quarterly change in the federal discount rate show a significant response of the expected sign in periods of unemployment crisis and an insignificant response in periods of no unemployment crisis. But the response of both budget surplus and federal discount rate to inflation, as we have measured it, is thoroughly insignificant inside and outside periods of 'inflation crisis'. This is only partly because we have used a poor proxy for the *ex ante* stance of budgetary policy. It is also because the administration fairly unequivocally deflated the economy (see Figure 4.1) in 1954 and 1961 when there was very little sign of an inflation or even of a balance of payments crisis. It is possible to bring forward *ad hoc* explanations for this,[48] but the harsh truth remains. In this particular field our model as at present conceived is not good enough.

I submit, however, that the overall data presented in Tables 4.4 and 4.5 suggest that the 'satisficing' model of economic policy-making shows sufficient promise to suggest that it should be improved rather than rejected. This we try to do in the next section by taking account of administrative and political considerations mentioned in Chapters 2 and 3 above, but not so far admitted into our model.

4.3 Extensions of the model: 'political' influences on policy-making

'Political' influences on policy-making

In the previous section we represented macro-economic policy-making as a simple administrative reflex: when things are 'unsatisfactory' the policy authorities do something; otherwise not. On pp. 94–95 above we argued that this was a reasonable way to model the policy-making process in the electoral mid-term: politicians do not need to worry overmuch about their party's popularity at this time, and even if they did, then as Chapter 2 demonstrated, the signals from the opinion-polls are too ambiguous and unstable to read aright. The administration[49] has full discretion to carry out the macro-economic policy it wants to carry out. In the run-up to an election it is a different matter. Politicians in the governing party begin to fight for ascendancy over the administration if it is not pursuing an 'appropriate' policy, which means – as the opinion polls make clear[50] – a temporary increase in personal disposable income. As Tufte has demonstrated, they usually win: in 19 out of 27 democracies for which evidence is available the growth of real disposable income was faster in election years than in other years.[51] That is certainly what has happened in Great Britain and the US, even if electorates these days are sufficiently wise to the idea of a 'pre-election boom' for it to be a good idea to induce that boom by stealth rather than mere tax cuts.[52]

The implication of this is that government macro-economic policy is likely to be more expansionary in election years than the simple 'administrative reaction function' (3.1) would predict, whether or not the economy is in crisis. Tables 4.6 and 4.7 demonstrate this to be the case. A 'dummy variable' representing a pre-election period[53] is added to the independent variables influencing government economic policy actions. Both in crisis and in non-crisis periods, it turns out to have a significant positive – that is, reflationary – influence on all policy instruments in the UK and on federal discount rate in the USA. Both the size and the significance of the election dummy as well as the response-coefficients are however generally greater in periods of economic crisis than at other times. In the United Kingdom, moreover, the level and significance of the response-pattern of policy instruments to the state of the economy and to election year is apparently greater when a Conservative government is in power than in years of Labour party government. We consider the implications of these findings at greater length in Chapter 7.

TABLE 4.6 Great Britain: partisanship and pre-election booms as influences on a 'satisficing' model

Equation no.	Dependent variable	Period	Constant	Regression coefficients on independent variables: Unemployment deviation from 'desired value'+	Balance of payments deviation from 'desired value'+	Election dummy++	r^2	D.W.
	Budget tax changes (£m)							
1.31		Whole period	−21	−0.45	0.13**	−4.90*	0.1313	0.3118
1.32		Crisis periods§	14	−0.61**	0.28	−8.66**	0.1801	0.3505
1.33		Non-crisis periods§	−47	−0.60**	0.077	−5.16	0.2394	0.3345
1.34		Labour administrations	59	0.15	−0.21	−5.71	0.0637	0.6252
1.35		Conservative administrations	−58	−0.67*	0.24**	28.9	0.3463	0.4864
	Public investment changes (£m)							
1.36		Whole period	18	0.071*	−0.16**	22.11**	0.3341	0.4736
1.37		Crisis periods§	10	0.11*	−0.20**	26.1*	0.3770	0.5032
1.38		Non-crisis periods§	15	0.039	−0.014	6.74	0.1483	0.3438
1.39		Labour administrations	19	0.10**	−0.017	12.9*	0.2010	0.6396
1.40		Conservative administrations	18	0.015*	−0.18**	18.4*	0.3788	0.4850
	Bank rate (%)							
1.41		Whole period	0.086	−0.00043	−0.0019**	−0.51	0.3358	1.3161
1.42		Crisis periods§	0.041	−0.00033	−0.0024**	−0.12*	0.3840	1.5822
1.43		Non-crisis periods§	0.12	−0.00071	−0.00052*	−0.097	0.1457	0.5389
1.44		Labour administrations	0.064	0.00037	0.00079	−0.023	0.0420	1.7043
1.45		Conservative administrations	0.10	−0.00045	−0.0022**	−0.14*	0.4301	1.2916

Notes

* Significant at 5% level.

** Significant at 1% level.

§ Crisis periods = the quarters 1947 I to 1947 IV; 1951 I to 1953 I; 1955 I to 1955 IV; 1958 I to 1959 II; 1960 I to 1960 IV; 1962 I to 1963 IV; 1964 I to 1965 I; 1966 I to 1969 I; 1971 I to 1973 II; that is, a fusion of the 'unemployment crisis' and 'balance of payments crisis' periods in Table 4.4 above. 62 observations. Non-crisis periods = all other periods between 1946 I and 1973 IV. 50 observations.

\+ 'Desired values' of unemployment and balance of payments are defined in Table 4.4 above.

++ 'Election dummy' takes the value 1 during the four quarters prior to an election, 0 at other times.

TABLE 4.7 United States: partisanship and pre-election booms as influences on a 'satisficing' model

Equation no.	Dependent variable	Period	Constant	Regression coefficients on independent variables: Unemployment, deviation from 'desired value'	Inflation, deviation from 'desired value'	'Election dummy'	r^2	D.W.
	Change in full-employment budget surplus ($ bn)							
1.46		Whole period	−0.30	0.00024	0.11*	0.017	0.0468	0.7124
1.47		Crisis periods§	0.078	0.00017	0.095	0.38	0.0828	0.6153
1.48		Non-crisis periods§	−0.20	0.0014*	−0.18	−0.09	0.1294	0.9749
1.49		Republican administrations	−0.16	0.0008	0.13	0.56	0.1015	1.0245
1.50		Democratic administrations	−0.46	−0.0003	0.10*	−0.38	0.0996	0.6231
	Change in federal discount rate (%)							
1.51		Whole period	0.082	−0.0001**	−0.001*	−0.006	0.0971	1.3165
1.52		Crisis periods§	0.23	−0.0002**	−0.026**	−0.13*	0.2667	1.3013
1.53		Non-crisis periods§	0.076	0.00006	−0.00029	0.095	0.0757	1.2079
1.54		Republican administrations	0.15	−0.0002*	−0.006**	−0.07	0.2465	1.6911
1.55		Democratic administrations	0.007	0.3×10^{-5}	−0.00089	0.12	0.0720	2.4379

Notes

* Significant at 5% level.

** Significant at 1% level.

§ Crisis periods = the quarters 1947 I to 1950 II; 1951 I to 1951 IV; 1954 I to 1955 II; 1956 I to 1961 III; 1969 II to 1973 IV; that is, a fusion of the 'unemployment crisis' and 'inflation crisis' periods in Table 4.5 above. 64 observations. Non-crisis periods = all other periods between 1946 I and 1973 IV. 48 observations.

\+ 'Desired values' of unemployment and inflation are defined in Table 4.5 above.

++ 'Election dummy' takes the value 1 during the quarters prior to a presidential election, 0 at other times.

Medium-term responses to crisis: 'search behaviour' among instruments

Superficially, then, it is possible to represent the behaviour of policy-makers in the post-war years in a rather mechanical way. If unemployment was at an 'unsatisfactory' level in relation to past performance the policy authorities stimulated the economy with all the instruments at their command (more violently in an election year): if inflation (or in Britain, the balance of payments) was at an unsatisfactory level in relation to past performance the policy authorities deflated the economy with all the instruments at their command (less violently in an election year). The end result was that the economy 'cannoned backwards and forwards like a billiard ball' as Jay has put it,[54] with the direction of policy being reversed every time that the economy strayed into a forbidden area. The process is graphically depicted in Figure 4.2.

Needless to say the policy authorities of the time did not see themselves as responding in such a mechanical manner. They might indeed, in the event of a crisis, *begin* their response by injecting money into the economy in inverse proportion to the perceived 'excess' or 'deficiency' of demand, as Keynes had taught;[55] but this was no more than an initial treatment of the symptoms. If the crisis persisted there was always an attempt to search for more fundamental remedies that might prevent the disease from recurring. All of this is entirely in accordance with 'satisficing' theory which sees the organisation as responding, not mechanically, but by means of a search process whose scope is graded to the severity and duration of the crisis which causes it.[56]

These more fundamental remedies were of three kinds. In the first place there were attempts to make the systems of fiscal and monetary policy serve more fundamental purposes than simply those of *ad hoc* stabilisation, such as the discretionary powers to vary income tax and federal investment spending taken out by the US President in the 1962 budget, which were designed to make fiscal policy act more quickly, and the instrument of 'selective employment tax', introduced in Britain in 1968, which was designed to direct resources from the services to the manufacturing

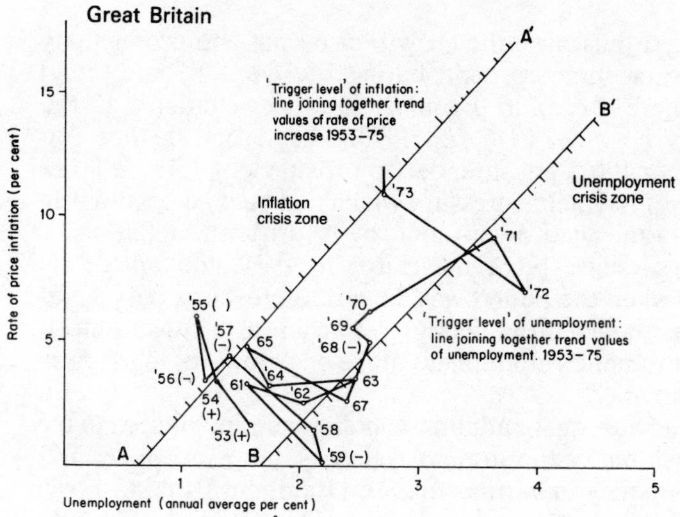

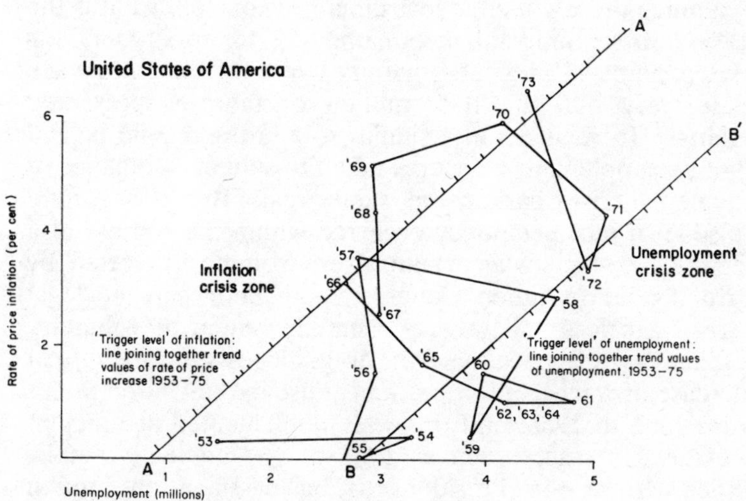

Figure 4.2 United States and Great Britain, 1953–75: observed values of unemployment and inflation with time trends on those levels (interpreted as 'trigger levels') superimposed

sector and thus raise the growth of output and productivity at the same time as contributing revenue. In the second place there were, in Britain, three devaluations of the currency between 1946 and 1973. The second of these, in November 1967, was intended to provide long-term relief to balance of payments pressure which had been intermittently present – and had been met by short-term deflationary measures – since 1963; the third, in 1971, took place by stealth, when the pound was floated to prevent a balance of payments deficit from acting, yet again, as a constraint on the government's attempts to move back towards high levels of employment.

The most frequent additional policy instrument used to try and break out of the stop-go cycle was, however, prices and incomes policy in various manifestations. In Britain, it was first adopted as an improvisation in 1961 by Harold Macmillan, to supplement the deflationary measures of the previous year. The Prime Minister thought of it as potentially a much more effective instrument of control: 'what is the use of our scraping and scrounging to get £50–£100 million of "economies"', he subsequently wrote, 'if the extra wage and salary bill of £1000 million or more is presented again?'[57] It was used in a similar role in the second half of 1966 to supplement measures taken to staunch a balance of payments crisis earlier the same year. But this second episode of incomes policy occurred within the context of a regime in which wage claims were voluntarily vetted by Britain's Trade Union Congress, and there were no legal curbs on prices and wages; a similar system of voluntary restraint by reference to norms or 'guideposts' for the rate of increase of wages and prices was in use in the United States form 1962 to 1968, and this was supplemented at times of pressure on prices such as 1967 by 'jawboning', that is, appeals from the President to businessmen and union leaders to restrain price and wage increases.[58]

In the early 1970s both Britain and America were under the control of conservative administrations opposed in principle to any interference with market forces: this included prices and incomes policy. When both administrations were forced to break with principle, in the summer of

TABLE 4.8 Great Britain: routine and non-routine responses to economic crises, 1946–73

Crisis and time of first manifestation	*Duration of crisis (quarters)*	*'Routine' response*	*Timing*	*'Non-routine' response*	*Timing*
Balance of payments, 1947 I	4	Budget tax change +£250 m	April and October 1947	Devaluation of pound	1949
Balance of payments, 1955 I	4	Tax change +£100 m Bank rate 3→4½%	October 1955	None	
Balance of payments, 1960 I	4	Tax change +£75 m Bank rate 4→6%	April 1960	Pay 'pause'	July 1961
Balance of payments/ unemployment (sequential), 1966 I	13	Tax changes +£298 m (budget) +£171 m (regulator) Bank rate 6→7%	April 1966	(1) Statutory wages freeze (2) Devaluation of £ sterling (3) attempts at industrial relations legislation	July–November 1966 November 1967 November 1969
Unemployment/ inflation (simultaneous), 1971 I	12	Tax changes −£701 m −£235 m −£1819 m	 March 1971 July 1971 March 1972	(1) Statutory incomes policy stage I: freeze stage II: '£1 + 4%' stage III: £2.25 per head or 7%, plus threshold increases (2) 'New monetary policy': (a) removal of control on bank lending (b) monetary aggregates adopted as target of monetary policy	 November 1972–March 1973 April–November 1973

TABLE 4.9 United States: routine and non-routine responses to economic crises, 1946–73

Crisis and time of first manifestation	*Duration of crisis (in quarters)*	*'Routine' response*	*Timing*	*'Non-routine' response*	*Timing*
Unemployment 1960 II	5	Cut in full employment budget surplus of $6.5 bn	Calendar 1962	(1) Granting of extraordinary Presidential powers to make temporary cuts in income tax and temporary increases in capital expenditure (2) 'Guideposts' on wages and prices	1962–3
Inflation 1966 I	4	No routine response; budget surplus cut		'Jawboning' on wages and prices	Spring 1967
Unemployment 1970 II, accompanied by crisis levels of inflation from 1973 I awards	15	Full-employment budget surplus cut $8.2 bn in 1971 $0.9 bn in 1972 $4.2 bn in 1973 Federal discount rate stable around 4½% until 1973 I, then gradually raised to 7½%		Mandatory limits introduced on wages and prices in each economic sector, within overall limit of 5½ %	15 August 1972

1972, they did so under the same stress – an inflation level climbing into double figures, with unemployment moving towards a postwar record at the same time – and in a remarkably similar manner: first a freeze, then a more flexible package in which different occupational groups could obtain differing rates of wage increase within an overall ceiling. This new way of presenting incomes policy was intended to avoid the faults of previous versions. Previous incomes policies, it appeared, had failed to restrain the growth of earnings except in the short term;[59] but nobody was satisfied with mere reduction of aggregate demand as a means of restraining inflationary tendencies in the economy as had been the case in the 1950s. So it was necessary to search for ways of modernising a policy tool whose performance had previously been unsatisfactory. The 'multi-phase' incomes policies implemented on both sides of the Atlantic from 1972 to 1974 were the consequence of this search. They represented the *coda* to a phase of economic policy-making in which the eventual response to each failure of conventional Keynesian interventions in the economy to achieve the desired result was to try and devise new and more sophisticated tools of policy.[60]

The sequence of these 'deeper-level' interventions is summarised in Tables 4.8 and 4.9. They demonstrate that as unemployment, balance of payments and inflation crises tended to become more severe over the 1960s and early 1970s the tendency was *first* to meet them by conventional fiscal and monetary methods, *then,* if the crisis persisted, to bring in the alternative tools of policy above described, each of which was introduced in a manner designed to avoid the faults apparent in its previous incarnation.

4.4 Epilogue

Sophisticated as the devices of Keynesian demand management might have become, nobody who contemplated the world economy in September 1973 – the month before the oil crisis struck it – could be happy with the way they were performing. In each successive boom since 1951 the peak level of inflation had been higher; in each successive slump since 1951 the peak level of unemployment had been higher also.[61] Not only this, but recent years had presented the unprecedented spectacle of unemployment and inflation rising simultaneously, a condition with which Keynesian techniques were – superficially – unable to cope. The economies of both Britain and America at this time – as Figure 4.2 bears witness – presented the apearance of a cow wandering back and forth between two electric fences, one of them labelled 'excessive unemployment' and the other labelled 'excessive inflation' or alternatively 'balance of payments crisis', but moving all the time towards the edge of a cliff labelled 'stagnation and hyperinflation'.

If such was indeed the position, then what was needed was not new methods for strengthening the electric fences, but rather a device which would attack the roots of the problem by bringing the cow away from the cliff-edge. The search for such a device, and its eventual implementation, occupies the whole of the next chapter.

Notes

1 United States, *Economic Report of the President and Annual Report of the Council of Economic Advisers* (1973), p. 71.
2 United Kingdom (1944), p. 1.
3 United Kingdom (1944), p. 5.
4 Dow (1964), p. 7.
5 *Economic Report of the President and Annual Report of the Council of Economic Advisers* (1949), p. 10. Author's italics.
6 See Table 4.1.
7 See Table 4.1. Dow (1964, p. 48) writes that the use of interest rates 'played no part in Sir Stafford Cripps' (Chancellor of the Exchequer (1947–50)) conception of democratic planning'. For the US see Friedman (1978), p. 12.
8 'pure hooey': Viscount Hinchingbrooke, *House of Commons Debates,* 10 April 1951, Col. 1105.
9 Winston Churchill. *House of Commons Debates,* 6 November 1951 cols. 77–80; *Economic Report of the President* (1953), pp. 1–5.
10 Also, both governments were rapidly dismantling post-war controls on prices and purchases at this time, and needed to deploy their existing budgetary instruments of policy with more flexibility if they

were to take the place of the instruments of control which had now disappeared from the scene. As early as 1948, the British government's *Economic Survey* for 1947 (para 27) had insisted on the need for macro-economic policy to carry out the kind of 'fine adjustments in the economic structure which controls cannot by themselves bring about'.

11 For more detail on these measures, see Dow (1964) pp. 75–6.

12 The 1953 *Economic Report of the President* declared (p. 14) that *full employment must be a constant objective of policy* (emphasis in original).

13 See Table 4.2. In January 1958 all three UK Treasury ministers – Peter Thorneycroft, Nigel Birch and Enoch Powell – resigned because they felt the deflationary measures had not gone far enough to balance the budget.

14 Dow (1964), p. 384.

15 Okun (1970), p. 40.

16 Dow (1964), p. 407.

17 The income tax rate could be moved up or down by 5 percentage points for a period of up to six months; capital improvements of up to \$2 billion could be authorised to terminate within 12 months. *Economic Report of the President* (1962), p. 17. This preventive rather than curative approach was known at the time as the 'new economics' (see *Annual Report of the Council of Economic Advisers* (1966), p. 44).

18 Inflation, in the state of thinking of the 1950s and 1960s, was definitely a subsidiary target of policy in Britain; see footnote 33 below.

19 *Economic Report of the President and Annual Report of the Council of Economic Advisers* (1964), p. 37.

20 Recall page 92 above.

21 Personal disposable income per head rose in 39 out of a possible 44 quarters between 1960 and 1970.

22 Okun records that in the late 1960s, 'for a brief moment even congressmen were using the word "professor" as a term of respect and approval'. (1970, p. 59).

23 *Economic Report of the President and Annual Report of the Council of Economic Advisers* (1968), p. 120. The implementation of the policy took the form of 'jawboning', or moral pressure by government officials on businessmen and trade union leaders, often involving in the latter case threats concerning the unemployment that might follow excessive wage increases. But these threats never had any legal sanction. See *Economic Report of the President and Annual Report of the Council of Economic Advisers,* (1967), p. 126.

24 *Economic Report of the President and Annual Report of the Council of Economic Advisers* (1971), p. 80.

25 See Figure 4.2.

26 United Kingdom (1944), p. 5; recall p. 88 above.

27 Lipsey and Parkin (1970) for Great Britain, and for the United States, Blinder (1979), Chapter 6.

28 The pattern of deflationary response was somewhat different in Britain and the US: see pp. 91–92 and 95.

29 This is a 'proportional control mechanism' in the terminology of Phillips (1954): the authorities react by changing their instruments when targets fall outside their 'satisfactory region', to a degree proportional to the size of the shortfall, but they keep their instruments unchanged at other times. In particular, there is no response to past levels of the error, or to the rate of change of the error, in this equation.

30 In this case of the three principal targets which we shall be considering in this chapter, that is, unemployment, inflation, and the balance of payments, this is the right way to write the inequality. In the case of targets which normally have to be pushed up to reach satisfactory levels (for example, growth of GDP) the inequality would have to be reversed.

31 The data set out in Table 4.1 and Figure 4.1 are the figures actually made available at the time, not those which are now accepted as correct estimates of the relevant macro-economic magnitudes in 1984. The idea is to set out those figures to which policy-makers actually responded, rather than those which are now believed to 'represent the truth'. Even this is not going far enough, since of course policy makers responded to a forecast of the target, not its actual value. For discussion of the consequences of using forecast values in the regression equation see Appendix III below.

32 In some years such as 1960 the balance of payments was in quite heavy deficit, but the reserves experienced a substantial increase. This no doubt owed much to 'window-dressing', for example, calling in of short-term foreign loans to offset a run on the currency.

33 In 1971, for example, price inflation rose to a record level since 1951, but there was no attempt to deflate the economy.

34 Rather, it was an attempt by President Johnson to finance the war in Vietnam without cutting back on social welfare programmes at home.

35 The words 'balance of payments' must be emphasised; deficits in America's overseas payments occurred on capital account only. The US balance of trade – see Table 4.1 – remained in surplus from 1945 until 1971.

36 Public investment is only a fairly small component of final demand by comparison with consumers' expenditure, and it is fairly difficult to change at short notice; Dow (1964), p. 221. However, public investment plans frequently were changed at short notice in response to a balance of payments crisis; for a narrative account of one empirical case, see Chapter 3, pp. 57–61 above.

37 The Chancellor of the Exchequer's *Financial Statement,* given out with each year's budget, forecasts the expected effects in both the coming financial year and a 'full year' of that budget's tax changes.

The latter differs from the former because some tax changes may not be implemented until some months after budget day.

38 A clearer picture of the budget changes that are autonomous is obtained if the inflation rate is held constant from one year to the next as well as the unemployment rate, since increases in inflation rates affect receipts much more promptly than expenditures. Also, it may make sense to hold the unemployment rate constant for particular strata of the population rather than for the population overall. The 1974 report of the Council of Economic Advisers recalculated the full-employment surplus and deficit according to these alternative assumptions.

Calendar year	*Actual surplus or deficit ($ billion)*	*Full employment surplus or deficit (−) under alternative assumptions*		
		4% unemployment	*4% unemployment, standardised inflation rate**	*Variable unemployment rate***
1969	8.1	8.8	4.0	4.9
1970	−11.9	4.0	4.0	0.3
1971	−22.1	−2.1	−1.3	−5
1972	−15.9	−7.7	−6.9	−10.4
1973	0.6	5.8	3.3	3.1
1974	−4.6	6.0	3.6	2.1

* Change in surplus or deficit between 2 succeeding years assumes that inflation rate is constant at level of first year.

** Assumes unemployment rates are constant at 1958 level in respect of four categories: males and females 16–24 and males and females 25 and over.
The overall unemployment rate rises to 4.6 per cent because the labour force is increasingly composed of groups (females, youths) having higher unemployment rates than older males.

39 See pp. 70–75 above, and for statistical detail on the level of inaccuracy, Appendix II below. As Tarschys puts the matter: 'Present deficits are not willed, They do not spring from conscious macro-economic designs but from the failings of budgetary policy.' (1982, p. 15).

40 To our knowledge, explicit numbers were only once attached to a policy target by the UK government during the period under examination, namely when the Treasury, in its submission to the Radcliffe Committee in 1959, stated that it aimed at a balance of payments surplus of £450 m. Neither for unemployment nor even for the growth of GNP were targets ever postulated; the 4% growth rate target put forward by the National Economic Development Council in 1962 was never explicitly accepted by government. The annual

Financial Statement and Budget Report never contained such targets.

In the US the position is somewhat different. The annual *Economic Report of the President* frequently names objectives and priorities. ('The first objective for 1948 must be to halt the inflationary trend', 'our immediate goal for 1950 should be to regain maximum unemployment', 'by all odds the country's main problem (in 1964) is persistent unemployment') but seldom attaches numbers to them. Exceptions are 1948 and 1952 when explicit targets for GNP were stated, 1962 when 'full employment' was defined as 4 per cent; and 1971, when the Council of Economic Advisers recommended a GNP target range of between \$1045 billion and \$1050 billion, 'which would be consistent with satisfactory progress towards the feasible targets of an unemployment rate in the 4½% zone and an inflation rate approaching the 3½% range'. (*Annual Report of the CEA* (1971), p. 78.)

41 Chapter 3 above, p. 66, and, for a fuller treatment, Appendix I below, pp. 214–218.

42 In past work (for example, Mosley, 1976) we have used a time trend over the entire period; but this was silly, as it implies that future values of a target variable have an influence on policy makers' decision about what is a satisfactory *current* value for that target! It is good to have this opportunity of setting past mistakes right.

43 This arises from difficulties in interpreting short-term movements in target variables; see Chapter 3 above, p. 66.

44 The reader will notice that when budget tax changes are the dependent variable, the correlation coefficients are generally low. One reason for this is clear. The regression exercises on which we report here use *quarterly* data. But discretionary budget tax changes are more often than not in Britain (and invariably in the USA) made only once a year. We have arbitrarily assumed in this exercise that the impact of budget tax changes is evenly spread across the four quarters. This is obviously not the case in practice, and it probably makes more sense in the case of this instrument to work with annual data. How much this improves the statistical results will be apparent if we report the results we obtained in a previous exercise for Great Britain for the years 1946 to 1971 (see Mosley, 1976):

Independent variable: unemployment (*percentage*, not absolute value as in Table 4.4)
Dependent variable: budget tax changes (£ million)

Equation	*Period*	*Constant*	*Regression coefficient*	*Correlation coefficient*	*Student's 't' statistic*
1.1	Whole period	– 27	– 494	– 0.53	3.38**
1.2	Unemployment crisis	612	– 499	– 0.90	4.32**
1.3	No unemployment crisis	– 380	262	0.41	1.63
	Independent variable: current balance of payments				
	Dependent variable: budget tax changes				
1.10	Whole period	12	– 0.7	– 0.57	4.12**
1.11	Crisis periods	134	– 1.28	– 0.54	3.23**
1.12	Non-crisis periods	– 264	– 0.49	– 0.47	2.05

Note
** Significant at 1% level.

These results tell – much more convincingly – the same story as those in Tables 4.4.

45 The measured relationship in the unlagged case (k = 0 in the notation of equation (3.1) above), is:

$$\text{budget change in taxes} = \underset{(1.80)}{-22} + \underset{(.32)}{0.27}$$

(current value of balance of payments), $r^2 = 0.0010$.
That the above relationship is lagged is already apparent from Figure 4.1 above.

46 See for example Keynes, *General Theory*, p. 378: 'I conceive that a somewhat comprehensive socialisation of investment will prove to be the only means of securing an approximation to full employment.'

47 See p. 95 above.

48 See Chapter 7 below.

49 In Great Britain, we mean by this phrase the Treasury in conjunction with the Cabinet; in the United States, we mean the President, advised by the CEA. See Chapter 3 above, pp. 45 and 66.

50 See Table 2.2 above, equation 18.

51 Tufte (1978), table 1.1 and pages 11 – 13, using data for the 1950s and 1960s.

52 Annual growth rates of personal disposable income calculated from Table 4.1 are:

	United Kingdom	United States
Election years	3.5	2.6 (presidential election years only)
Non-election years	2.6	2.0

In early election years, such as 1955 and 1959 in the UK, the strategy of a pre-election boom was sufficiently fresh for it to be engineered by means of tax cuts in the budget. Governments now fear that this kind of crude electioneering may rebound on them, and orchestrate pre-election handouts with rather more finesse, for example by timing social welfare payments so that they arrive in the month before a presidential election as in the USA in 1972 (see Tufte (1978), pp. 39–44; or by arranging for large public-sector pay awards in election year, as in the case of the 'Clegg awards' in the UK in 1979. For development of this argument, see Chapter 7 below, pp. 187–194.

53 It takes the value 1 during the four quarters prior to an election, 0 at other times.

54 Jay (1976) p. 21.

55 These initial responses are the ones depicted in Tables 4.4 to 4.7.

56 See Appendix I below, pp. 214–218 and Downs (1967), pp. 169–84.

57 H. Macmillan, *At the End of the Day, 1961–1963* (London: Macmillan, 1973), p. 36.

58 For more details of the 1967 episode see Okun (1970), p. 76.

59 Academic studies first circulated in the late sixties, for example Lipsey and Parkin (1970) suggested that the effect of incomes policy was to 'twist the Phillips curve anticlockwise', that is, to bring about lower rates of inflation at high levels of employment for the short period that the incomes policy was in force. After incomes policies were taken off there was a catching-up period during which earnings rose to the levels to which they would probably have risen if the policies had never been imposed.

60 However, the search continues, in exile; see the discussion of 'tax-based incomes policies' in Chapter 8 below, pp. 206–207.

61 Cf. Table 4.3 above.

5 Years of Experience: the 'Monetarist Experiment' and the Medium Term, 1974–82

We used to think that you could just spend your way out of a recession and increase employment by cutting taxes and boosting Government spending. I tell you in all candour: that option no longer exists. And insofar as it ever did exist, it worked by injecting inflation into the economy. And each time that happened unemployment rose. The cosy world which we were told would go on for ever, where full employment could be guaranteed by a stroke of the Chancellor's pen, is gone. JAMES CALLAGHAN, *UK Prime Minister 1976–1979, to Labour Party Conference, 29 September 1976.*

When I first went to the Exchequer in March 1974 and was told to produce a budget in three weeks, the centre of the budget was something called the Budget Judgement which was a guess of how much demand the government should put into the economy or take out. But governments are very bad at guessing this now ... The estimate I was given for the PSBR when I came into office turned out to be 4,000 million pounds too low. That was 5.6 per cent of gross domestic product in 1974, a bigger error than any fiscal change in demand ever brought about by any budget ... These genuine difficulties in managing demand led people all over the world to look for an easier way of running the railroad, and I suggest because some of them had been in the Air Force during the Second World War, they looked for an automatic pilot. They wanted to 'leave it to George'. DENIS HEALEY, *UK Chancellor of the Exchequer 1974–79, City-Association Lecture, March 1981.*

The 1970s have been an incredible decade for the US economy – years in which Murphy's Law replaced Okun's Law as the most reliable empirical regularity in macroeconomics. ALAN S. BLINDER, *Economic Policy and the Great Stagflation*, p. 25.

5.1 Summary history of the period

In 1974 the lamps went out on the pattern of policy-making which had dominated the western world for a period of thirty years. For the simple rule, 'reflate if unemployment is excessive, and deflate if the balance of payments is in crisis' was unworkable in an environment where both unemployment and the payments deficit, and for good measure inflation too, stood at postwar record levels and still rising. Such was the position in both Britain and America in 1974 as the oil price increases of that year[1] hit the economy at precisely the point when the latest and most frenetic of postwar booms was beginning to burst of its own free will. Such 'stagflation', as it soon came to be known, presented what we defined in Chapter 3 as a 'major crisis' for the government, involving not only the alteration of existing instruments but the creation of new instruments and/or targets. A new policy regime did eventually emerge. But it was not a clear-cut response to the policy dilemma of 1974. Dissatisfaction with the prevailing short-term budget-dominated pattern of economic policy-making had been brewing long before 1974, and when that discontent acquired political and intellectual weight in the crisis of 1974 it took a long period of trial (or 'search', in the terminology of previous chapters) and error, before it was translated into a positive and stable set of operating rules. When an organisation of any sort is faced with a completely new problem, rather than a routine one such as a balance of payments crisis, it has by definition no precedent to guide it in its search; and when the searchers are in addition divided concerning the principles which ought to direct the search, as became increasingly the case when the Keynesian or 'Butskellite'[2] consensus over the conduct of economic policy broke up, the transition to a new equilibrium is apt to take a long time. Arguably, it has not been attained even yet.

Throughout the 1960s economists were agreed, as we have seen, that government stabilisation policy had not exactly covered itself with glory. Most of them, as we have seen, recommended at the time that it should tighten up its act: produce better forecasting systems, respond more quickly and gently to discrepancies between forecast and desired levels of target variables, and make more use of automatic stabilisers (such as social welfare payments) and medium-term instruments (such as incomes policy). But a growing body of opinion came to insist that the system of making economic policy by 'fine-tuning' should be dismantled rather than improved. The level of uncertainty attaching to the impact of any policy instrument, on this view, was too great for any given policy measure to have an acceptable likelihood of achieving its intended effect.[3] This argument carried the implication that the Government could do more to prevent macroeconomic instability by sitting on its hands than by trying to 'steer' the economy in the conventional manner.

This view was put forward in two contrasting sets of clothes. On the one hand there was the view of the 'new Cambridge' school that since the private sector spends (within a relatively short period) nearly all it earns, it was not likely to be a source of destabilising shocks to the economy. These could therefore only come from overseas or from within Government itself; so government should abstain from its accustomed practice of trying to control personal consumption expenditure through the budget and confine itself instead to counteracting disturbances of foreign origin.[4] On the opposite hand, there was the 'monetarist' view that the key variable in determining the level of economic activity was the nominal quantity of money, and that if the rate of growth of this variable could be kept steady by the central bank, then the rate of growth of economic activity would stay stable too, and no further discretionary intervention by the state in the economy would be necessary.

All of this, of course, consisted of the mere scribblings of academic economists, who moreover were instructing the state to abdicate a part of the control over events which the Keynesian revolution had appeared to give it. It is safe to assume that these teachings would never have found their way into practical policy-making, had the policy-makers themselves not been boxed into a corner by their predicament of 1974. But in that year it became apparent as never before that the 'Phillips curve' – the negative relationship between unemployment and inflation which had appeared to offer a stable menu for policy choice for so many years – was drifting outwards; see Figure 4.2. For several years the British and American economies had presented to the onlooker the likeness of a swimmer, swimming frantically from one side of the beach (excessive inflation) to the other (excessive unemployment) but all the time drifting offshore. What was needed in this environment, clearly, was a policy to bring the victim back towards the shore. The Keynesians had tried one such policy during the 1960s – namely incomes policy – without much apparent success. The monetarists offered an alternative.

Their first and most controversial step was a value-judgement, namely that the medium-term control of inflation was the only target of policy with which macroeconomic policy need concern itself. On its own this was a questionable objective,[5] but it could be made more attractive by asserting that since each Phillips curve only held good for a given set of inflationary expectations amongst employers and workers, a long-term cut in the inflation rate would pull the Phillips curve inwards and thus *reduce unemployment as well.*[6]

Once this basic objective had been asserted, all else followed. If the rate of growth of prices had to be brought down over the medium term, then by the quantity theory of money the rate of growth of the money stock had to be brought down over the medium term. If the growth of the money stock was to come down, then government deficits – which, if met by borrowing from the banks, constituted a major element in the growth of the money stock – had to come down as well. If government deficits were to be regulated by reference to the growth of the money stock, that precluded them from being used for any other purpose, such as for example to achieve a target level of employment. And if the growth of the money stock was to serve as an intermediate target of policy, that precluded interest rates – the price at which that money stock could be borrowed – from being used as an instrument. Thus, the shift from a 'Keynesian' to a 'monetarist' paradigm for the making of economic policy involved four separable elements, as set out in Table 5.1.

TABLE 5.1 Alternative paradigms of macro-economic policy-making

Characteristic / *Scenario*	*'Keynesian'*	*'Monetarist'*
Target variable	Employment, with side conditions concerning the level of balance of payments deficit (or inflation) that can be afforded	Inflation
Time period over which targets are to be attained	Short-term (i.e., major part of objectives to be attained within one or at most two years)	Medium-term (i.e. five years or more)
Order of precedence amongst instruments	Fiscal policy determines the stance of monetary authorities	State of monetary growth in relation to target determines what the budgetary authorities are able to 'give away'
Monetary instrument	Interest rates (plus auxiliary instruments such as controls on bank lending)	Monetary aggregates

The transition from the first pattern to the second lasted throughout the decade of the seventies. We tell the story first for Britain and then for the United States.

In Britain, the first thing to change was the instrument of monetary control. The Bank of England had shifted around 1970, *sub rosa*, from using minimum lending rate as its primary instrument of policy to watching monetary aggregates.[7] In itself, this was nothing revolutionary: so long as the budgetary policy which the Treasury wished to pursue did not force the growth of the money stock outside the tolerance limits which the Bank of England had set for it, all that was involved was a change of means, without the fundamental ends of policy being altered. But this change in the Bank's operating procedures created a slipway down which more basic changes in the policy-making mechanism could be the more easily introduced.

In 1974 these followed under the stress of 'stagflation'. The Expenditure Committee of the House of Commons, having been lectured by representatives of both the 'New Cambridge School'[8] and by a leading monetarist[9] on the failure of fine-tuning methods of control, with particular reference to the delayed and excessive deflation of the economy in 1970/71 followed by a delayed and excessive reflation in 1972/73, concluded that: *'Short-term considerations tend to predominate in Treasury thinking and we are inclined to think that they predominate too much, with adverse effects on the economy'.*[10]

The Committee asserted, in particular, that there should be a target for the public sector borrowing requirement and that in managing the economy changes in the level of public expenditure should be used only as a tool of last resort.[11] Both of these points, although entirely contrary to Keynesian principles as these had previously been understood, were common ground between the New Cambridge School and most monetarists.[12] The following year the Chancellor, Denis Healey, made it clear that he had taken this message to heart, indeed that he had gone further and rejected the whole idea of year-by-year countercyclical budgeting. In his budget speech he made the following break with the principles of the previous thirty years: 'The budget judgement is conventionally seen as an estimation of the amount of demand which the government should put into the economy. For many reasons I do not propose to adopt this approach today.'[13]

Mr Healey made it clear that although unemployment was expected to rise sharply in 1975, he did not propose to stimulate demand in his budget of that year. In justifying this behaviour he referred to the excessively high public sector borrowing requirement and its expected influence on the balance of payments,[14] thus making clear the influence of the 'New Cambridge' School on his thinking. However, he did not abandon hope of incomes policy; a voluntary norm for the rate of increase of prices and incomes, to be administered by the Trades Union Congress, remained in force throughout his tenure as Chancellor, and more than once he explicitly linked the amount he could 'give away' in his budget to the amount of restraint which the TUC was able to impose on wages.[15]

Under the stress of the 1976 reserve crisis the Bank of England announced explicit monetary targets and the Treasury made it clear that the PSBR and, hence, public expenditure, would have to be cut in order to enable these targets to be more easily achieved. We have already examined, in Chapter 3 above, the process by which these cuts in expenditure were made.[16]

The transition to the 'new' methods of policy-making was now three-fourths complete, in the sense that fiscal policy was now subordinated to monetary policy and both were subordinated to long-term anti-inflation goals. But the Labour government still kept faith with the full-employment goal enunciated in the 1944 White Paper and with incomes policy as a means for achieving it.[17] All that remained to complete the transition was for the incoming Conservative government of 1979 to abandon both the target and the instrument. Sir Geoffrey Howe, the Chancellor, formally did this in his 1979 budget speech. His excuse for doing so was the claim that any government-induced change in aggregate demand would affect exclusively prices and in no way influence the long-term level of employment or real income:

> this prospect (the reduction in the public sector deficit) cannot be taken to mean that the Budget is, in the traditional language of neo-Keynesian economists, perversely contractionary. To make that claim is to argue that an alternative course of fiscal policy would produce more growth and more employment. I believe that argument to be profoundly wrong. To aim at a significantly higher PSBR – in other words, to ease the stance of fiscal policy – would serve only to fuel the fire of inflation. In the end, we should have less growth, less employment, and even higher prices'.[18]

Short-term fiscal policy was formally killed by this statement; medium-term monetary policy replaced it. In March 1980 the Treasury announced a 'medium-term financial strategy' – a set of monetary growth targets – covering, not only the following year, but the three subsequent ones as well. The targets are set out in Table 5.2.

TABLE 5.2 United States and Great Britain: 'target' and actual growth rates for money supply, 1975–82

United Kingdom					United States				
Date target announced	*Period*	*Sterling M_3[1] target range*	*Sterling M_3 out-turn*	*Error*[3]	*Date target announced*	*Period*	*M_3 target range*[2]	*M_3 out-turn*	*Error*[3]
December 1976	April 1976–April 1977	9–13	7.7	– 1.3	October 1976	1976 IV to 1977 IV	9–11½	12.2	+0.7
March 1977	April 1977–April 1978	9–13	16.0	+ 3.0	January 1977	1977 I to 1977 IV	9–11½	12.3	+0.8
April 1978	April 1978–April 1979	8–12	10.9	—	October 1977	1978 I to 1978 IV	8–10	11.2	+1.2
November 1978	October 1978–October 1979	8–12	13.3	+ 1.3	October 1978	1978 IV to 1979 IV	6–9	9.2	+0.2
June 1979	June 1979–April 1980	7–11	10.3	—					
November 1979	June 1979–October 1980	7–11	17.8	+ 6.8	October 1979	1979 IV to 1980 IV	6½–9½	10.7	+1.2
March 1980	February 1980–April 1981	7–11	22.2	+11.2	November 1980	1980 IV to 1981 IV	6½–9½	10.8	+1.3
March 1981	February 1981–April 1982	6–10	13.5	+ 3.5	November 1981	1981 IV to 1982 IV	6½–9½	10.5	1.0
March 1982	February 1982–April 1983	5–9[4]; 8–12[5]	13.4	+ 1.4	November 1982	1982 IV to 1983 IV	6½–9½	11.0	+1.5

Notes

1 'Sterling M_3' consists of notes and coin held by the public, private sector sterling sight deposits ('current accounts'), plus private and public sterling time deposits ('deposit accounts').

2 United States M_3 consists of currency plus all demand deposits on which cheques can be written plus all time deposits plus certain miscellaneous categories of liquid assets such as Eurodollar deposits and money market mutual fund shares.

3 'Error' is the difference between the out-turn and the top or bottom of the target range.

4 Target announced in March 1980.

5 Target announced in March 1982.

Sources United Kingdom, *Third Report from the Treasury and Civil Service Committee,* Session 1980–81, vol 1, page xiv, and *Financial Statement and Budget Report* for 1981 and 1982. United States, Annual issues of *Economic Report of the President and Annual Report of the Council of Economic Advisers.*

This strategy was to act as a navigational beacon to which all short-term fiscal policy adjustments would be subordinate. In the words of Denis Healey, quoted at the beginning of this chapter, British policy-makers wanted to throw the difficulties of intricate short-term calculations overboard and 'leave it to George'. But 'George', as we shall see, was himself to let them down almost from the moment of his incarnation.

In the United States, as in Britain, the shift to the 'new' methods of economic management came in two stages. In 1975, faced with the dilemma of 'stagflation', the Administration chose to set the control of inflation as its first objective, and to bring this about by gradually reducing the size of the budget deficit over several years.[19] It offered *temporary* tax cuts in 1975 and the first half of 1976, but most observes agree that they had little stimulative effect.[20] Meanwhile the Federal Reserve failed to increase the money stock during 1974 at a rate which would have offered hope of pulling the economy out of recession, and indeed lowered its ranges of tolerance for the growth of money supply during each of the four quarters of 1974. This enhanced the deflationary stance of government policy.[21] In the process, the Federal Reserve adopted explicit targets for the rate of growth of the money supply for the following year.[22] But unemployment continued to be a nominal policy objective of the Carter Administration, and a voluntary incomes policy, less complex than the version which had failed in 1972–74, was reintroduced in 1978.[23] Only in 1980 were both abandoned by the Reagan Administration, paralleling the British move of a year earlier.

No sooner had this new pattern of policy-making become established than it had to be relaxed. For the basis of the new policies was control of the money supply, and the money supply was seldom under effective control. As Table 5.2 demonstrates, the monetary targets set in both countries over the last seven years have been very frequently exceeded in spite of having been expressed in terms of a rather broad range of tolerance, with a particularly embarrassing episode in the UK in 1980 during which sterling M_3 grew by more than twice the permitted maximum. The indications are that the demand for money function, which monetarists had proposed with some relish as a guiding light for policy during the fluctuations of the savings function in the early 1970s, had itself become just as unstable.[24] But whatever the cause of this volatility in the growth of the money supply, its consequence was a relaxation, in 1982, in the monetary policy of both countries. In the UK Budget of March 1982 the target rate of growth for sterling M_3 for 1982–83 was raised from 5–9 per cent to 8–12 per cent from a base which was already well above its end-of-year target,[25] and in October 1982 the Federal Reserve announced that it would make no attempt to bring the monetary aggregates, currently running above the top of their target ranges, back within their tolerance limits.[26] Ironically, inflation fell dramatically in 1982 at precisely the time that the authorities were having to admit their failure to control the variable which they themselves had declared to be its principal cause, namely the growth of the money supply. Why this should have happened is an appropriate question for a macro-economic textbook, not the present work, although there is some discussion in Appendix II below. The question which at present concerns us is rather: is it possible to continue to explain the behaviour of the policy authorities during 1974–82 in terms of the 'satisficing' model of our previous chapter?

5.2 The model to be tested

Amidst all the mayhem described above, certain things did not change between 1945–73 and 1974–82, in particular the decision-making mechanisms described in Chapter 3. Macro-economic policy continued to be jointly made by the Treasury and the Cabinet in Great Britain, and in the United States by the President's Council of Economic Advisers in conjunction with Congress. It continued to be made without any specification of an objective function or statement of the relative weight to be allotted to the different targets of policy, for the compelling political reasons mentioned in our first chapter. An atmosphere of

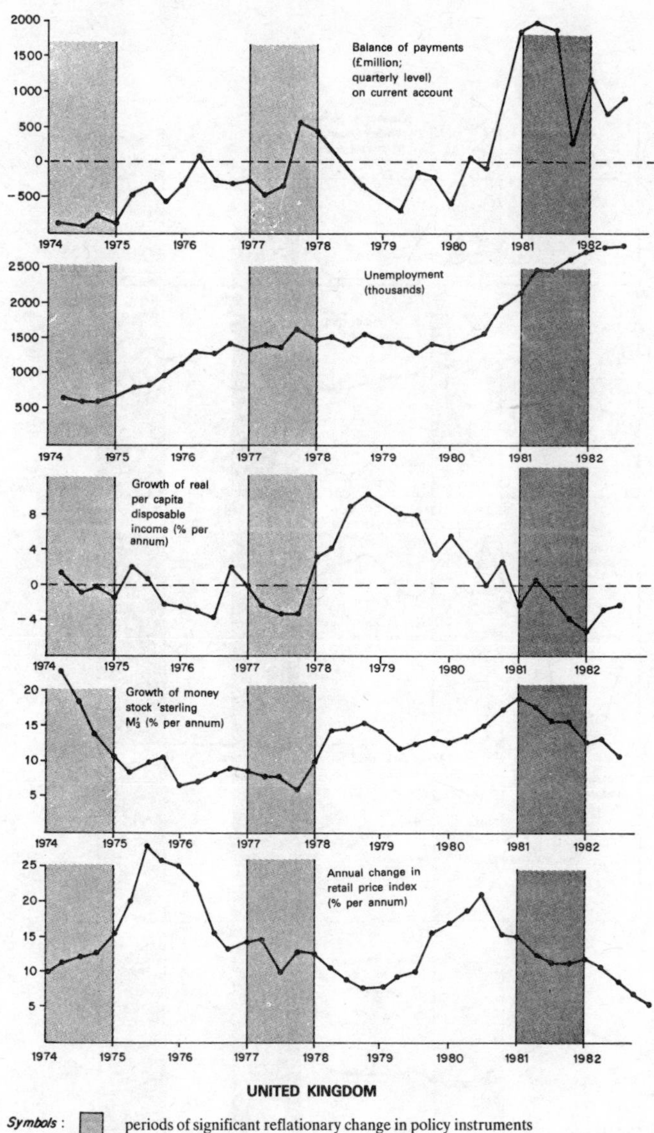

Symbols: periods of significant reflationary change in policy instruments

periods of significant deflationary change in policy instruments

For meaning of 'significant' see Table 4.2 above, pp. 100-101.
Source for all data: Tables 5.3 and 5.4.

Figure 5.1. Movements in targets of economic policy, 1974–82.

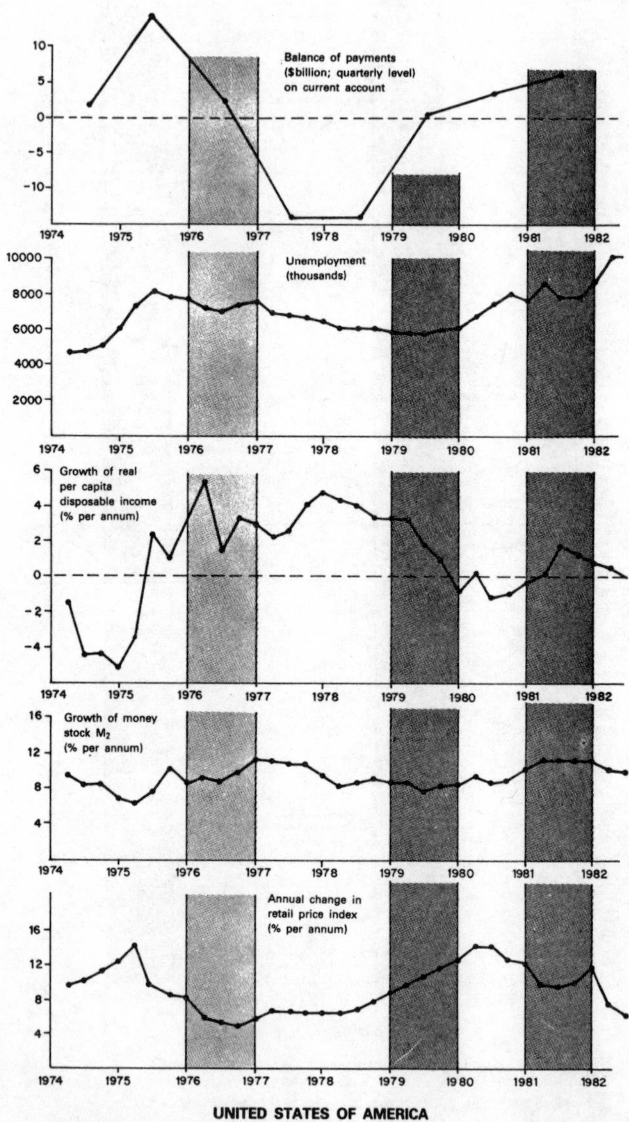

Figure 5.1 United Kingdom and United States 1974–1982: Movements in possible targets of economic policy, with periods of significant change in economic policy stance superimposed.

economic policy as an *ad hoc* response to crisis persisted,[27] in spite of an avowed shift towards medium-term objectives of policy. Desired values of target variables continued to be adjusted in response to disappointing performance, as we have just seen in the case of the money supply. In short, we see little reason when examining the period 1974–82 to depart from our basic hypothesis of 'satisficing' behaviour on the part of the policy authorities, that is,

$$\triangle x_{i(t)} = \alpha + \beta\,(y_i - y^*_i)_{t-k}$$ when $y_i > y^*_i$ (i.e. y_i has not been brought down to its satisfactory level)

$$\triangle x_{i(t)} = 0$$ at other times

where x_i represent instruments, y_i represent targets and y^*_i represent the desired values of targets. However, the *identity* of the principal instruments and targets did change. We have already seen this demonstrated in impressionistic terms, but the picture will become still clearer from an examination of Figure 5.1, which sets out, by analogy with Figure 4.1, the major 'reflationary' and 'deflationary' changes in policy in relation to the principal target variables of the previous period, plus the growth of the money supply.

From Figure 5.1 it is apparent that

(i) unemployment is no longer a significant target of macro-economic policy; the first great surge of unemployment in both the UK and the US in 1975 met with a policy response that could not be described, even by its proponents,[28] as a stimulus to the economy (it appears as 'neutral' on the rough criteria of Table 5.4) and the second big increase in unemployment, in 1980–81, met a response that began neutral and turned to outright deflation in 1981.

(ii) The balance of payments is not a significant target of policy either in an era of floating exchange rates. The 1981 deflation was perpetrated when both Britain and America were in substantial surplus.

TABLE 5.3 Movements in possible targets of economic policy, 1974–82

	United Kingdom							United States of America						
	Unemployment excluding school leavers		Per capita growth rate of		Current balance of payments	Change in: money stock	Retail price index, %	Unemployment, not seasonally adjusted		Growth rate of real per capita disposable income	Current balance of payments	Change in money stock		Consumer price index %
	(thousands)	(percentage)	GDP, %	Real personal disposable income %	(£m)	(sterling M_3), %		(thousands)	(percentage)		($ billion)	M_2	M_3	
1974	599	2.6	−1.6	−1.4	−3427	16.4	16.1	5101	4.9	−3.4	2.1	7.2	7.6	10.9
1975	929	3.9	−0.9	0	−1732	8.8	24.2	7862	2.7	0.9	18.2	8.3	11.1	9.9
1976	1269	5.3	3.0	−0.8	−1202	8.2	16.5	7302	7.1	3.3	4.4	11.2	12.1	6.2
1977	1376	5.7	1.8	−1.5	−224	7.8	15.8	6831	7.4	3.5	−14.1	9.4	12.2	6.5
1978	1375	5.7	2.6	8.2	764	14.7	8.3	6034	5.9	3.8	−14.0	8.6	10.4	7.5
1979	1302	5.4	1.6	6.8	−2319	12.5	13.4	5917	5.9	1.3	1.4	8.3	8.3	11.2
1980	1647	6.8	−2.3	1.2	2737	16.4	18.0	7637	7.1	0.5	0.4	10.4	10.7	13.5
1981	2539	10.6	−2.3	−2.3	6066	16.0	11.9	8273	7.6	2.4	4.6	11.4	11.5	10.2
1982	2793*	11.7*	1.6*	−0.6*	5378*	9.3*	8.6*	10678*	9.8*	0.1*	2.3*	9.8*	11.0*	6.1*

Note
* All data for 1982 are provisional.

Sources All United Kingdom statistics are taken from *current* issues of *Economic Trends,* and all United States statistics are taken from *current* issues of the *Economic Report of the President and Annual Report of the Council of Economic Advisers*. Note that the figures displayed here are not the best estimate of the target variables in question available at the present time (winter 1983–4), but the best estimates available at the time when policies were constructed to respond to the current values of these target variables. For a note on the discrepancy between these two sets of data, see Appendix V below.

TABLE 5.4 Main acts of economic policy, 1974–82

	United Kingdom								United States of America						
	Fiscal			*Monetary*	*Incomes Policy*[3]	*Other*	*Stance of policy (see note 4 below)*		*Fiscal*				*Monetary*	*Incomes policy*[2]	*Stance of policy (see note 4 below)*
	Budget change in taxes (£m)	*Change in public investment*[2] *(£m)*		*Central bank minimum lending rate (%)*					*Federal budget surplus ($ billion)* *Actual level*	*Actual change*	*'Full employment' level*	*'Full employment' change*	*Federal discount rate (average of end-of-quarter levels)*		
1974	1387	742	Supplementary special deposits scheme	12¾–11½	Off[3]		+		4	10	2.2	14.4	7.5	Off[3]	..
1975	1251	598		11¼–9¾–11¼	On[3]		..		–75	–79	–4.6	–6.8	7.8		..
1976	–970	422		11–9–15–14¼			..		–56	19	–11.6	–7	5.6		+
1977	–1507	–597		14–9–7			+		–51	4	–18	–6.4	5.0		..
1978	–2585	–196		6½–10–12½			..		–44	13	–13	5	5.6	On[3]	..
1979	425	561		14–17	Off[3]		..		–27	17	9.8	22.8	8.1		–
1980	235	577		17–16–14		Medium-term financial strategy; end of exchange control	..		–68	–41	–18.3	–28.1	11.2	Off[3]	..
1981	2649	–1196		14–12			–		–72	–4	–6.3	(12)	13.2		–
1982	–3283*	–18*		..[1]					–111*	NA	NA	NA	11.0*		

Notes

* All data for 1982 are provisional.

1 From 20 August 1981 the Bank of England suspended the announcement of minimum lending rate.

2 Gross domestic capital formation of the 'general government' sector (currently table 56 of *Economic Trends*)

3 The incomes policy abandoned by both the UK and US governments in 1974 was a compulsory policy; the incomes policies introduced in the UK from 1975 to 1979 and in the US from 1978 to 1980 were voluntary policies. For more detail see pp. 128–131.

4 The stance of policy is defined as 'reflationary' (symbol +) if two or more instruments were changed by more than one standard error in a reflationary direction (e.g. reduction in taxes, or reduction in central bank lending rate). It is defined as 'deflationary' (symbol –) if two or more instruments were changed by more than one standard error in a deflationary direction (e.g. increase in taxes, or increase in central bank lending rate). If policy cannot be defined as reflationary or deflationary according to these criteria, the symbol .. is entered.

Sources: United Kingdom Budget change in taxes: United Kingdom, *Financial Statement and Budget Report,* annual. The figure given in column 1 is the expected yield in a 'full year' of tax changes as given by the Chancellor of the Exchequer in this *Report.* All other data: from successive annual issues of *Economic Trends and National Institute Economic Review.* United States: all data from successive annual issues of the *Economic Report of the President and Annual Report of the Council of Economic Advisers.*

(iii) Rather, the main target of policy is price inflation. In Britain, as a rough rule, there are expansionary budgets whenever inflation is below 12 per cent or so, and contractionary budgets at other times. In the United States, the statistical picture is less clear, but the quotations from the previous section leave no doubt that the control of inflation was the principal objective of the Administration's macro-economic policy. In both countries the authorities announced an intention to adapt their fiscal and monetary policies to the observed rate of change of the money supply as a leading indicator, and cause, of changes in the rate of inflation.

In the light of these considerations we propose to test the basic 'satisficing' hypothesis (Equation 3.1) for the time period 1974–82 in the form:

(5.1) change in instrument variables per time period $= \alpha + \beta$ [deviation of inflation or money supply from desired value] (crisis periods)

$= 0$ (non-crisis periods)

(5.2) 'desired value' = mid-point of current central bank target range (money supply); average value of inflation over last three years (inflation rate)

The results of this exercise are displayed in the two parts of Table 5.5. They should be interpreted with great caution. Not only is the period under scrutiny rather short – it contains 34 quarterly observations, which is just above the bare minimum for the sensible application of regression methods – but it was also a period of constant experiment and search for a better way of running the economy, hence one should not expect the reaction function to be stable over time.[29]

These caveats apply particularly to the analysis of budget tax changes over the entire period. These show a significant

TABLE 5.5(a) Great Britain: empirical results for 'satisficing' equation (5.1), 1974–82

(1) Independent variable: inflation rate, measured $\dot{p}-\dot{p}^*$, †

Equation no.	*Dependent variable*	*Period*	*Constant*	*Regression coefficient*	*Correlation coefficient*	*Student's T statistic for regression coefficient*
	Budget tax changes (£m)					
5.1		Whole period	−43	36.2	0.59	4.12**
5.2		Crisis periods‡	56	20.2	0.30	1.42
5.3		Non-crisis periods‡	7	60.0	0.86	5.44**

(2) Independent variable: growth of money supply (sterling M_3), measured as a deviation from the mid-point of its announced target range for that year (see Table 5.2)

Equation no.	*Dependent variable*	*Period*	*Constant*	*Regression coefficient*	*Correlation coefficient*	*Student's T statistic for regression coefficient*
	Quarterly change in Bank rate (%)					
5.4		Whole period	−0.93	0.017	0.16	1.85*
5.5		Crisis periods‡	−0.15	−0.048	0.23	1.04
5.6		Non-crisis periods‡	−0.73	0.47	0.90	6.70**

Notes

* Significant at 5% level;

** Significant at 1% level.

† $\dot{p}$ = actual value of inflation at any time; $\dot{p}^*$ = 'desired' value of inflation at that time, interpreted as the average value of inflation over the previous twelve quarters; see p. 103.

‡ Crisis periods = the quarters 1974 II to 1977 II, and 1979 III to 1981 I, i.e. those for which inflation was – and remained for three quarters or more – greater than its 'desired value', as defined above. 22 observations.

Non-crisis periods = all other quarters during the period 1974 I to 1982 II. 12 observations.

Sources: Tables 5.3 and 5.4.

TABLE 5.5(b) United States: empirical results for 'satisficing' equation (5.1), 1974–82
(1) Independent variable: inflation rate, measured $\dot{p}-\dot{p}^*$,†

Equation no	*Dependent variable*	*Period*	*Constant*	*Regression coefficient*	*Correlation coefficient*	*Student's T statistic for regression coefficient*
Change in full-employment budget surplus ($ billion)						
5.7		Whole period	−0.23	0.34**	0.41	2.56
5.8		Crisis periods‡	−0.98	0.33*	0.42	2.05
5.9		Non-crisis periods‡	0.95	0.53**	0.68	2.94

(2) Independent variable: growth of money supply (M_3), measured as a deviation from the mid-point of its announced target range for that year (see Table 5.2)

Equation no	*Dependent variable*	*Period*	*Constant*	*Regression coefficient*	*Correlation coefficient*	*Student's T statistic for regression coefficient*
Change in federal discount rate (%)						
5.10		Whole period	0.14	0.011*	0.17	2.12
5.11		Crisis periods†	−0.15	0.089**	0.25	2.79
5.12		Non-crisis periods‡	0.32	−0.04	0.09	1.10

Notes
* Significant at 5% level.
** Significant at 1% level.
† $\dot{p}$ = actual value of annual increase in consumer prices at any time; $\dot{p}^*$ = 'desired' value of annual increase in consumer prices at that time, as measured by the average value of consumer price inflation in the preceding twelve quarters; see p. 103.
‡ Crisis periods = the quarters 1974 (I) to 1975 (IV) and 1978 (III) to 1982 (III), i.e. those periods for which inflation was in excess of its 'desired value' as defined above; 23 observations.
Non-crisis periods = all other quarters during the period 1974 (I) to 1982 (II). 11 observations.

Sources: Tables 5.3 and 5.4.

positive response to the level of inflation in both countries, as expected. But the response is stronger and more significant in 'non-crisis periods' than in 'crisis periods', contrary to the predictions of our theory. The problem arises because we have imposed a fixed model on to a changing environment. Firstly, as policy decisions came to be made more and more within a medium-term rather than a short-term framework in the 1970's, the asymmetry of response between 'crisis periods' and 'non-crisis periods' could be expected to diminish. Secondly, the new approach of fixation on the inflation rate only came in gradually, as we have seen. In 1974 the inflation and balance of payments crisis which followed as the first oil price increase was met in Britain by borrowing, not by deflation,[30] and the policy responses of that year emerge on our classification as midly stimulative. Similarly in the United States in 1975/76 there were cuts in taxes.[31] In other words, during the first inflation crisis of 1974–5, the policy response was not the sharp and decisive one which the model predicts. The policy-makers were still feeling their way, and they were still concerned about the level of unemployment, if only as a side condition. Things were very different during the second inflation crisis of 1979–81, partly for political reasons which are analysed on pp. 187–189 below.

Caution is also necessary, however, in interpreting the monetary policy reaction functions set out in the bottom half of Tables 5.5(a) and 5.5(b). These again show a policy response which is of the expected sign, but barely significant, and in Britain it is also weaker in crisis than in non-crisis periods. This indeed calls for explanation, since if a strict monetarist policy is being followed the response of interest rates to a monetary overshoot should be automatic: the moment such an overshoot is announced, the central bank will sell financial assets to the money markets, reducing liquidity, driving up the entire structure of interest rates and bringing the money supply back under control. Hence the correlation between bank rate and money supply should be very high, whereas in fact it was low. What was in fact happening?

Appearances suggest that central bank discount rates

continued to be used, right through the period under examination, against targets other than the money supply. Thus in Britain in the autumn of 1976, when money supply for once was running well within its target range, the Bank of England's minimum lending rate was abruptly raised from 9 to 15 per cent to staunch an outflow of foreign exchange reserves and to discourage excessive private borrowing. In the United States in the fourth quarter of 1980, with both M_2 and M_3 well within their target range, Federal Reserve discount rate was raised from 11 to 13 per cent. In general, the policy authorities often seem to have allowed interest rates to rise in response to increases in public sector borrowing on the assumption that these would otherwise lead to damaging increases in the money supply; but since the empirical link between the public sector deficit and the money supply was loose during the period under examination,[32] it is often not possible to see any relationship between ex post changes in central bank lending rates and *ex post* growth of the money supply.

It is possible to improve on these results by using the *forecasts* of inflation and money supply which policy-makers actually used as independent variables rather than the published *ex post* values which have been used here. The task is attempted in Appendix III. But even after this modification has been made we must accept that for the 1970s the sharp distinction which once existed between the authorities' behaviour in 'crisis' and 'non-crisis' periods no longer exists. They acted during that decade as if there were a persistent inflationary crisis and nothing else to worry about – on the economic scene. But the political imperatives of the previous period were no less insistent in the 1970s, as was the pressure to try and bring more fundamental instruments of policy to bear as the macro-economy. We consider these in the next section.

5.3 Extensions of the model

Governments which wish to ride the political business cycle in the 1970s and 1980s need to be cannier than their

TABLE 5.6 Great Britain and United States: increases in per capita GDP around and away from election times, 1974–82

Great Britain *(general elections in Feb. and Oct. 1974, and May 1979)* *Average increase in per capita disposable income*	*%*	*United States* *(presidential elections in November 1976 and November 1980)* *Average increase in per capita disposable income*	*%*
1973: I to 1974: I and 1978: II to 1979: II	4.6	1975: III to 1976: III and 1979: III to 1980: III	2.1
Average, 1974: I to 1982: II	1.2	Average, 1974: I to 1982: II	1.5

Source As for Table 5.3.

forebears. Blatant tax-cutting budgets, such as those of 1955 and 1959 in Great Britain and 1972 in the US, may even be counter-productive these days, as they are sure to be exposed as election ploys by politicians and popular newspapers[33] of the opposite persuasion. But if an increase in personal disposable income can be engineered with greater finesse, then the evidence suggests that this will still help the government's opinion-poll rating.[34] In none of the four nationwide elections covered by this chapter – the American presidential elections of 1976 and 1980 and the British general elections of 1974 and 1979[35] – was there any of the euphoria which characterised the occasions previously mentioned. But it still remains the case that personal disposable income per head, in three of these four cases, rose unusually fast, much faster then than at other times. The figures are shown in Table 5.6.

Each of these exercises escaped being labelled as a pre-election gambit. The increase in the British standard of living in 1978/79 was accomplished through a series of pay awards to different professional groups in the public sector based on an elaborate comparability formula (the 'Clegg awards').[36] The American improvement in 1976 was

TABLE 5.7 Great Britain and United States: partisanship and pre-election booms as influences on a 'satisficing' model, 1974–82

Equation no	Dependent variable	Period	*Regression coefficients and independent variables:* Constant	Inflation, deviation from 'desired value'† (expected sign +)	'Election dummy'† (expected sign −)	r^2	D.W.
USA: Change in full employment budget surplus ($ billion)							
5.13		Whole period	−0.58	0.54*	−2.12*	0.2207	0.9048
5.14		Republican administrations (18 observations)	−0.40	0.18	−2.43*	0.1727	0.9345
5.15		Democratic administrations (16 observations)	0.98	0.57**	−0.95	0.4739	1.4245
Great Britain: Budget tax changes (£ million)							
5.16		Whole period	−34	35.7**	−31.1	0.3484	0.7498
5.17		Labour administrations (25 observations)	499	40.6**	−1604	0.8258	1.2092
5.18		Conservative administrations (9 observations)	−201	−68	(294)‡	0.1413	1.8525

Notes

* Significant at 5% level;
** Significant at 1% level.
† 'Desired values' of inflation are defined in Table 5.5(b) above.
‡ 'Election dummy' takes the value 1 during the four quarters up to a general election (presidential election in US), 0 at other times.

achieved by a spontaneous recovery from recession gently enhanced by tax cuts. The American attempt to prolong the output boom of 1978 into 1979 and 1980 was eventually swamped by higher-than-expected levels of inflation. None of them was sufficient to win the election for the incumbent party. The important thing for our present purposes, however, is that these little nudges to demand happened, and that they bounce the technocratic policy reaction function (3.1) off course. The results of including the standard 'pre-election dummy variable' in that reaction function are illustrated in Table 5.7; they are presented in respect of budgetary policy only, as it is less likely that monetary policy is consciously manipulated for electoral purposes.

Somewhat surprisingly the results of Table 5.7 suggest a stronger response – coefficient of the budget surplus (tax changes in UK) to inflation in the case of the 'left-wing' parties (Labour in the UK and the Democrats in the US) than in the case of their 'right-wing' opponents. But in view of the shortness of the sample period, these results are of little significance.

Other responses to crisis: 'search behaviour' among instruments

In Chapter 4 we noted that economic crises of exceptional severity had been met not only by the application of conventional measures of fiscal and monetary policy but also by a search for other measures – usually in the field of industrial structure,[37] overseas trade, and above all prices and incomes policy – designed to treat the underlying causes of the crisis in the medium-term rather than the immediate symptoms in the short. In the current period, as fiscal and monetary policy were themselves switched on to a co-ordinated medium-term basis, governments lost some of their room for manoeuvre with the existing medium-term instruments. For example, any policy for the exchange-rate that would appear to make the achievement of monetary targets more difficult was now out.[38] However, attempts to supplement the government's fiscal and monetary approaches continued on both sides of the Atlantic through-

TABLE 5.8(a) Great Britain: routine and non-routine responses to economic crisis, 1974–82

Crisis and time of first manifestation	*'Routine' (fiscal and monetary) response*	*Timing*	*'Non-routine' response*	*Timing*
First oil-price inflation, 1973 IV/	Sharp increases in minimum lending rate	November 1973; October 1976		
1974 I	Deflationary budget	March 1975	(1) 'voluntary' prices and incomes policy (until early 1979)	July 1975
			(2) Tying of Budget judgement to level of wage increases	March 1976
Second oil-price inflation, 1979 III	Series of deflationary budgets within context of 'medium-term financial strategy'	1979, 1980, 1981	'Supply-side measures': (1) cuts in direct taxation	March 1979
			(2) loosening of restrictions on privately rented sector of housing market	March 1980
			(3) industrial relations legislation	Sept. 1982
			(4) taxation of unemployment benefit	March 1982

TABLE 5.8(b) United States: routine and non-routine responses to economic crisis, 1974–82

Crisis and time of first manifestation	*'Routine' (fiscal and monetary) response*	*Timing*	*'Non-routine' response*	*Timing*
First oil-price inflation, 1974 I	Deflationary budget; tightening of growth limits for monetary aggregates	1974	Voluntary pay and price 'standards'	October 1978
Second oil-price inflation, 1979 III	Deflationary budget with expenditure cuts, closure of tax loopholes,	1981 1982	'Supply-side measures': cuts in marginal tax rate, more generous tax treatment of capital depreciation	February 1981
	increases in federal discount rate	continuous through 1979 III–1981		

out the 'years of experience'. As time went on and left-ward-leaning administrations were replaced by rightward-leaning ones, the character of these interventions changes sharply, as summarised by Table 5.8.

The new generation[39] of compulsory, multi-stage prices and incomes policies introduced by Mr Heath and President Nixon in 1972–3 had been widely condemned for not only failing to restrain the boom of those years, but actually making it worse.[40] When a third vintage of such policies was brought in in Great Britain in 1975 and in the US in 1978 to deal with the wage-inflationary consequences of the oil-price increases, they were made voluntary in order to avoid antagonising the labour movement. The vocabulary of such policies was mollified to suit the new tone of conciliation: what had previously been referred to as 'limits' for pay and price increases now became 'standards' in the US and 'norms' in the UK and the policies themselves were described, respectively, as an 'accord' and an 'agreement'. Much reliance was placed on educating union leaders in what was felt to be macro-economic reality: the higher the level of wage increases, the greater the likely increase in unemployment. For a while, particularly in Britain in 1978, this approach seems to have been successful.[41] But in 1979, under the stress of renewed inflation, it began to crumble. Union leaders had seen that the wage/unemployment tradeoff, while inescapable for the country as a whole, could be escaped by individual unions who enjoyed sufficient power to raise wages whilst pushing their costs in terms of job losses on to other employees. The story is told that in February 1979 Prime Minister Callaghan invited the leader of Britain's largest trade union[42] to 10 Downing Street and asked him to reconcile his members' claim for a 20 per cent wage increase with his own frequently expressed demand for inflation to be brought down to 2 per cent. 'My members', the union leader is alleged to have replied, 'are not interested in such macro-economic considerations'.[43]

When conservative administrations took over in Britain and the United States in 1979 and 1980 they started from a different set of assumptions. For them, unlike their predecessors, labour movements were not groups with whom it was natural to have a special relationship which made the negotiation of pay and prices agreements a relatively low-cost exercise. We argued in Chapter 3 above that when confronted with a major crisis which could not be resolved by 'routine' changes in instruments, a search process would be initiated which would cause other instruments to be brought in *starting with those whose use involved the smallest political and financial costs.*[44] For the Conservative party in England, imposing an incomes policy involves enormous political costs, particularly when the previous one has demonstrably failed. Far smaller, for such an administration, are the costs involved in legislation which appears to increase the incentive to work and to remove the barriers to higher productivity.[45] Hence, in the last three years, the great wave of what is known as 'supply-side legislation'; cuts in income tax,[46] cuts in company taxation,[47] measures to make trade unions legally liable for costs caused by strike action,[48] measures to make unemployment benefit taxable,[49] removal of restrictions on the eviction of tenants from privately rented housing.[50] What effect on the real economy all of these measures have had is too early to say. But they represent an important symbolic move away from the principle that economic growth is demand-led and should be promoted by stimulating aggregate demand.

5.4 Epilogue

In the 1950s and 1960s we likened the economies of Britain and America to a cow, wandering backwards and forwards between two electric fences. One of those fences was the government's automatic response to above-normal unemployment, and the other was its automatic response to balance of payments crises (or inflation), as documented in Chapter 4. In 1974 both economies seemed well on their way to wandering over the cliff of ever-accelerating inflation and unemployment. What has happened since?

What has happened, as Figure 5.2 demonstrates, is that the electric fence preventing the economy from wandering into the pasture called 'record levels of unemployment' has

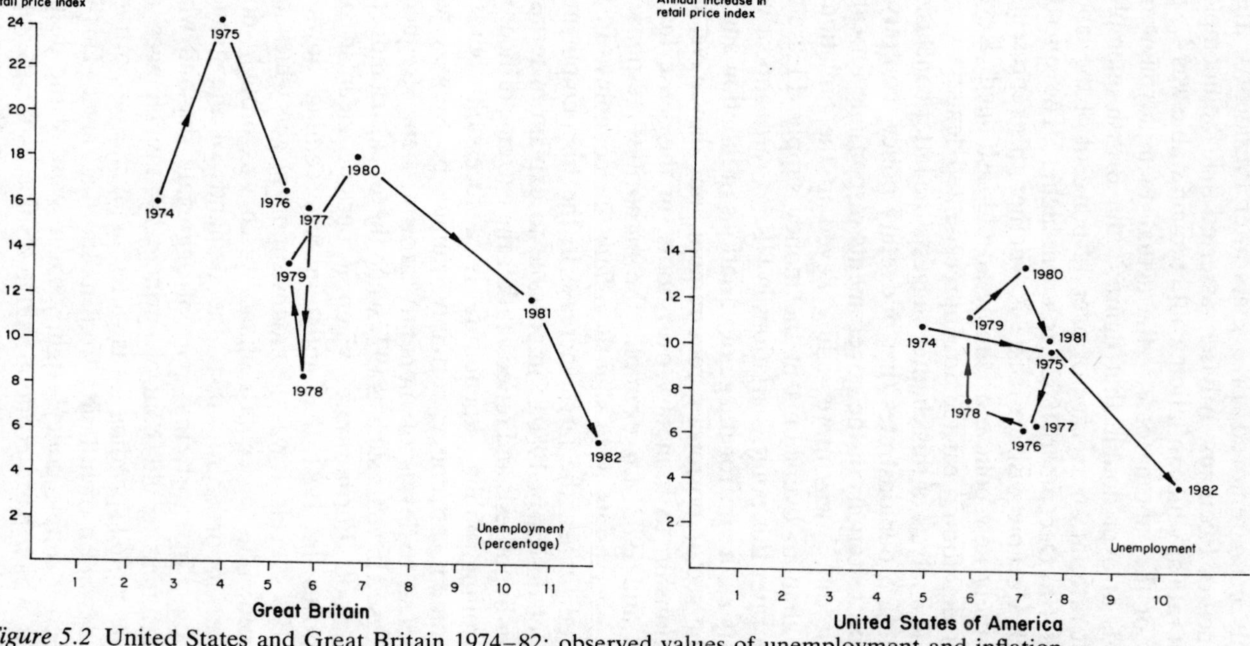

Figure 5.2 United States and Great Britain 1974–82: observed values of unemployment and inflation

simply been removed. Five years after President Carter's Council of Economic Advisers asserted that the unemployment rate at which inflation would remain stable was 4.9 per cent of the labour force,[51] the actual unemployment rate stands at over double that figure;[52] the British unemployment rate, at an average of over 12 per cent of the labour force (in December 1982) is even higher. The question which we now wish to tackle is whether this represents a genuinely new policy, or simply an old-fashioned (Keynesian) deflation[53] carried to unprecedented lengths.

The analysis of this chapter suggests the latter conclusion. Table 5.5 demonstrates that budgetary policy, contrary to the protestations of the governments responsible for carrying it out,[54] was more tightly keyed to the 'inflationary gap' than to overshoots in the money supply. Figure 5.3 elaborates this point. Variations in UK tax rates appear very nearly as the mirror image of variations in inflation and the public sector borrowing requirement, but they have little relationship to monetary overshoots, in the sense that in 1978 and 1982, for example, the authorities' response to such overshoots is to slightly *reflate* the economy. In the United States, the large increase in the high-employment budget deficit in 1980 is impossible to explain in terms of either hypothesis and reflects rather the extreme difficulty of controlling public expenditure in a recession; but that instrument of policy certainly cannot be viewed as a response to levels of monetary growth, being frequently increased in years such as 1977 when there is also a monetary overshoot. Furthermore, when it became clear in both countries in 1982 that inflation was coming down to pre-1970s levels, it was the money supply targets which were relaxed, not aggregate demand which was brought down further in order to satisfy the demands of the financial strategy. In short, that part of aggregate demand which government could control – principally tax changes and public capital spending – was varied in inverse proportion to the deviation of inflation from its 'normal' level. This was indeed a simple policy – rightly so, in view of the disturbances which basic economic relationships had experienced during the decade.[55] But it was new only in the sense that

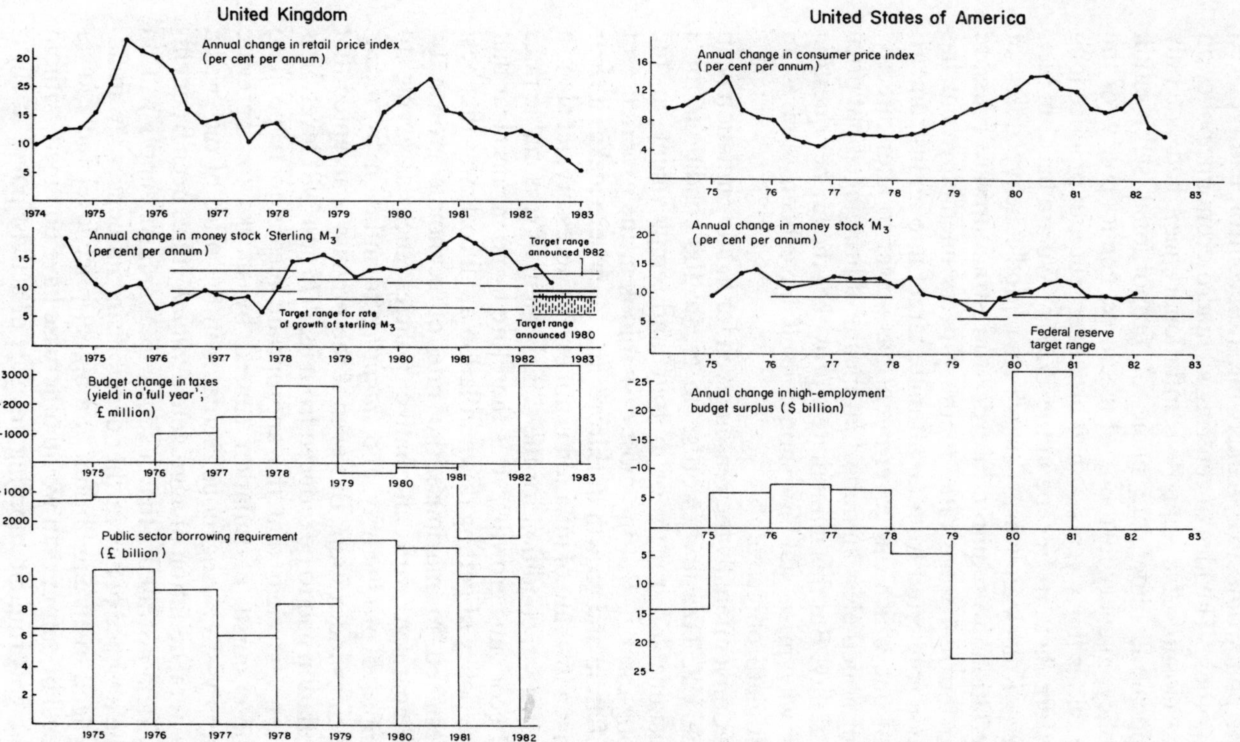

Figure 5.3 Inflation, money supply and fiscal changes: United Kingdom and United States, 1974–82

one policy objective, namely inflation control, had replaced all others. The idea of centring all macro-economic policy on the closure of a supposed 'inflationary gap' had not only appeared, under the name of proportional stabilisation policy, in every textbook of macro-economics policy for the previous thirty years; it had also been put into practice long before then, in Europe in the 1920s.[56] We are back, in fact, in a Kaleckian world, in which periodic heavy doses of deflation are required in order to restrain upward pressure on the real wage rate. In the process unemployment has been converted from an ultimate target into an instrument: not one which the government has power to alter directly, but nonetheless an important means of bringing about price stability. But this immediately provokes the further question of why price stability should itself have been seen as an ultimate objective.

Conventionally the reason given for fighting inflation is, in the UK Treasury's words, 'to create the conditions for a sustainable growth of output and employment in the long-term'.[57] But the most casual look at the experience of inflation and growth in Europe and elsewhere makes it clear that a low rate of inflation is not even a necessary, let alone a sufficient, condition for the achievement of reasonable rates of economic growth.[58] It is therefore by no means clear that the policy of getting down inflation at all costs was that best designed to maximise the rate of economic growth by comparison with alternative policies such as trying to improve productivity and *adapting* to inflation by means such as indexation. But even if the premiss is accepted that inflation had to be reduced from its 1975 and 1981 levels, it is even less clear that the appropriate means to respond to these bursts of inflation caused by shocks to aggregate *supply* – i.e. exogenous increases in the price of oil – was a general deflation of aggregate *demand*. It has been frequently demonstrated[59] that a shock to aggregate supply will, in the absence of any further destabilising influences, eventually lead to an equilibrium at a higher price level and a lower level of output than would otherwise have obtained, without the government adopting any sort of activist policy at all. If the government however intervenes by deflating demand, this will simply move the economy 'along the Phillips curve' – that is, increase the level of unemployment, and depress the level of inflation, in relation to what they would otherwise have been. But this additional step will not normally be – and certainly does not seem to have been in 1981 – necessary to get the inflation rate to stabilise. Once the critical rate of unemployment is passed at which expectations stabilise – the non-accelerating inflation rate of unemployment (NAIRU) or, as it has sometimes been called, the natural rate of unemployment – then any further deflation is quite redundant from the point of view of controlling prices, and will serve only to redistribute income from those who do not have jobs to those who do. Unemployment, in both the US and the UK, is now running at approximately twice the best available estimates of its 'natural' level.[60]

In terms of strictly technical criteria of growth-maximisation, then, the macro-economic policies followed in the UK and US since 1974 seem to overshoot the mark quite absurdly. But it is of the essence of this book's argument that such criteria do little to explain the policies actually followed. Criteria of political and administrative rationality do much more. A policy of keying the government's macro-economic stance to inflation and the public sector deficit is simple and avoids frequent policy reversals; this makes the policy popular with administrators. And in political terms, the data of Chapter 2 showed that the idea of an attack on inflation appears to have become increasingly popular with at any rate the British electorate, probably not because voters see any link between inflation rates and their personal welfare but rather because the popular media have educated them to characterise inflation in terms of a threat of anarchy and chaos.[61]

For the moment, therefore, it is possible for a sort of political rationality to triumph over economic rationality, as long as the public obsession with this one target of policy lasts. But the likelihood is that the backlash against this process has already begun in the United States,[62] and that it will soon spread to the rest of the western economy.[63] We explore the consequences of this argument further in Chapter 8.

Notes

1 The oil price increases began in the autumn of 1973, but most of their effect did not feed through to the economy until the following year.
2 'Butskellism': a term coined in Britain in the 1950s to denote the similarity of views between R.A. Butler, Conservative Chancellor of the Exchequer 1951–5, and Hugh Gaitskell, Labour Chancellor of the Exchequer 1950–1 and Leader of the Opposition 1955–63. Both believed thoroughly in Keynesian demand management (and the protection and expansion of the welfare state and the mixed economy).
3 This argument was strengthened by the increasing volatility of the basic relationships on whose stability the forecasts of macro-economic modellers depend. An important example is the ratio of savings to GDP, which is the basis for calculation of the conventional national income multiplier. This ratio stayed relatively stable in Britain throughout the 1950s and 1960s; then, after the first increase in oil prices, it rose remarkably in all countries. Following the second oil crisis in 1979, it jumped up again in Britain and throughout Europe, but fell in the US – it was below 3 per cent in 1980. Nobody properly understands the cause of these gyrations. But they have made the practice of 'fine-tuning' the economy seem increasingly unwise.
4 More details on the teachings of the 'new Cambridge school' is contained in Blackaby (1979), pp. 138–9; Bispham (1975); and in particular in the memorandum by Cripps, Godley and Fetherston to United Kingdom (1974).
5 The conventional argument for making inflation a target of policy is that high inflation means a constantly changing rate of inflation, and that a constantly changing rate of inflation depresses the rate of investment and prevents business contracts from being concluded. (see for example the defence of its current policies by the United Kingdom Treasury in United Kingdom (1981), Vol III, pp. 68–73, paras 4–8.) But empirical support for this argument is never given; the UK Treasury, in the passage cited, supports it only by a quotation from Hicks about the advantages of price systems being allowed to acquire the 'sanction of custom'. See also note 58 below.
6 Much economic discussion of the 1960s had assumed that a negative relationship (or 'Phillips curve') such as that set out in the diagram below could remain, and had remained, stable over a long period of time as long as the rate of change of unemployment did not vary.

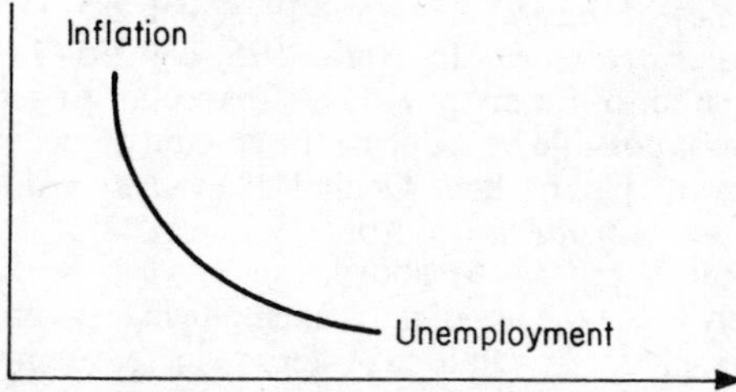

But in the late 1960s the relationship began to shift northeastwards (see Figure 4.2). The conventional interpretation put on this trend was that expectations of future inflation held by employers and union leaders had risen during this period, causing the rate of inflation corresponding to a given level of unemployment to rise. On this analysis, any Phillips curve would only hold good as long as inflationary expectations remained stable. If inflation could be brought down, many people argued, inflationary expectations would fall in their wake; if this could be achieved, it would bring the Phillips curve down again, and reduce both inflation and unemployment at the same time.

7 At this stage it was a 'confidential internal objective' of the Bank of England (see Savage, 1979). In the early years of the 'Keynesian revolution' it had been asserted that the demand for any monetary aggregate (otherwise put, its velocity of circulation) was unstable for reasons such as, in particular, the existence of a speculative demand for cash. But a large empirical literature (see for example Goodhart (1975), Laidler (1971), Laidler and Parkin (1970)) was built up in the 1960s to demonstrate that a stable demand-for-money function existed both in the US and the UK. This literature provides the rationale for the subsequent use of monetary aggregates as instrument variables.

8 Cripps, Godley and Fetherston; see United Kingdom (1974), Minutes of Evidence, pp. 1–27.

9 Professor David Laidler; see United Kingdom (1974), Minutes of Evidence, pp. 48–63.

10 United Kingdom (1974), report, page xii. Italics in original.

11 United Kingdom (1974), report, page xi.

12 United Kingdom (1974), minutes of evidence, pages 1–27 and 48–63. It was probably critical for the acceptance of these points by a Labour-dominated Expenditure Committee and government that the 'New Cambridge School' was itself, unlike the monetarists, Labour Party-orientated. 'Monetarism' has always been a dirty word in the Labour Party, even though a Labour government adopted economic policy-making to monetarist principles under another name. The New Cambridge School's influence was, in this sense, the Trojan horse through which monetarism made its entrance into the policy-making circle in Britain.

13 Denis Healey, *Hansard,* 15 April 1975, col 282.
14 Denis Healey, *Hansard,* 15 April 1975, col 285–7.
15 'I am prepared to use my powers as Chancellor to get the next pay limit as low as possible by reducing the amount of income tax which is taken from the pay packet.' Denis Healey, *Hansard,* 5 April 1976, col. 272; see also *idem,* 15 April 1975, col. 281.
16 See Chapter 3, pp. 57–61 above.
17 'I absolutely reject the use of mass unemployment as an instrument of policy (and) pledge myself to take steps to increase employment once our inflation rate has settled down to the international average.' Healey, *Hansard,* 15 April 1975, col. 321.
18 Sir Geoffrey Howe, *Hansard,* 12 June 1979, cols 243–4.
19 *Economic Report of the President and Annual Report of the Council of Economic Advisers* (1975), p. 128.
20 The small reflationary effect of the 1975–6 tax cuts has been attributed to the hypothesis that taxpayers did not see them as an increase in their 'permanent income', and hence did not increase their spending much. See Blinder (1979), pp. 150–78.
21 This behaviour is described and heavily criticised by Blinder (1979), pp. 185–94.
22 *Economic Report of the President and Annual Report of the Council of Economic Advisers* (1977), p. 80.
23 *Economic Report of the President and Annual Report of the Council of Economic Advisers* (1980), p. 4.
24 Conventional monetary theory uses the identity

$MV = PQ$ M = nominal quantity of money
P = average price level at which transactions take place in a given time period
Q = physical volume of transactions in that time period
V = 'velocity of circulation' of money stock

which is true by definition, to generate the *theory* or *conditional proposition* that providing velocity (V) remains constant over time, then the rate of growth of prices (P) will be approximately equal to the rate of growth of the money supply (M) less the rate of growth of physical output (Q). Is the original premiss of this proposition correct? Evidence for both Britain and the US in the fifties and sixties suggested that velocity – or, otherwise put, the demand for money – was impressively stable – see the references cited in note 7. But UK velocity fell dramatically below its slightly upward trend in 1973/74 and 1981/82 (see United Kingdom (1981), vol III, p. 77 and Budd in Kay (1982), pp. 24–5); and US velocity fell dramatically in 1982 (see Brittan, 1982). This increase in 'speculative demand for money' may be a temporary response to a high risk of loss on non-cash assets, or it may be something else. But whatever the cause it makes changes in the money stock embarrassingly unreliable as predictors of inflation and other target variables.

25 Sir Geoffrey Howe, Budget Statement, *Parliamentary Debates* 9 March 1982, col. 733.

26 See Anatole Kaletsky, *Financial Times,* 7 September 1982. The announced target ranges for 1982 were: 2.5 per cent to 5.5 per cent for M_1; 6 to 9 per cent for M_2; and 6.5 to 9.5 per cent for M_3.

27 See the episode described on pp. 57–61 above.

28 Cf. Denis Healey's words when introducing the 1975 UK Budget, quoted on p. 128 above.

29 We regress the budgetary change in taxes against inflation and changes in minimum lending rate against the money supply, on the assumption that budgetary policy is conceived as a medium-term instrument for getting inflation down and monetary policy is conceived as a short-term instrument for correcting deviations in the monetary aggregates. The accuracy of this assumption is considered in Figure 5.2.

30 See Savage (1982) for a narrative account of this episode.

31 See page 131 above.

32 The public sector borrowing requirement is itself an important component of the money stock: formally,

change in sterling M_3	= change in PSBR	+ sales of public sector debt by non-bank private sector	+ sterling lending to UK private sector	+ external and foreign currency counterparts	+ change in net non-deposit liabilities

However the statistical link between the PSBR and the money stock is not very strong. Savage (1979, p. 50) estimated the statistical relationship between quarterly changes in sterling M_3 and the public sector borrowing requirement in Britain over the period 1970–8 to be:

$$(\pounds M_3) = \underset{(656)}{1364} + \underset{(0.14)}{0.44}\ \text{PSBR}, \quad r^2 = 0.43$$

where: $\pounds M_3$ = nominal money supply (sterling M_3), in £million,
PSBR = public sector borrowing requirement in £million, number of observations = 36.
Standard errors in brackets.

33 See Mosley (1982) p. 18 for an example of such exposure in the British popular press.

34 See Chapter 2 above, Table 2.3, equations I and III for entire period.

35 Certainly this is what the statistical results suggest: attempts to fit a 'pre-election dummy' to equations such as those in Table 5.7 with bank rate as dependent variable yielded insignificant results.

36 For more detail of this, see Chapter 7 below, pp. 188–189.

37 Measures as diverse as Selective Employment Tax and the Regional Employment Premium in the UK come into this category (see Table 4.8 above).

38 See for example evidence by HM Treasury to the House of Commons

Treasury and Civil Service Committee: United Kingdom (1981), vol II, p. 201.

39 To be distinguished from the short-term emergency wage freezes used, for example, by Mr Macmillan in 1961.

40 See for example Blinder (1979), p. 132.

41 Inflation was kept down to 8 per cent in the middle of a minor boom. Much of the success of the policy was ascribed to the working relationship between Jack Jones, general secretary of the Trades Union Congress, and the ruling Labour Party.

42 Moss Evans of the Transport and General Workers' Union.

43 Quoted in *Sunday Times,* 'Insight' report, March 1979.

44 See pp. 64–66 above and for further extension of the argument, Appendix I below.

45 This legislation was made more popular by the development of the hypothesis known as 'crowding-out', which purports to demonstrate that an increase in the relative share of the public sector in GNP depresses the output of the private sector. It has not yet been properly confirmed or refuted, with different models showing different results (see for example Laury, Lewis and Ormerod, 1978).

46 E.g. Great Britain (1979) and US (1981).

47 E.g. United States in 1981.

48 E.g. Great Britain in 1982.

49 E.g. Great Britain (1982) and US (1981).

50 E.g. the creation of 'short-hold tenancies' in Great Britain in 1980.

51 *Economic Report of the President and Annual Report of the Council of Economic Advisers* (1977), p. 51.

52 10 per cent, as communicated to the OECD in December 1982.

53 The phrase is Denis Healey's; see for example Healey (1981), p. 15, which substitutes the word 'conservative' for 'Keynesian'.

54 See for example United Kingdom (1981), vol 2, p. 87: 'The Government has deliberately not set its targets in terms of the ultimate objectives of price stability and high output and high employment because... these are not within its direct control. It has instead set a target for the growth of money supply, which is more directly under its influence, and has stated that it will frame its policies for taxation and public expenditure to secure a deceleration of money supply without excessive reliance on interest rates.'

55 In evidence to the Treasury Committee enquiry of 1980–1 a leading economist in that ministry stated: 'we seek for policies which are robust in the fact of alternative views of the world, on the grounds that we are in fact fairly ignorant'. (A.J.C. Britton, in United Kingdom (1981), vol II, p. 98).

56 See Tomlinson (1982), also T. Sargent, 'Managing moderate inflations: a comparison of the Poincaré and Thatcher policies', University of Minnesota, unpublished paper, 1982.

57 Paper by HM Treasury, 'Objectives of Economic Policy', in United Kingdom (1981), vol II, p. 86.

58 The following figures for nine major industrial countries during the

		1970	1971	1972	1973	1974	1975	1976	1977	1978	1979	% change 1980
US	GDP	−0.1	2.9	5.8	5.4	−1.3	−1.0	5.6	5.1	4.4	3.2	−0.2
	RPI	5.9	4.3	3.3	6.2	11.0	9.1	5.8	6.5	7.7	11.3	13.5
JAPAN	GDP	11.7	5.1	9.3	10.0	−0.3	1.4	6.5	5.4	5.9	5.6	4.2
	RPI	7.7	6.1	4.5	11.7	24.5	11.8	9.3	8.1	3.8	3.6	7.7
GERMANY	GDP	6.0	3.2	3.7	4.9	0.5	−1.8	5.2	3.0	3.3	4.5	1.8
	RPI	3.4	5.3	5.5	6.9	7.0	6.0	4.5	3.7	2.7	4.1	5.5
FRANCE	GDP	5.7	5.4	5.9	5.4	3.2	0.2	5.2	2.8	3.6	3.2	1.8
	RPI	5.2	5.5	6.2	7.3	13.7	11.8	9.6	9.4	9.1	10.8	13.6
UK	GDP	2.2	2.7	2.2	7.5	−1.2	−0.8	4.2	1.0	3.6	0.8	−1.6
	RPI	6.4	9.4	7.1	9.2	16.0	24.2	16.5	15.8	8.3	13.4	18.4
ITALY	GDP	5.3	1.6	3.2	7.0	4.1	−3.6	5.9	1.9	2.6	4.9	4.0
	RPI	5.0	4.8	5.7	10.8	19.1	17.0	16.8	18.4	12.1	14.8	21.2
SWITZERLAND	GDP	6.4	4.1	3.2	3.0	1.5	−7.3	−1.4	2.4	0.3	2.2	4.1
	RPI	3.6	6.6	6.7	8.7	9.8	6.7	1.7	1.3	1.1	3.6	4.0
AUSTRALIA	GDP	6.2	5.4	3.0	5.3	2.6	2.4	3.6	0.9	1.7	3.0	2.7
	RPI	3.9	6.1	5.8	9.5	15.1	15.1	13.5	12.3	7.9	9.1	10.2
BRAZIL	GDP	8.8	13.3	11.7	13.9	9.8	5.7	9.0	4.7	6.0	6.4	7.8
	RPI	22.3	20.2	16.5	12.7	27.6	28.9	42.0	43.7	38.7	52.7	82.8

Source: OECD.

Casting our net wider and examining the relationship between inflation and growth we find, for the 80 countries for which growth and inflation statistics are available for the 1970s in the World Bank's latest *World Development Report*, the following statistical relationship.

Growth rate of real GDP = 3.29** − 0.089 annual rate of inflation
(average 1960–77) (12.13) (0.74) (average 1960–77)
$r^2 = 0.0076$ (T-statistics in brackets)

It is not possible to infer from these data that there is any connection between countries' growth rates and their inflation rates.

1970s suggest little relationship between growth (GDP) and inflation rates (RPI):

59 Two useful references are Gordon (1975a) and Blinder (1979), Chapter 1.

60 US unemployment is now over 10 per cent against an estimated 'natural' level of around 5 per cent (see note 51 above). UK unemployment is now over 12 per cent against an estimated 'natural' level of around 7 per cent, or 2 million (Minford and Peel, 1981, p. 115).

61 Gordon (1975b), p. 829 and Budd, in Cairncross (1982), pp. 55–6, both imply that voters' attitude to the economy is conditioned by the most searing economic event that has occurred during their lifetimes, and that the Great Unanticipated Inflation of the 1970s has replaced the unemployment of the 1930s in this role for most people. But this leaves unexplained, to my mind, the question of why so many people should have been seared by the former event, given that it did not, in itself, appear to have had much effect on their well-being. For further discussion see Chapter 8 below, pp. 208–209 and in particular note 19.

62 See Chapter 3 above, pp. 73–75.

63 The famous 'clockwise loops around the Phillips curve' (which, as Figure 5.2 demonstrates, were as much a feature of the post-1974 economy as of the happy days beforehand) can be explained in terms of this schema:

First cycle

Phase	*Occurrence*	*Consequences for inflation and unemployment*	*Timing*
1	Supply shock, 'stagflation'	$U\uparrow$, $\dot{P}\uparrow$	1974 (US), 1974/5 (UK)
2	Government-induced demand deflation	$U\uparrow$, $\dot{P}\downarrow$	1975 (US), 1976 (UK)
3	Political pressure for reflation	$U\downarrow$, $\dot{P}$ constant or falling	1976/7 (US), 1977/8 (UK)
4	Inflationary consequences materialise	U constant, $\dot{P}\uparrow$	1979
Second cycle			
1	Supply shock, 'stagflation'	$U\uparrow$, $\dot{P}\uparrow$	1980
2	Government-induced demand deflation	$U\uparrow$, $\dot{P}\downarrow$	1981/2
3	Political pressure for reflation	$U\downarrow$, $\dot{P}$ constant or falling	Second half 1982 through 1983

Part 3
IMPLICATIONS

6 What Difference Does It All Make? Policy Reaction Functions in a Macro-Economic Model*

6.1 Introduction

The main macro-economic models currently in use, such as the Treasury, London Business School[1] and National Institute models in the UK and the Federal Reserve and Wharton models in the US, treat economic policy as exogenous, that is, they assume that tax changes, interest rate changes and other economic policy interventions arise from sources outside the macro-economy itself. This is obviously unreasonable: the whole of Chapters 4 and 5 have been devoted to demonstrating that economic policy instruments *do* respond in a fairly systematic way to the state of the economy, even if the form of the response has been changing over the last ten years. In this chapter we consider the implications for economic forecasting and for macro-economic analysis of taking account of this kind of systematic response.

* Much of the research described in this chapter was done in conjunction with Richard Cracknell in the summer of 1981 and I am grateful for his permission to reproduce it here. There is a fuller report on our work in Mosley and Cracknell (1981, 1984). We are both grateful to Peter Smith of Southampton University for help in setting up our model.

6.2 United Kingdom: estimating a reaction function for 1960–80

The technique which we use is very simple: we compare the performance of a simple macro-economic model of the United Kingdom with and without 'policy reaction functions' inserted. The word 'performance' is here to be understood in two senses: on the one hand, we are interested in whether the ability of the model to explain past developments in the economy is improved by the insertion of a policy reaction function; on the other, we also want to know whether inserting such a reaction function alters our estimate of the response of inflation to the money stock, or of unemployment to the imposition of a wages policy, or any of the other basic multipliers on which the forecasts and ultimately the manifestos of the rival schools of economic policy are based.

We begin by explaining our choice of model and of reaction function. The *model* on which our experiments were carried out is the teaching version of the Southampton econometric model known as SPARTAN; a flow diagram of the model is set out as Figure 6.1. With 25 behavioural equations and 15 identities, it is much smaller than all the major macro-models of the UK economy (it contains less than one-tenth as many relationships as the Treasury model); but it needed to be this small to be represented in the simple diagram of Figure 6.1. At the same time the model is, we believe, sufficiently realistic to include the essence of the major relationships affecting economic policy and sufficiently broad in scope to incorporate the critical economic aggregates. It is a 'Keynesian' model in the strict sense that variations in real output are caused exclusively by variations in the various components of final demand; but it contains, as any model must which claims to have a bearing on present-day debates about economic policy, scope for the financial sector to exert an independent influence on the economy. The model is set out in full as Appendix IV.

The reaction function used here is essentially a composite of those used in Chapters 4 and 5. The policy instruments

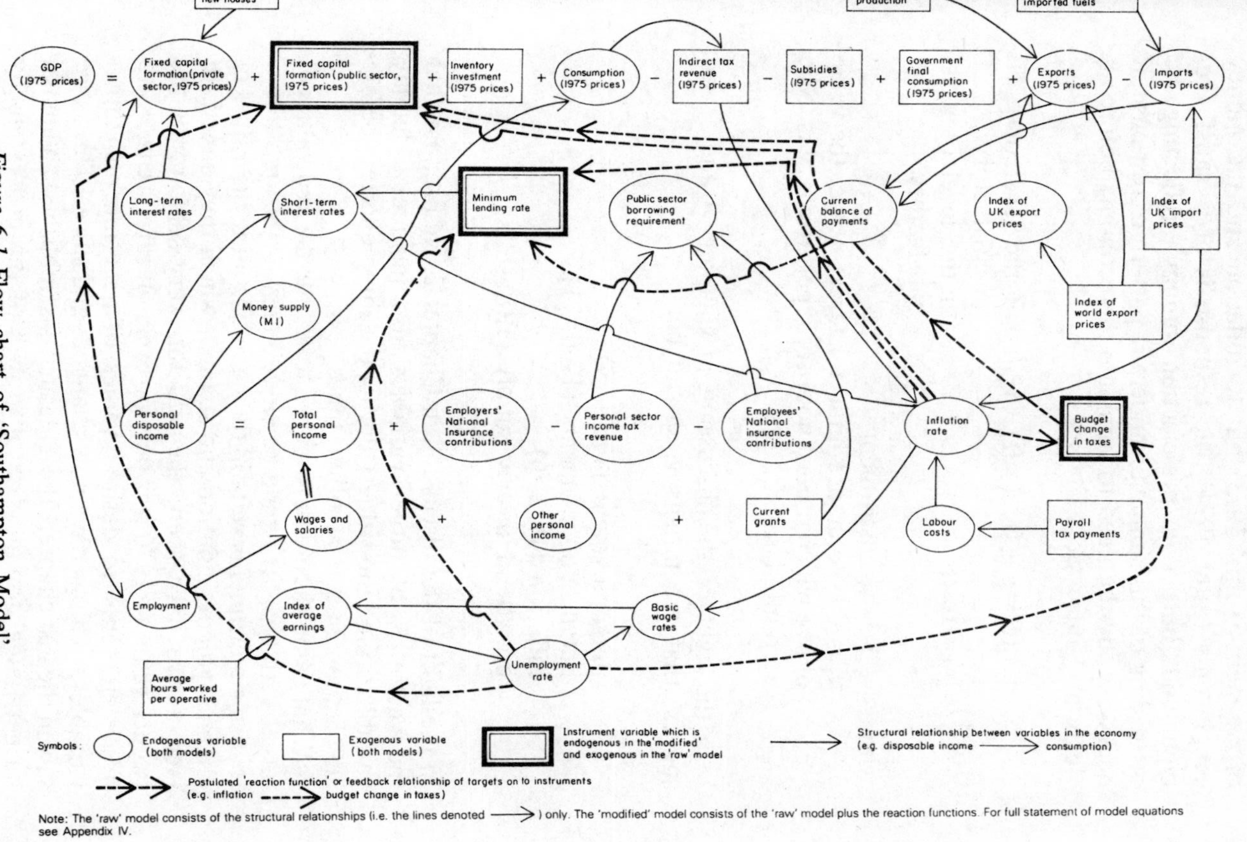

Figure 6.1 Flow chart of 'Southampton Model'

respond to 'crisis levels' of unemployment and the balance of payments (until 1973) but to inflation and the money supply only (after 1974); the response is of a 'satisficing' type; and there is a 'pre-election dummy', reflecting the overriding of this simple technocratic pattern of response, if necessary, by the need to stimulate the economy before an election. Hence we write:

$$(6.1)\quad \begin{cases} x_i(t) = \alpha + \beta \sum_{j=1}^{n} (y_j(t) - y^*_j(t)) & \text{if the level of } y_j \text{ is unsatisfactory} \\ x_i(t) = 0 & \text{if the level of } y_j \text{ is satisfactory} \end{cases}$$

where: x_i is any instrument
y_j is the 'tolerance limit' for target y_j, i.e. the value above which it must not rise[2] if performance is to be accounted satisfactory

In the light of the discussion in Chapters 4 and 5, we suggest that the targets y_j should be:

unemployment (1960–79)
balance of payments (1960–71)
inflation (1971–6)
growth of money supply (1976–80)

In the light of the discussion in Chapter 2, we propose that the vector $\bar{y}_j$ of target variables also include a dummy variable taking the value 1 during the three quarters before an election and 0 at other times.

What value should be attached to y^*, the desired values of target variables? It would be easy to answer this question if British governments were in the habit of stating the values of unemployment, inflation and so on at which they aimed. In fact, as we have seen, they do this very seldom. In the twenty years to 1976 it is only possible on rare occasions to find statements of desired values of governments' target variables.[3] Things have now changed, and since 1976, as we saw in the last chapter, the Treasury has published an annual 'target range' for the rate of growth of the money supply (sterling M_3). Thus for this variable we use the mid-point of the range as a measure of y^*; for the others, in the absence of any official statement, we shall use the mean value of each target variable over the previous twelve quarters as a measure of its desired value. This is consistent with the frequently observed fact that the levels of unemployment and inflation which have triggered off government policy action have progressively increased over time.

As examples of x_i, the instrument variables, we considered public sector capital expenditure, minimum lending rate, and the annual budgeted value of tax changes.[4] The measured reaction functions, as estimated by ordinary least-squares on 82 quarterly observations from 1960: I to 1980: II, were as set out in Table 6.1. In the case of public investment and the budget change in taxes it can reasonably be said that a statistically significant relationship has been established between the instrument and the targets. Taxes are reduced when unemployment is high, and raised when the balance of payments is in deficit, or when inflation or the growth of the money supply exceed their 'target levels' during the period when those variables were effective as targets of policy; in all cases except the money supply the effect is significant. Public investment is raised when unemployment is high and cut when the balance of payments, inflation or the money supply exceed their target levels; again the effect is significant for all target variables except the money supply. Changes in bank rate respond in a quite different way; they display a generally weak association with all target variables *except* the balance of payments and the money supply, although this latter association is not surprising since attempts to raise bank rate automatically imply restrictions on the money supply and vice versa. All the instruments of policy analysed, finally, are moved in a generally expansionary direction during the period before an election, although in the cae of bank rate the effect is not statistically significant.

For the budget change in taxes and bank rate, at least, the reaction functions set out in Table 6.1 give rather low correlation coefficients in relation to previous exercises in this genre, and before we proceed further it is worth spelling out why this is so. First and foremost, we are regressing *changes* in instruments against *deviations from trend* of targets, rather than, as is traditional, absolute values of

TABLE 6.1 Policy reaction functions: results of regression analysis

Dependent variable	Regression coefficients on independent variables (see under 'symbols' below for definition)							
	Constant	'Unemployment dummy'	'Balance of payments dummy'	'Inflation dummy'	'Monetary growth dummy'	Election dummy'	r^2	DW
(1) Annual change in value of government public investment (current £m)	68.9 (1.79)	0.16** (2.70)	−0.15 (1.29)	−10.3** (3.44)	−1.29 (0.32)	91.82* (1.91)	0.5978	1.0281
(2) Annual change in value of minimum lending rate (bank rate) (per cent)	0.31 (0.59)	−0.0011 (1.47)	−0.002** (2.32)	−0.41 (0.98)	0.052* (1.97)	−0.21 (0.33)	0.1181	1.4852
(3) Budget change in taxes (current £m)	−1.09 (0.83)	−0.39** (3.71)	−0.12 (0.59)	39.2** (3.82)	8.36 (0.62)	−32.9** (2.20)	0.3875	1.5066

Notes
Numbers in brackets beneath coefficients are Student's t-statistics.
** denotes significance at 1% level; * denotes significance at 5% level.
Symbols
'Unemployment dummy' = the deviation of unemployment, in thousands, from its average for the previous 12 quarters *if and only if it exceeds this value,* during period 1960:I to 1979:II.
'Balance of payments dummy' = the deviation of the balance of payments, in current £m, from its mean value for the previous 12 quarters, *if and only if it exceeds this value,* during periods 1960:I to 1971:IV.
'Inflation dummy' = the deviation of the consumers' expenditure deflator, in per cent, from its mean value for the previous 12 quarters, *if and only if it exceeds this value,* during periods 1972:I to 1976:IV.
'Monetary growth dummy' = the mid point of the announced annual target growth rate for sterling M_3, as taken from annual *Financial Statements,* during the period 1976:I to 1980:II.
'Election dummy' = 1 during the three quarters before an election, 0 at other times.
These independent variables are assumed only to be 'effective' as targets during particular periods on account of 'fashions' in central government economic policy-making. For a justification of the periods chosen, see text, pp. 94–95 and 135–138 above.

Sources: Economic Trends Annual Supplement, 1983 edition, except the announced target range for the growth of sterling M_3, which is taken from HM Treasury, *Financial Statement and Budget Report,* annual.

instruments against absolute values of targets.[5] Our own procedure, we believe, gives a better picture of the reaction-mechanism actually at work; but the conventional procedure which it replaces automatically reaps a high r^2 because all the variables which it is regressing are subject to a strong upward time trend. Secondly, the 'satisficing' specification which we have chosen for equation (1) assumes that changes in an instrument variable will be *zero* if the targets to which it responds are not 'in crisis'. This strong assumption would, we believe, be perfectly reasonable if the instruments of economic policy listed in Table 6.1 were used purely as instruments of stabilisation policy. This, however, is not the case; budget changes in taxes are used to raise revenue, public investment disbursements may reflect past commitments as much as the current state of the economy, and so on. For these reasons we do not find it at all surprising that only a smallish proportion of the variance in instrument values can, with our present methods, be explained by the levels of targets. This does not mean that our present methods cannot be improved on: we return to this question in section 6.4 below.

6.3 Inserting the reaction function into the model

We now proceed to examine the performance of our macro-model with and without reaction functions inserted. Firstly let us consider the *tracking performance* of the 'raw' and 'modified' models, that is, their ability to account for variations in the level of certain key indicators of social welfare. In particular we shall be interested in tracking performance with respect to the following list of variables:

GDP at current prices
consumption } at 1975 prices
investment } at 1975 prices
exports } at 1975 prices
personal disposable income } at 1975 prices
unemployment rate
wage rates at current prices
balance of payments on current account

Table 6.2 sets out the values of certain indicators of tracking performance for each of these indicators using the 'raw' and 'modified' models. These are the Theil U-statistic and the RMSE, or root mean square error.[6] On the strength of these indicators the 'modified' model is better at

TABLE 6.2 Relative tracking performance of 'raw' and 'modified' models, 1964:I to 1980:II

Variable	*Theil U-statistic:*		*Root mean square error:*	
	In 'raw' Southampton model	*In 'modified' Southampton model (incorporating reaction functions from Table 6.1 above)*	*In 'raw' model*	*In 'modified' model*
GDP at current prices	0.65	0.56	8.10	7.19
Personal disposable income at 1975 prices	0.82	0.71	31.60	26.04
Consumption at 1975 prices	0.39	0.85	98.80	97.22
Investment at 1975 prices	4.55	3.64	65.40	68.83
Exports at 1975 prices	0.68	0.66	15.03	14.05
Balance of payments on current account	2.35	1.39	92.24	66.19
Wage rates at current prices	0.88	0.94	28.43	38.65
Unemployment	0.72	0.71	22.57	21.65
Price index (deflator used for consumers' expenditure)	0.38	0.42	10.45	11.92

simulating the behaviour of consumption, GDP, personal disposable income, the current balance of payments, unemployment and exports, though in the case of the last two variables the improvement is only marginal. It is worse than the 'raw' model at simulating wage and price inflation and more or less equivalent at simulating the behaviour of private sector investment. A graphical presentation of the tracking performance of the raw and 'modified' models in respect of personal disposable income over the sample period is given in Figure 6.2. In general terms the 'raw' model performs better at the beginning and end of the period (where the reaction functions of the modified model predict more deflation in response to the monetary and price increases of 1979/80 than actually took place) and the

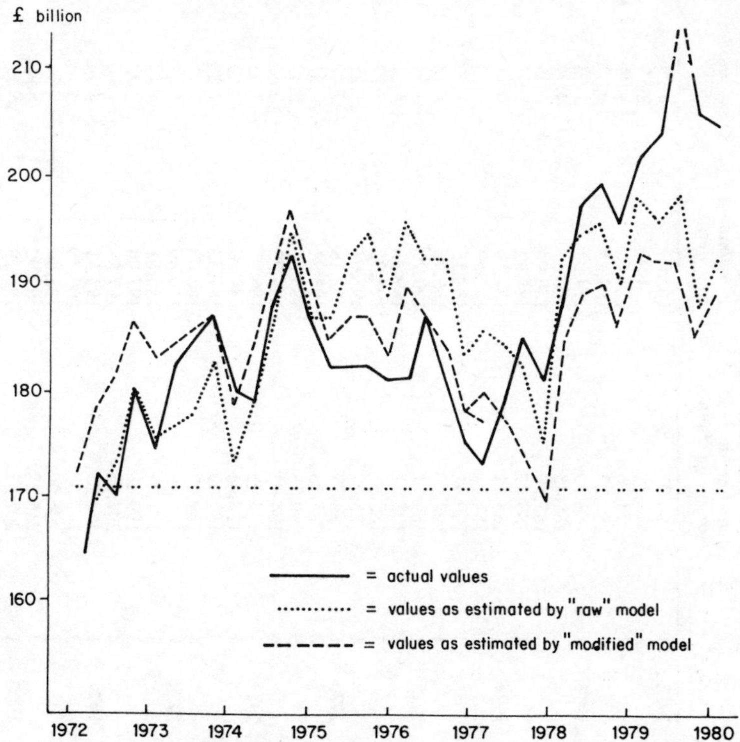

Figure 6.2 'Raw' and 'Modified' models: relative tracking performance, 1972–80, for real personal disposable income *(for table of actual and estimated values see overleaf)*

Table of actual and estimated values for Figure 6.2.

Year	Quarter	*Actual value of personal disposable income at 1975 prices (£ billion)*	*Value of 1975 PDY as estimated by 'raw' model*	*Error as estimated by 'raw' model*	*Value of 1975 PDY as estimated by 'modified' model (£ billion)*	*Error as estimated by 'modified' model*
1972	1	162.71	167.00	−4.29	179.15	−16.44
	2	176.38	174.01	2.37	186.37	−9.99
	3	173.66	176.74	−3.08	189.11	−15.45
	4	183.22	183.21	0.01	191.62	−8.40
1973	1	178.20	179.33	−1.13	187.22	−9.02
	2	185.43	180.49	4.94	188.76	−3.33
	3	187.59	180.94	6.65	189.39	−1.80
	4	189.47	185.82	3.65	190.75	−1.28
1974	1	183.11	177.10	6.01	182.30	0.81
	2	182.14	182.69	−0.55	189.03	−6.89
	3	190.47	188.55	1.92	193.04	−2.57
	4	194.79	196.76	−1.97	197.56	−2.77
1975	1	189.71	190.29	−0.58	191.88	−2.17
	2	185.71	189.93	−4.22	189.48	−3.77
	3	185.88	194.85	−8.97	193.50	−7.62
	4	185.77	197.02	−11.25	193.75	−7.98
1976	1	184.77	192.18	−7.41	187.70	−2.93
	2	185.13	197.94	−12.81	193.83	−8.70
	3	190.18	195.67	−5.49	190.52	−0.34
	4	184.63	195.23	−10.60	188.38	−3.75
1977	1	178.98	186.93	−7.95	180.33	−1.35
	2	177.46	189.06	−11.60	182.43	−4.97
	3	182.99	187.55	−4.56	180.51	2.48
	4	189.17	186.06	3.11	177.12	12.05
1978	1	184.55	179.49	5.06	170.58	13.97
	2	191.37	195.61	−4.24	186.58	4.79
	3	199.28	197.06	2.22	188.14	11.14
	4	201.96	197.88	4.08	188.17	13.79
1979	1	198.25	193.51	4.74	185.43	12.82
	2	203.59	200.46	3.13	193.03	10.56
	3	206.00	198.04	7.96	191.58	14.42
	4	216.22	199.92	16.30	190.23	25.99
1980	1	207.87	191.29	16.58	181.92	25.95
	2	206.56	194.77	11.79	185.55	21.01

Table 6.3 Certain impact multipliers in the 'raw' and 'modified' model

*'Raw' model**

Response in £ million after [5 years / 10 years / 15 years] of a sustained 5 per cent increase in: / *on:*	*Exchange rate*	*Public expenditure (all exogenous elements) at 1975 prices*	*Index of world export prices*
GDP at 1975 prices	– 22.7 – 13.4 – 22.5	180.1 165.0 178.4	5.8 16.2 26.8
Personal disposable income at 1975 prices	– 28.1 – 24.7 – 33.8	63.2 60.5 78.0	21.4 24.6 31.5
Balance of payments on current account	– 34.8 – 37.8 – 62.0	– 39.3 – 49.3 – 45.9	34.8 39.3 52.5
Public sector borrowing requirement	2.53 2.06 2.96	70.9 76.5 91.4	– 1.5 – 1.8 – 3.2
Employment (in thousands)	0.4 1.5 3.0	18.1 17.8 15.2	1.06 1.44 2.16
Index of consumer prices (percentage)	0.002 0.001 0.002	0.005 0.005 0.004	0.002 0.003 0.001

*'Modified' model**

Response in £ million after [5 years / 10 years / 15 years] of a sustained 5 per cent increase in: / *on:*	*Exchange rate*	*Public expenditure (all exogenous elements) at 1975 prices*	*Index of world export prices*
GDP at 1975 prices	– 17.6 – 14.1 – 11.9	165.1 152.0 149.1	4.6 15.3 19.9
Personal disposable income at 1975 prices	– 26.1 – 26.2 – 20.4	57.6 59.2 63.3	18.2 20.1 25.6
Balance of payments on current account	– 32.5 – 36.9 – 39.7	– 37.1 – 39.2 – 46.0	28.4 35.5 42.2
Public sector borrowing requirement	2.02 2.02 2.14	61.3 65.1 77.2	– 1.3 – 1.2 – 3.0
Employment (in thousands)	– 0.5 1.7 3.3	21.7 20.1 18.2	1.06 1.45 2.13
Index of consumer prices (percentage)	0.003 0.002 0.002	0.006 0.007 0.003	0.002 0.002 0.001

Notes

* The 'raw' model is the Southampton model as set out in Appendix 1 of Mosley and Cracknell (1981), with all policy instruments exogenous. The 'modified' model is the raw model modified by the inclusion of policy reaction functions (1), (2) and (3) from Table 6.1.

'modified' model performs better in the middle of the period.

Secondly, let us compare the response of the main targets of economic policy to the main instruments and exogenous variables in the 'raw' and 'modified' models. Table 6.3 sets out the value of the 'dynamic multipliers' of the exchange rate, public sector capital formation and export prices on the main endogenous variables analysed in Table 6.2, that is, the extent to which those endogenous variables would alter if the exchange rate, public investment and export prices were increased separately by 5 per cent from their base value. The general finding which emerges from this table is that the multiplier is, in general, lower in the modified than in the raw model.[7] The common sense behind this finding is as follows: if some policy instruments are assumed to be systematically responsive, in a contra-cyclical direction, to the state of the economy rather than to be exogenously determined outside the model, then the scope which genuinely exogenous shocks have to influence the course of the economy is *pro tanto* reduced.

Consider in detail the case of public expenditure. The conventional way of looking at the behaviour of this variable is as set out in Figure 6.3: 'leakages' (which may include feedbacks from the monetary sector and the price level) are

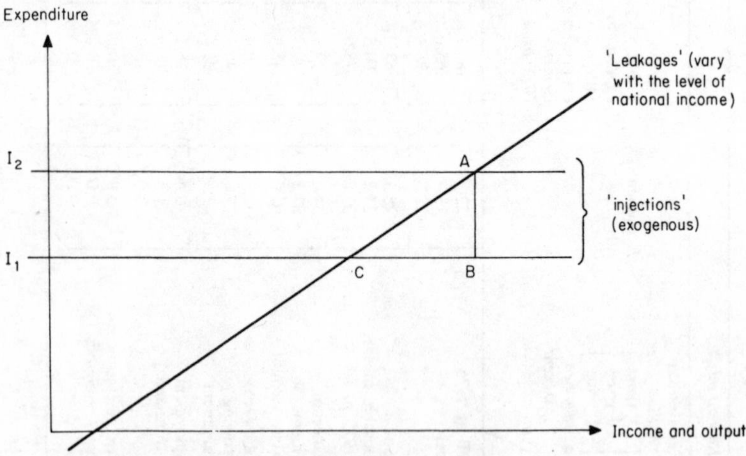

Figure 6.3 Conventional national income model

responsive to the level of nominal national income, 'injections' are exogenously determined, and equilibrium national income is determined by the intersection of the two functions. If there is an autonomous change in injections, such as public expenditure (represented by the shift from I_1 to I_2 on Figure 6.3) then the 'multiplier' of the autonomous injection on national income is the ratio BC/AB.

If a part of public expenditure is now assumed to be not exogenous, but rather to respond to the state of the economy, then two things will happen. First, the amount of expenditure that is genuinely 'discretionary' in any time period will fall: this will limit the extent to which the injections schedule can shift upwards in any time period, but will not affect the size of the multiplier. Secondly, however, the leakages schedule will become more elastic with respect to the level of national income as automatic leakages that were previously excluded from the model (viz the deflation of demand when the balance of payments, inflation level, or money supply, according to the time period that is considered, is 'in crisis')[8] are now incorporated in it.[9]

We can see the implications for forecasting of the omission of reaction functions if we look back to Figure 6.2, which shows the behaviour of British personal disposable income between 1975 and 1980 as it was; as it was estimated by the 'raw' Southampton model; and as it was estimated by our 'modified' model with reaction functions added. The principal thing that appears from this diagram (apart from the tendency of both models to over-estimate positive changes in GDP) is that GDP as estimated by the 'modified' model is in general less volatile than GDP as estimated by the 'raw' model. In years when the Treasury timed its policy interventions right a balance of payments deficit (before 1971) or an inflation overshoot would be followed by a deflationary response from the policy authorities; this response would be automatically captured by the 'modified' model, lowering the observed multipliers, but would appear purely as an exogenous variable in the 'raw' model. As a result, the path of real income would be smoother in the 'modified' than in the 'raw' model. In years, on the other hand – particularly election years – when the Treasury appeared to 'time its policy intervention wrong', then the ex-post response of policy would by destabilising, and the path of real GDP would be smoother in the 'raw' than in the 'modified' model.

We have, in short, evidence of an *intended* 'built-in stabilising' mechanism on movements in the level of real national income additional to the stabilising influence traditionally supposed to be exerted by the interest rate.[10] The existence of this mechanism may help to explain why the calculated value of the national income multiplier, in most econometric models of the British economy, falls a long way short of the value which is traditionally ascribed to it in textbook models.[11]

6.4 Discussion

Whether any of the analysis conducted above matters from the point of view of the *policy authorities* – as distinct from outside observers – depends on three things. Are the policy authorities free to depart from the pattern of their own previous behaviour, so that a reaction function such as we have estimated in previous chapters may be expected to hold into the future? Can they forecast the level of their own policy instruments? Are their policy actions perfectly co-ordinated? If the answer to all of these three questions is yes, then policy authorities do not need to know anything about reaction functions in order to make forecasts of the future state of the economy. We shall argue, however, in what follows that the actual answers are yes; no; and no (particularly in the United States).

It is, of course, true that the Treasury, for example, is physically free to alter the pattern of its reaction whenever it wishes. One Treasury paper on forecasting puts the matter as follows:

> Modellers outside government often use estimated reaction functions to determine government policy. For example in a fixed exchange rate regime a reaction function to determine minimum lending rate would probably relate it to the current balance or the level of the foreign exchange reserves. Such devices are generally not necessary for analyses

carried out inside the Treasury because if necessary policy makers can be consulted directly about their intentions, a procedure not open to outside modellers.[12]

There is no doubt that policy-makers can change their 'intentions' whenever they wish; for instance – the case considered in the last chapter – by refusing to allow any cut in tax rates whatever the level of unemployment. What they cannot do without a long political struggle and a long time-delay is to express those intentions in any form more precise than that of a conditional prediction, for example, 'public investment will depend on the level of inflation'. As public investment is an exogenous variable independent of the level of inflation in the Treasury model (see the flow chart in Figure 6.4) the scope for inaccuracy in forecasting the level of 'policy makers' intentions' and in respect of public consumption would seem to have been arbitrarily increased by specifying that variable as exogenous rather than as subject to a reaction function. There is some evidence that British public expenditure projections have gone wrong in the last three years (for example, in the sense of inaccurately predicting that the real level of public expenditure would not rise over the period 1979–82) partly because of their neglect of relationships of this type.

The argument so far has been conducted on the basis of a unitary stabilisation authority, which if an accurate assumption, would entitle us to talk as if only one reaction function actually mattered. This is a tolerably accurate assumption for the United Kingdom, where as we saw in Chapter 3 it is difficult for Parliament, the Bank of England or even the Cabinet to frustrate a line of policy on which the Treasury has determined.[13] But it is very far from being a true picture of the United States where Congress can, and often does, throw out the President's budget and where the Federal Reserve can, and often has, acted at cross-purposes to the fiscal authorities.[14] In this kind of environment it is necessary not only for the individual authorities within the policy-making circle to be aware of their *own* reaction functions, but also for the fiscal authorities to be aware of the Federal Reserve's likely reaction-pattern and vice versa,

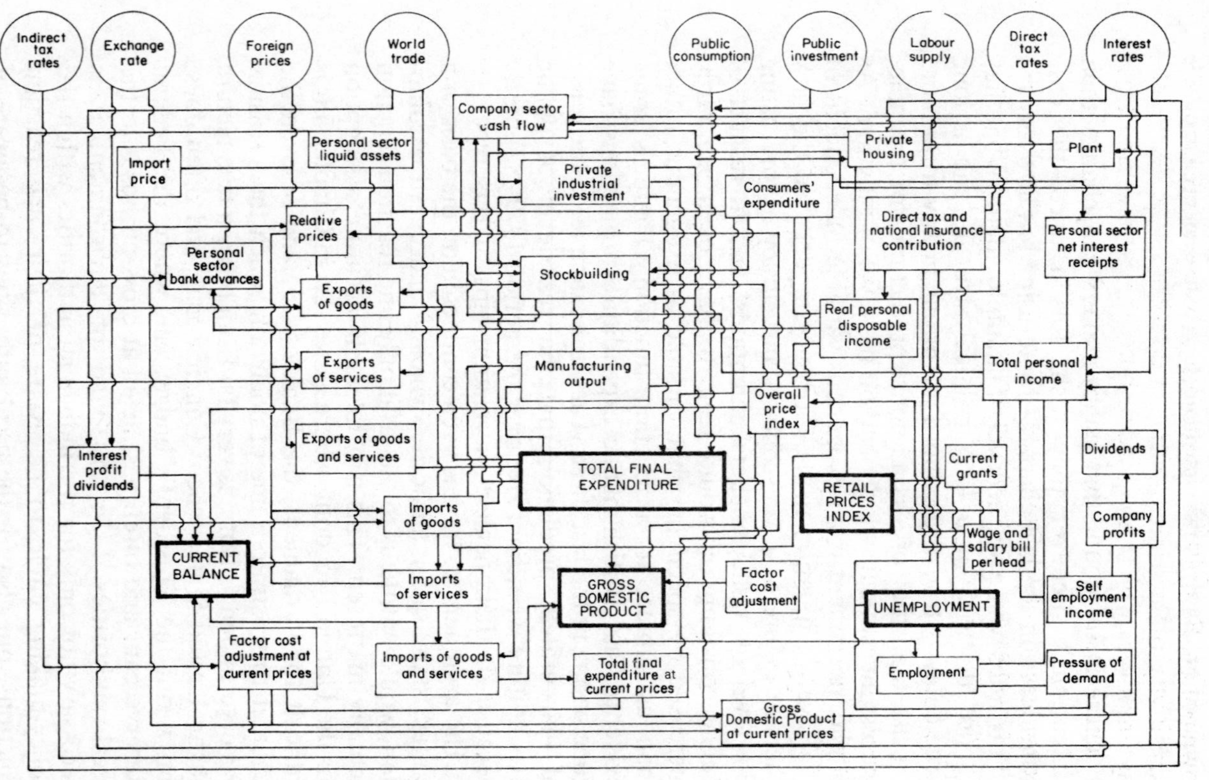

Note: target variables are in heavy boxes; exogenous variables are in circles

Figure 6.4 Flow chart of the Treasury macro-economic model

otherwise each party will over-estimate the potency of its own policy. Fair (1978) has recently investigated in detail the sensitivity of measures of the effect of fiscal policy to the assumptions which are made about the behaviour of the Federal Reserve and concludes that:

In the simulation (of an increase in the real value of goods purchased by the government) in which the behaviour of the Federal Reserve is endogenous, the Fed responds to the increase in economic activity by increasing the bill rate. The simulation is thus less expansionary than the experiments in which the bill rate remains unchanged.

In summary, (our results) show that fiscal policy effects are quite sensitive to assumptions about the behaviour of the Fed. The most expansionary case is where the government deficit is financed by an increase in nonborrowed reserves (sc. bank credit), and the least expansionary case is where the Fed keeps the money supply unchanged.'[15]

The implications of this chapter, therefore, are threefold. Firstly, if the plausible idea of 'policy reaction functions' is accepted, it then becomes necessary to define the concept of a policy instrument more carefully; for an 'instrument' is by definition something which the government can manipulate at will, not something which responds in a predetermined way to the state of the economy. On an extreme view, all acts of taxation, spending and money creation would be dictated by the state of the economy, none of them would be genuinely exogenous, and, the concept of a 'policy instrument' would disappear. We do not advocate any such extreme view here; the question of what can be reasonably defined as an 'instrument' is further explored in Appendix II. But we have consistently argued that some variables conventionally thought of as policy instruments, in particular the annual budget change in taxes and the level of government capital expenditure, do show some systematic response to the state of the economy and are thus not instruments in the true sense at all. To the extent that this is so, the government's freedom to manoeuvre is less than it is conventionally represented. Traditionally the Treasury has been seen as the driver of a car, freely able to manipulate accelerator or steering-wheel as he wishes, in order to keep the car moving along the road at the desired speed. But if policy reaction functions exist at all, then some of these controls will have a life of their own and will respond to the position of the car, whatever the driver does.

Secondly, if a policy reaction function is inserted into an existing macro-model, this makes a difference to its predictions: a 'modified' model which contains policy reaction functions predicts, in the particular case which we have considered, better than a 'raw' model which excludes them in the case of six out of eight key target variables.

Thirdly, if a policy reaction function is inserted into an existing macro-model, this makes a difference to its estimated policy effects: a model 'modified' by the addition of policy reaction functions in general exhibits lower policy effects or 'multipliers', for those policy instruments which remain exogenous, than a 'raw' model.

There is however scope for further research and for refinement of the view of policy-making presented here in a number of areas. First, it would no doubt be possible to improve on the reaction functions eventually used: we believe that the ones used here represent an advance on previous work in the sense that they embody both 'technocratic' and 'political' responses to the state of the economy and also fashions in the use of certain policy instruments, but they exhibit low correlation coefficients, and the lag-structure could probably be adjusted so as to improve matters. Second, it would be possible to incoporate reaction functions of this sort in more elaborated models of the British economy such as the Treasury and London Business School models in order to see whether, as in the case here described, predictive performance is once again improved. Finally, so far as we are aware, no actual estimated policy reaction functions have been inserted into econometric models outside the US and UK. It would be useful to see how well the optimistic early results for those countries reported by Fair (1978), and now here by ourselves, stand up in comparative perspective.

Notes

1 Some versions of the London Business School model treated Bank of England minimum leading rate (when it existed) as endogenous.

2 Below which it must not sink, in the case of the balance of payments.
3 See footnote 40 to Chapter 4 above.
4 See pp. 94–95 and 135–138 above.
5 The traditional approach is adopted by, for example, Fisher (1968), Pissarides (1972), Friedlaender (1973) and Frey and Schneider (1978b).
6 The definition of these statistics is:

Theil U-statistic = $\sqrt{\dfrac{\sum_{t=1}^{n}(a_t-p_t)^2}{\sum_{t=1}^{n}a_t^2}}$ where a_t, p_t are percentage first differences of 'observed' and 'tracked' values of the variable respectively, and n is number of observations.

RMSE = $\sqrt{\dfrac{\sum_{t=1}^{n}(A_t-P_t)^2}{\sum_{t=1}^{n}(A_t-\bar{A})^2}}$ where A_t, P_t are actual values of 'observed' and 'tracked' values of the variable respectively, and n is number of observations.

7 In 41 of 54 cases set out in Table 6.3, the response of the endogenous to the exogenous variable is lower in the modified than in the raw model. The multipliers of the exogenous variables on GDP and personal disposable income are almost invariably lower in the 'modified' than in the 'raw' model. In the case of employment and prices – where the predictive performance of the 'modified' model, see Table 6.2, is rather poor – the multipliers tend to *rise* as one passes from the 'raw' to the 'modified' model.
8 See p. 166 above.
9 This may be formally demonstrated as follows:
If an analyst models the macro-economy as

(1) $C_t = a + bY_t + u_t$ — C = consumption, Y = income, u = random element in consumption

(2) $Y_t = C_t + I_t + G_t$ — I = investment, G = government expenditure

then, if he treats government expenditure as autonomous, he will infer that the reduced-form equation for income is

$$Y_t = \frac{a + I_t + G_t}{1-b}$$

whence the multiplier of government expenditure on income is

(3) $$\frac{dy_t}{dG} = \frac{1}{1-b}$$

If in fact government demand G_t responds to 'errors' in the target variable Y according to a reaction function such as we have used above:

$$G_t = \bar{G}_t - g(Y_t - Y^*_t) + v_t \qquad \bar{G} = \text{'uncontrollable' government expenditure}$$
$$g = \text{reaction coefficient}$$

the reduced form for income will be

$$Y_t = \frac{a + \bar{G}_t + I_t + gY^*_t + u_t + v_t}{1 - b + g}$$

whence the true multiplier for income will be

$$\frac{\delta Y_t}{\delta G} = \frac{1}{1 - b + g} \tag{4}$$

If the true multiplier is (4) whereas the analyst measures it as (3), then his estimate will be biased upward to an extent determined by the size of the reaction-coefficient g.

10 This stabilising influence is traditionally symbolised by the 'IS/LM' representation of the macro-economy; see for example Chrystal (1982), Chapter 1.

11 Laury, Lewis and Ormerod (1978), p. 56, report that:

In a symposium on UK models held in 1972, Bispham, using the NI model of 1972/73, reported a real GDP multiplier of 0.98 after eleven quarters with respect to a sustained shock to current government expenditure, while the version of the model reported here gives a multiplier of 0.68 after eleven quarters. Ball, Burns and Miller reported a real multiplier of 1.11 after twenty-four quarters for the 1972 version of the LBS model against 1.06 in this simulation. Treasury results with a model of similar vintage reported by Evans and Riley show a real multiplier of 1.33 after sixteen quarters compared to 1.09 in the present version. The lower multiplier values found for the current versions of the NIESR and Treasury models are partly due to the higher import propensities which occur when the estimation period is extended to include more recent experience.

Conventional macro-economic textbooks, of course, tend to use arithmetical examples in which the value of the national income multiplier is anything between 2 and 10 depending on the marginal propensity to 'leak' income out of the economy.

12 Mowl (1980), p. 5.

13 An area in which this may not be true concerns the exchange rate. At present (January 1983) the pound is under pressure on the foreign exchanges and it is not clear, even to the Treasury, how far the Bank of England will intervene to protect it by buying pounds with its reserves of foreign currency.

14 See the discussion of Chapter 3, pp. 67–69 above; Blinder (1979), pp. 185–194 and Goldfeld and Blinder 1972, p. 193.

15 Fair (1978b) p. 1174.

7 The Political Business Cycle

7.1 Introduction

We have argued throughout this book that the response of economic policy instruments to the state of the economy in a democracy is essentially technocratic in the electoral mid-term but political during the run-up to an election. However, the political element in the process has in our statistical estimations been vulgarised into a simple government-induced boost to disposable income during the year before the election. The evidence from Chapters 4 and 5 is that this boost still happens; but there is more to the political element in policy-making than this, and in this chapter we review the main controversies in the theory of the political business cycle.

The literature provides two entirely distinct explanations of why governments may deliberately destabilise an economy for political reasons. According to one story the government deliberately *reflates* the economy in the period before an election in order to win electoral support. According to the other story the government deliberately *deflates* the economy whenever aggregate demand becomes excessive in order to prevent a squeeze on profits. In the first case the essential stimulus to the political business cycle comes from the demand side of the 'market' for government policies and in the second case it comes from the supply side. We shall therefore refer to the two approaches as 'demand-side' and 'supply-side' explanations respectively.

7.2 Demand-side explanations: the 'pre-election boost'.

Most demand-side explanations of the cycle share the following characteristics. Firstly, 'the government' (assumed to be unified) is a vote-maximiser.[1] Secondly, the electorate is short-sighted and therefore cannot 'see through' a pre-election boom.[2] Thirdly, the consequences of the pre-election boom take a long time to feed through into inflation, by which time the election is over and the boom has (the government hopes) served its purpose.[3] There is substantial difference betwen these writers in the way they construct the government's objective function and in the time horizon over which they see maximisation as taking place.[4] But as they all lead to the same prediction, namely that government economic policy will be more expansionary during the run-up to an election than at other times irrespective of the objective condition of the economy, it is impossible to choose between them on the basis of their explanatory power, and the choice between these different sub-hypotheses becomes purely a matter of taste.

TABLE 7.1 Great Britain: changes in budget surplus and personal disposable income in election years

Date of election	*'Incumbent' government*	*Change in real personal disposable income per capita in previous 12 months (%)*	*Change in taxes in previous budget (£m; value in a full year)*
(a) 1953–74			
May 1955	Conservative	6.9	– 150
October 1959	Conservative	5.0	– 350
October 1964	Conservative	3.1	101
March 1966	Labour	6.7	298
June 1970	Labour	4.6	– 202
February 1974	Conservative	– 4.0	– 462
Annual average for entire period		2.7	– 110
(b) 1974–82			
May 1979	Labour	8.2	425
Annual average for entire period		1.1	– 266

Note The second general election of 1974 is not included in the analysis.
Sources As for Tables 4.1, 4.2, 5.3 and 5.4.

There are two reasons, however, why it may be worth taking the matter a little further here. The first is that even though the prediction of a pre-election stimulus to the economy is common to this entire family of political business cycle theories it is not – as we discovered in Chapters 4 and 5 – always right. The second is that the motivational assumption by which one explains the cycle *does* have relevance for any proposals which one may make to diminish its intensity.

We can begin by taking a second look at data already presented in Chapters 4 and 5. Tables 7.1 and 7.2 set out the changes in policy instruments and in personal disposable income – the only thing which correlates at all systematically with government popularity[5] – in postwar pre-election periods in the UK and the US respectively. Average growth

TABLE 7.2 United States of America: changes in budget surplus and personal disposable income in presidential election years.

Date of election	*'Incumbent' presidential candidate*	*Change in real personal disposable income per capita in previous 12 months (%)*	*Change in full-employment budget surplus in previous calendar year ($bn)*
(a) 1948–74			
1948	Truman	3.4	6.2
1952	Stevenson	1.1	– 1.8
1956	Eisenhower	2.6	6.2
1960	Nixon	0.0	12.9
1964	Johnson	5.6	– 3.0
1968	Humphrey	2.8	– 19.1
1972	Nixon	3.3	– 0.9
Annual average for entire period		2.3	– 0.5
(b) 1974–1982			
1976	Ford	3.3	– 7.0
1980	Carter	– 0.9	– 28.1
Annual average for entire period		1.5	– 0.7*

Note * 1974–80 only; no data for 1981 and 1982.

Sources As for Tables 4.1, 4.2, 5.3 and 5.4.

rates have been separately calculated for the period before and after 1974 to reflect the slow-down in world productivity growth which began around this date.

We consider first the case of the United States, where the date of the presidential election is fixed by the constitution and where the administration in consequence has no freedom of manoeuvre in timing the election. It is apparent from Table 7.2 that on the evidence of the past thirty years there is a two-out-of-three chance (literally six out of nine) that the budget will be more than usually reflationary in an election year, and there is also a two-out-of-three chance that the annual increase in take-home pay will be higher than normal in a presidential election year. The pattern of election-year reflation is weakest in the years before 1960, and it is probably no coincidence that these were the years when confidence in the *administration* (as distinct from the academic community) concerning the ability of fiscal policy to bring lasting increases in prosperity was weakest.[6] In 1980, for the first time since the war, there was a *decline* in real personal disposable income in a presidential election year, but this year in fact contained a stimulus to the high-employment budget deficit of $28 billion,[7] the greatest that had yet been encountered. That this quite intentional boost to the economy did not feed through into real take-home pay was due, so far as one can see, purely to a recession of a depth which the President's economic advisers had not anticipated[8] accompanied by postwar record levels of inflation.

In Britain the constitutional position is different, in that the government can choose when to call a general election during a five-year period following the previous one. The budget change in taxes is 'unexpectedly' reflationary in only four cases out of seven. In the three cases when it was not, namely the spring of 1964, 1966 and 1979, there is clear evidence that the balance of payments was acting as a constraint on the government's ability to reflate.[9] The second of these cases is particularly interesting, since it provides an example of the British government doing what is not possible in America, namely to choose a moment of economic *crisis* to appeal to the nation's loyalty. This is a case which cannot be fitted into the standard theory of the political business cycle, in which a boom is always arranged to coincide with the election. In March 1966 the strategy came off for the ruling Labour party; in February 1974, when the experiment was tried again by the Conservative party amidst the crisis imposed by petrol scarcity and a miners' strike, it failed.

In Britain, a deliberate stimulation of *personal disposable income* is far more likely to accompany an election than a tax-cutting budget. Above-normal increases in real take-home pay occurred in six election years out of seven, the solitary exception being February 1974 when, as in America in 1980, a very generous preceding budget was swamped by a move into recession and inflation at the same time. This makes perfect political sense. Voters, as we have seen, welcome increases in their real take-home pay.[10] But they are likely to be more welcoming to increases which they see as lasting than to increases which they see as temporary. Budgets, given the quaint British system in which secret decisions are pulled out of a locked despatch box once a year amid a blaze of publicity, are particularly likely to be seen as providing the latter, and to be stigmatised as such by that part of the popular press which supports the opposition.[11]

Hence the budget – these days – may in fact be the *least* sensible way of trying to stimulate take-home pay. What is needed is a boost which will promote the necessary sense of well-being but can avoid being labelled as a political gimmick with transitory effects on welfare. A classical example of such a boost is 1979 in the United Kingdom. That year inflation was rising, the balance of payments was in deficit, and a tax-cutting budget would have looked irresponsible. The budget that Mr Healey intended to present in early April in fact never went through in its originally intended form, as the Government had by that time been defeated in a confidence motion, and had to agree its Budget with the Opposition; but it is clear that it would have been broadly neutral, apart from the indexation of tax allowances, rather than stimulative.[12] Something however had to be done in the light of the coming election. And indeed, behind the scenes, the following things were happening:

(i) The large pay increases recommended by the Top Salaries Review Board, which had reported in June 1978, were being paid in full, after much debate in Cabinet,[13] over a phased period of two years.

(ii) An 'underpinning' of £3.50 per week was offered on Cabinet instructions to local authority manual workers to enable them to receive more than would have been available under the 5 per cent pay norm then prevailing.

(iii) Following a brief strike and work to rule by some civil servants, a very large pay award to all categories of civil servants was agreed in February 1979. The bottom grade of the principal's scale,[14] which at that time stood at £6791 per annum plus £524 London weighting, was raised by this agreement to £7402, rising to £7742 in August and £8850 plus £780 London weighting in January 1980. This meant that civil servants in this representative grade were being promised a pay increase of 31.6 per cent in 1979 against an inflation rate which at that time stood at 9.6 per cent (but was forecast to rise). The outturn was an inflation rate of 13.4 per cent,[15] or a real income gain of over 18 per cent, for the lucky young administrator.[16]

(iv) Also in February an independent commission was established to study comparability of pay in the public and private sectors under the chairmanship of Professor Hugh Clegg. The intention was that the establishment of this commission would appease the resentment felt against, in particular, the civil servants' rise by groups such as doctors, teachers, policemen and the armed forces. It was intended that this Commission should report by August 1979 – that is, *before* the deadline for a general election, which was in October – but any hope of using the report for electoral purposes was thwarted by the government's defeat on a confidence motion in March of 1979.[17]

The combined effect of these measures, in conjunction with the fact that the peak of the boom in private sector production had not been reached, was to secure an increase in real per capita disposable income, over the twelve months to the election in May 1979, of 8.2 per cent[18] in spite of the absence of any budgetary stimulus. Even this was not enough to win the election for the Labour party. Its popularity deficit in relation to the Conservative opposition, as measured by the Gallup Poll, fell from minus 20 per cent in February at the peak of that winter's strike wave to minus 2 per cent in May,[19] but it was a case of one of those damned spurts which did not come in the nick of time.[20] The central point remains. The improvement in personal standards of living which achieved all this was achieved not by open and deliberate handouts in the Budget which could be labelled as overt electioneering but by decisions in which the Government could pose as a passive actor and thereby escape that charge. In fact it was very far from a passive actor, since in all of the four cases mentioned above the decision was debated, and could have been thrown out, by the Cabinet; but by keeping a low profile the Cabinet could hope to avoid the change of vulgar electioneering. In the run-up to the following election, the whole process began again. Because of a risk of an overt breach in the medium-term financial strategy, the Budget could not be very expansionary and confined such expansion as there was to marginal increases in the level of tax allowances and reliefs for house-owners.[21] But in the two months before the election there were announcements that the planned programme of closures in the steel industry was to be stretched out over a longer period than anticipated,[22] that the Serpell report, which proposes similar rationalisations on British Railways, would be implemented 'in due course' and not immediately,[23] and that the real value of the central government grant to local authorities was to be increased. It requires little imagination to see that here, once again, the government was helping to shape pre-election economic welfare not by acting overtly but, much more desirably, by not acting. The *content* of a pre-election economic package, in other words, is if anything more important than its size: it must produce a feeling of well-being in the electorate without being presented *as* a package. Invisibility is everything.

All of this has a good deal of bearing on the frequently encountered proposition that the political business cycle would die if people could be educated to see pre-election spurts as mere symbolic gestures which simply raise inflation and have no long-term effect on their real income. The point is not simply that an astute government can avoid ever allowing a pre-election economic package to be so represented. It is also that not even the best economists in the world are able to tell them what the precise effects of such a package would be. Estimates of the present shape of the 'short-term' Phillips curve differ wildly,[25] from those who see any stimulus to aggregate demand as being purely inflationary in the short term to those who see it as having big effects on employment over any time period that a government need worry about. The Labour party claim that a £10 billion boost to the economy would create at least 2 million additional jobs; a hard-line 'new classical monetarist' would deny that such a measure could create any additional jobs.[26] Many different models are in competition with one another, but none of them provides an acknowledged 'best forecast' against which to test such claims. Amidst such a cacophony of discordant voices, it is crazy to expect voters, however educated, to come to a unanimous or 'rational' judgement about what the effects of a pre-election boost will be and to punish the government for its 'irresponsibility'.[27] Macro-economics simply is not an exact enough science to make this possible. Hence it is a safe bet that future governments will keep the mechanism of the political business cycle going for some years to come. Pre-election boosts are not always recognised as such; they are usually good for the popularity ratings; and their long-term consequences cannot be clearly foreseen. So they will probably continue, even if the pressure of external circumstances sometimes causes them to fail in their objective.

7.3 Supply-side explanations; big business and macro-economic policy

We now consider the proposition that governments may spontaneously choose to puncture a boom in the economy in the interests of businessmen. Some writers see this as a response to a 'profits squeeze': Boddy and Crotty, for example, argue on the basis of American evidence that businessmen are likely to ask for a deflation of demand in the boom because 'halfway through the typical expansion the economy experiences a pronounced decline in the ratio of profits to wages'[28] since prices in the boom rise less fast than wages. But Kalecki's own position was more circumspect. He conceded that *in the short term,* booms would be 'less likely to reduce profits than to increase prices',[29] and that any deflationary measures might have harmful short-term effects for businessmen. But, he argued, such deflationary measures could yield *longer-term* benefits: they would restore discipline amongst the labour force, make the sack into an effective threat,[30] and to the extent that they enlarged the relative size of the private sector of the economy, they would make the government more dependent on the confidence of businessmen for achieving its economic targets.[31] The test of both these approaches, however, is the proposition that some indicator of the state of business welfare can influence the direction of macro-policy *independently* of conventional targets of economic policy such as inflation or the balance of payments; for if this is not the case, then these 'radical' theories are empirically no different from the 'stimulus-response' approaches to policy which we examined in Chapters 4 and 5. We now embark on such a test.

Figure 7.1 plots the course through time of profits and days lost due to industrial disputes (the most obvious triggers for a 'supply-side' political business cycle) and also inflation and the balance of payments, and Table 7.3 gives summary details of each of the deflationary episodes which qualified as 'significant' by the criteria of Chapters 4 and 5. The first thing which is apparent from this table is that changes in the share of profits in GNP are a very poor predictor of deflationary episodes: in the United States, only half of such episodes are associated with a fall in the profit share, and in Britain it is only three out of seven. More often than not, in other words, profits are actually *rising* even as a percentage of national product when governments embark on deflationary policies. This particular Marxian proposition

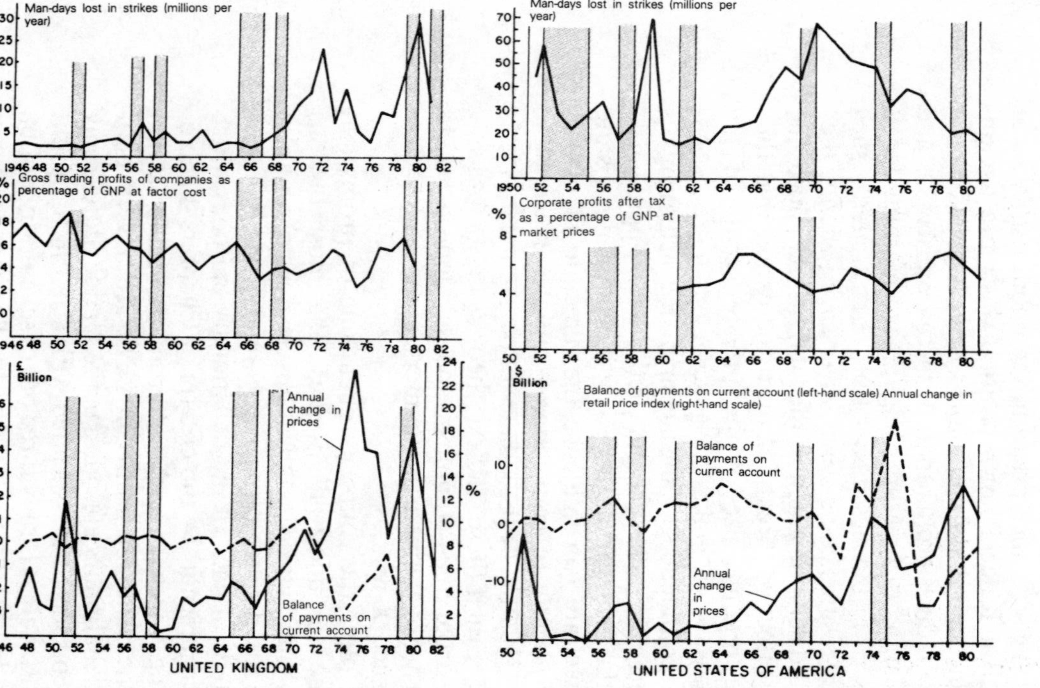

Figure 7.1 United States and United Kingdom: industrial disputes, profits and state of the economy in relation to deflationary episodes, 1946–82

Sources United Kingdom: inflation and balance of payments – Tables 4.1 and 5.3 above. Company profits – *Economic Trends Annual Supplement* (1983), table 38. Man-days lost in strikes – *Annual Abstract of Statistics,* various. United States of America: inflation and balance of payments – Tables 4.1 and 5.3 above. Corporate profits and man-days lost in strikes – OECD, *Main Economic Indicators,* various issues.

Symbols ▒: *periods of 'significant deflationary change' in policy instruments as defined on pp. 101 and 137.*

TABLE 7.3 United States and Great Britain: characteristics of postwar deflations

Great Britain				*United States*			
	Was episode associated with:				*Was episode associated with:*		
Date of deflationary episode	*Increase in man-days lost due to industrial disputes?*	*Fall in share of profits in GNP?*	*Deterioration in balance of payments (before 1974)? or inflation (after 1974)?*	*Date of deflationary episode*	*Increase in man-days lost due to industrial disputes?*	*Fall in share of profits in GNP?*	*Deterioration in inflation?*
1951	Yes	No	Yes	1951	Yes	Yes	Yes
1956	No	Yes	No	1955–6	Yes	No	Yes
1958	Yes	No	Yes	1958	Yes	Yes	Yes
1965–6	Yes	Yes	Yes	1961	No	No	No
1968	Yes	No	No	1969	No	Yes	Yes
1979	Yes	No	Yes	1974	No	Yes	Yes
1981	No	Yes	No	1979	No	No	Yes
				1981	No	Yes	No

Source Time lost in industrial disputes and share of profits in GNP: as for Figure 7.1. Balance of payments and inflation: Tables 4.1 and 5.3. Changes in variables are measured as the difference between the stated year's average value of that variable and the previous year's average.

therefore appears empirically doubtful for the years under examination.[32]

In the United States the alternative Marxian hypothesis of an association between deflationary episodes and industrial militancy appears equally weak – the association is only apparent in four cases out of eight, and in none of these cases does it explain something which is not already explained by the trend in the inflation rate. In Britain, however, five out of seven deflationary years since 1951 have also been years of increased work stoppages due to industrial disputes. There is an identification problem here, of course, since booms tighten the labour market, which leads both to a higher probability of strike action being successful in raising wage settlements and also to inflation. But there are three cases at least, 1956, 1968 and 1981, where Britain took deflationary action even though there was no deterioration in the balance of payments position since the previous year;[33] the second of these years, only, is also correlated with an increase in industrial militancy. Let us look a little more closely at these episodes.

The deflation of 1956 was the Conservative government's response to a run on the gold and foreign exchange reserves. Since 1951 the Conservative government had been gradually removing controls on the export and import of capital, and since sterling was in widespread use as a reserve currency at this time, the British economy was thus doubly exposed to unexpected movements in the reserves which bore no relation to the underlying balance of payments position. One such occurred in the summer of 1955, and another in the wake of the Suez fiasco in autumn 1956.[34] There was a continuing net export of capital over this period, which Dow ascribes to a growing belief among investors that British finances were 'unsound'.[35] Between them these sterling crises account for much of the tough budgetary action in the spring of 1956 and the increases in Bank rate later on in the year. They mark the beginning of a debate between those who favoured responding in this way to a financial crisis and those who favoured an adjustment in the external value of the pound.

By 1968, our second episode, this debate had for the first

time since 1949 been resolved by a devaluation of the pound, in the previous November. The balance of payments improved throughout the year, but the improvement did not appear as such until after the event,[36] which left the Chancellor, as he felt, no option but to continue with a deflationary policy until such time as the devaluation might take effect on the foreign balance. In addition to this there were runs on the reserves in December 1967 and March 1968,[37] and the result was what a standard commentary on the economic policy of that period describes as 'perhaps the most formidable deflationary budget since the war'.[38] A ceiling on bank lending was fixed in May; in November, with things still seeming to be 'getting worse rather than better',[39] there was an additional tightening of control on bank lending, and the introduction of an import deposit scheme.[40] Meanwhile there was, as previously noted, an increase in industrial militancy. This consisted in large part not of strikes officially called by trade unions, but of strikes called at plant level in the defiance of the unions. This caused the government, as noted in Table 4.8 above, to divert its attention from incomes policy to legislation on unofficial strikes, for which it was ultimately unable to get sufficient support within its own party. The macro-economic measures described above could, on the evidence of this raw data, be interpreted as a Kaleckian counterpart to this legislation designed to 'restore discipline in the factories'.[41] But it is difficult to find evidence to support this view. The Confederation of British Industry (CBI) felt that the Chancellor's Budget of 1968 was too harsh (whereas its attempts to introduce order into industrial relations law were not harsh enough),[42] and by the summer of the following year were openly supporting a change of government.[43] It is hard to interpret British economic policy of 1968 as anything but a reaction to a balance of payments positon which at the time seemed worse than it really was.

It is even harder to find support coming from the industrial lobby in the case of the third British deflation not 'justified' by the inflation or balance-of-payments position, that of 1981. In the previous autumn the Director of the CBI had made his famous promise of a 'bare-knuckled fight'[44] with the government over its refusal to do anything to reduce the level of interest rates, and after the harsh Budget of 1981 the CBI persisted in its demand for a reduction of the National Insurance Surcharge, even at the cost of a 'temporary' increase in the public sector borrowing requirement.[45]

If these deflations, then, were not demanded by the industrial lobby, nor necessitated by the state of the government's target variables, the question remains what did prompt them. One is tempted to find the answer in pressures by the financial sector, whose inter-linkage with industry happens to be much looser in Britain and the US than in most other advanced capitalist countries. As Frank Longstreth emphasises:

> The major British clearing banks have for a long period kept to short-term overdraft loans to industrial customers, avoiding shareholdings and long-term loans as well as any involvement in industrial management, promotion or restructuring. While there has been a fairly dramatic growth in institutional shareholding in the past two decades, the predominant effect of the Stock Exchange and other financial institutions of the City has been to reinforce a short-term attitude towards profits, earnings and investments in manufacturing firms. This economic dominance of financial capital is mirrored by a position of super-privileged access and influence on the part of the City as regards the political system. For the major part of the post-war period, as in earlier times, the political influence of the City and the Bank of England has weighed on the side of liberalism, whether in the drive for convertibility in the 1950s, the defence of sterling in the 1960s or the convertion to monetarism in the 1970s, policies which explicitly or implicitly undercut the corporatist alternative.[46]

We have now witnessed episodes from each of those three phases of policy. It was in the last of them, perhaps, that the split between industrial and financial interests opened widest. In March 1981, by contrast with the CBI attitudes above described:

> one broadly-based poll of normally discrete financiers confirmed this picture. Published in March 1981 it found nearly 80% of the senior managers in banks, money markets, investment houses, the stock market, insurance companies etc. in strong agreement with government strategy. At a point when industrialists were complaining rather loudly of the effects of a high exchange rate, as many as 40% thought the level ($2.28 to the pound) about right or too low . . . .[47]

It does seem, then, that the government does sometimes spontaneously deflate the economy in a manner not required by the state of the prevailing target variables nor, therefore, explained by the 'satisficing' response pattern set out in Chapters 4 and 5. But to the extent that this happens, it seems to happen for reasons quite separate from the desire of Kalecki's capitalists to undermine the 'self-assurance and class-consciousness of the working class'. It seems rather, to be a short-term attempt by the government to retain the 'confidence' of the financial community at times when this has been called into question.

7.4 Conclusions

There are, then, two kinds of political pressure which may deflect economic policy-making from its pursuit of the administration's current economic target variables. The first is a pressure believed to come from the mass electorate for a stimulus to personal disposable income. The second is a pressure believed to come from businessmen for a periodic deflation of the economy. We have found evidence of response to both these pressures, but not in the form suggested by the literature. The stimulus given to the economy in the year or so before an election seems often nowadays to take the form of an *indirect* stimulus to personal income rather than an overt gesture such as a tax-cutting budget which could be interpreted as an insult to the floating voter's intelligence. Given the lack of unanimity amongst experts concerning the economic effects of such measures, however, there seems little likelihood that any future government will get a clear enough signal that they have 'backfired' to persuade it to desist from such measures in the future. Stimuli to purchasing power in advance of an election, then, are probably an inescapable feature of the political landscape in countries where the government is democratically elected, until such time as there is consensus regarding the likely effects of economic policies.

Deflation of the economy in years when there was no inflationary or foreign payments crisis – a much commoner phenomenon in Britain than in America – also occurred but seems to have had little to do directly with falling profits or industrial unrest, and indeed often to have been opposed by the business lobby. In Britain, at least, it seems generally to have been a response to pressure from financial interests to provide proof, following a run on the currency, that the economy was being administered on principles of 'sound finance'. This phrase means very little in an objective sense; but it has enormous emotive value for those who sustain the structure of credit. In our final chapter we speculate further on the limitations which it imposes on macro-economic management.

Notes

1 MacRae (1977), p. 241; Nordhaus (1975), p. 174; Mosley (1978), p. 377; Chappell and Peel (1979), p. 329.
2 Nordhaus (1975), p. 172; Mosley (1978), p. 383; Fair (1978a), pp. 159–73; MacRae (1977), p. 241.
3 MacRae (1977), p. 243; Nordhaus (1975), p. 170; Blinder (1979), p. 30; Tufte (1978), p. 33
4 These differences can be summed up as follows:

Voters' rate of discount of the past within an election year	*Government's time horizon*	
	Next election	*Infinite*
Complete	Lindbeck (1976)	Frey and Schneider (1978)
Positive finite	Nordhaus (1975)	Frey and Lau (1968)
No discounting	MacRae (1977)	

5 See Chapter 2 above, pp. 30–33.
6 Tufte (1978, pp. 16–18) suggests in addition that during the Eisenhower years (when the link between election years and governmental stimulation of the economy was weakest) the president may have had sufficient trust in his personal popularity to make pre-election stimulation of the economy unnecessary.

7 In Table 7.2 it appears as a cut of that amount in the full-employment budget surplus.

8 The (January) 1980 report of the Council of Economic Advisers states:

> The expected recession is likely to be mild and brief. Declines in GNP should not extend much past mid-year, and economic growth will resume later this year, albeit slowly at first. (p. 67)

In fact growth of real GNP remained around or below zero not only throughout 1980, but throughout 1981 and 1982 as well.

9 The balance of payments deficits in question were, for the first two quarters of the year:

1964	−£109 m
1966	−£107 m
1979	−£884 m

In the first of these cases, the government's failure to do more than it did about the balance of payments problem is believed to have helped lose it the election of October 1964.

10 See Chapter 2 above, Table 2.2 and pp. 33–37.

11 Here is one piece of 'exposure' of this sort:

> WHO ARE THEY TRYING TO KID?
> We DON'T want a Budget designed to win votes
> We DO want honesty from our politicians.
> (*Sun,* 10 March 1970)

For other examples, see Mosley (1982), p. 18.

12 See Barnett (1982) pp. 181–3.

13 For the details of which, see Barnett (1982) pages 160–1. When the Labour government was defeated at the general election of May 1979 the incoming Conservative government honoured these pay awards.

14 The Principal grade is the fifth grade down from the top in the administrative civil service.

15 Table 5.3.

16 I was one at the time!

17 The Clegg Commission did report in the summer, and did award inflationary pay increases, which the incoming Conservative government allowed to be paid in full.

18 Per capita disposable income at 1975 prices was measured by the Central Statistical Office at £3730 in the second quarter of 1979 against £3446 in the second quarter of 1978.

19 *Gallup Political Barometers 1977–1980,* cols 2 and 3.

20 'A government is not supported a hundredth part so much by the constant, uniform, quiet prosperity of the country as by those damned spurts which Pitt used to have just in the nick of time' Brougham, 1814, cited by Tufte (1978), p. 3.

21 The boost to demand in the budget of 15 March 1983 was under £2 billion, largely confined to an increase in the value of tax allowances on individuals and on mortgages.
22 Patrick Jenkin, *Hansard,* 20, December 1982, cols 672–6.
23 David Howell, *Hansard,* 20, January 1983, cols 489–91.
24 For example, Oppenheimer in Harrod (1978); MacRae (1975); Minford and Peel (1981), page 12.
25 In evidence to the House of Commons Treasury and Civil Service Committee inquiry on *Monetary Policy,* Professor Laidler suggested that on his model an increase of 1 per cent in unemployment might reduce the inflation rate by 5 per cent (United Kingdom 1981, vol. I, p. lxxiv) whereas the Treasury suggested that over four years a lasting fall in inflation of 1 per cent would have to be bought at the cost of an increase in unemployment of 2½ per cent, or otherwise put, that an increase of 1 per cent in unemployment might reduce the inflation rate by 0.4 per cent. This implies a Phillips curve twelve times as flat – that is, twelve times less responsive to policy-induced changes in unemployment – than the one in Professor Laidler's model.
26 The *Alternative Economic Strategy* (Labour Co-ordinating Committee, London, 1980), p. 52, describes the bringing down of unemployment to 2½ per cent over five years as 'an objective by no means impossible to achieve' and on p. 54 suggest this be done by means of a £10 bn boost to public spending; for the contrary view, see Chapter 5 above, footnote 18. It is very difficult to compare the effects of (say) a £10 bn boost to demand in different econometric models because the assumptions which are made regarding the values of exogenous variables (in particular policy variables) differ as between models, over and above the differences in assumptions about individual behaviour.
27 For further discussion, see Chapter 8 below, pp. 204–206.
28 Boddy and Crotty (1975) p. 5, quoting Albert Burger, 'Relative Movements in Wages and Profits', *Federal Reserve Bank of St. Louis Review* 55 (February 1973), pp. 8–16.
29 Kalecki (1943), p. 326.
30 Kalecki (1943), p. 326; see Chapter 1, p. 7 above.
31 Kalecki (1943), p. 325; and Feiwel (1974), pp. 26–7.
32 Kalecki had himself conceded that this would be likely (see note 29 above). It is significant that Boddy and Crotty, the main proponents of the hypothesis of 'deflation as a response to profits squeeze' do not make a direct empirical test of this hypothesis, but infer its accuracy from the fact that profits tend to decline in the second half of the boom.
33 In 1956 and 1981 there was not even a balance of payments deficit of any sort.
34 Dow (1964), pp. 88–96.
35 Dow (1964), p. 96.
36 Successive Central Statistical Office estimates and forecasts of the current balance of payments were: (in £ million)

Date of estimate	*Calendar 1967*	*Calendar 1968*
November 1967	−350	−375
May 1968	−514	−375
November 1968	−404	−506
Current estimate:	−315	−271

Source Blackaby (1979), p. 48, and Table 4.1 above.

For further discussion of the policy implications of statistical revisions of this sort, see Appendix V below.

37 Blackaby (1979), pp. 44 and 45.

38 Blackaby (1979), p. 46; presumably written in 1977.

39 Blackaby (1979), p. 49.

40 Blackaby (1979), p. 47.

41 Kalecki (1943), p. 326.

42 *Industry Week* (CBI journal) 5 April 1968, p. 6 and 10 May 1968, p. 3.

43 *Industry Week* (CBI journal), 11 July 1969, pp. 8 and 9.

44 Reported in *Financial Times,* 11 November 1980.

45 See *Financial Times,* 3 and 4 November 1981. This demand persisted in the CBI's representations to the Government in respect of its 1982 and 1983 Budgets; for the former, see Table 3.2 above.

46 Longstreth (1983), p. 9.

47 Longstreth (1982), p. 52, citing *inter al. Guardian,* 2 March 1981.

8 Conclusions

The maintenance of full employment requires that we should be not only good but clever. ... It may turn out, I suppose, that vested interests and personal selfishness may stand in the way. But the main task is producing first the intellectual conviction and then intellectually to devise the means.
J.M. Keynes in a letter to T.S. Eliot, cited in R. Kahn, *Essays in Employment and Growth*, Cambridge University Press, 1972.

As a highly technical subject which nonetheless touches on the lives of billions of people, macro-economic policy has been beset by attempts to make it comprehensible by means of simple analogies. At different times, the job of economic policy-makers has been described as being like: steering a ship;[1] climbing a mountain;[2] weeding a garden;[3] servicing a central heating system[4] and healing a sick patient.[5]

All of these analogies have some merit but it is probably the medical one which can be taken furthest. The economic policy-maker, like the doctor, is trying to achieve what are often multiple objectives, by means of a variety of instruments whose linkage with the targets is by no means stable or predictable. Like the doctor, the economist finds sickness easier to define than health, but even the signs of sickness are often difficult to evaluate, with the implication that intervention may come too late. And like the doctor, the economist may over-prescribe once the diagnosis is clear, and court the accusation that he has aggravated the very condition he is in business to cure. Given this twofold risk both doctors and economic policy makers tend to be forced into what we have here called 'satisficing' or 'rule of thumb' behaviour – that is, the development of those decision rules in response to crisis which run the least risk of causing serious damage. In this book we have argued that in the economic sphere, this pattern of decision-making remained essentially unaltered throughout the postwar period in Britain and America, even though the guiding rule of thumb was changed in the mid-seventies. But once one looks at the results of policy the medical analogy starts to crumble. For although no-one would dispute that doctors have in the aggregate had a beneficial effect on the national health over the last fifty years, it would be a bold man who would assert that the astronomical increase in the number of economists over that period[6] has had any effect whatever on any of the major indices of economic welfare. To be sure, not all economists agree with what is going on at the moment, of which more shortly. But it is the case that the one advance in the reach of central economic policy-making which has taken place in that period, namely the governmental commitment to full employment, has now been quite explicitly repudiated, and unemployment is now at levels which, for the old at least, are now actually higher than those of the 1930s.[7] If state interference in the macro-economy does not actually make anyone any happier or better off, the whole business might as well be abandoned. It is therefore germane to ask whether, on the evidence made available in this book, the job of 'economic management' could be done better, should be done as at present, or should simply be jettisoned. The problem is that there is no agreement concerning what the job involves.

Postwar economic policy has been based on an attempt to juggle three balls in the air: full employment, price stability, and political democracy. In this it has failed: we have not been 'good' enough, in Keynes' words, to keep all the balls in the air at once. The result has been what we described in Chapter 1 as a process of 'search'. But different groups, in conducting their search, have operated on different value-premisses concerning which of these objectives was the most expendable. One ideological group has tended to treat the postwar pledge to full employment as the least vital link in the chain and these are conventionally labelled 'monetarists';[8] another group has continued to treat high employment as important and these are conventionally labelled 'Keynesians'. But each of these has its own model of the way the world works, which *follows from*, rather than existing in a separate chamber from, its view of the way the world ought to be. If one considers the choice between

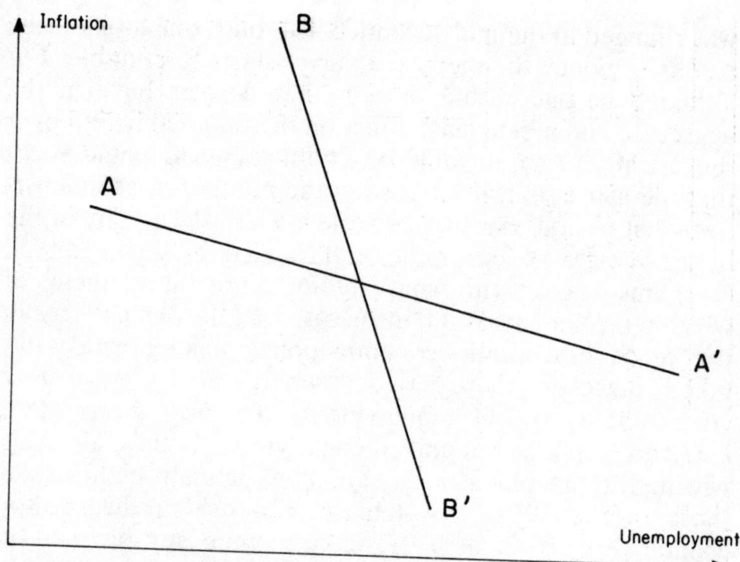

Figure 8.1 Alternative views of the world

inflation and unemployment, 'Keynesian' economists are likely to see a world in which markets adjust slowly to disequilibria and expectations adjust slowly to changes in the external world, producing a Phillips curve such as AA′ in Figure 8.1, which moves slowly clockwise, whereas 'monetarist' economists will see a world in which markets clear instantaneously and expectations quickly converge on a true picture of the world, producing a Phillips curve such as BB′ which quickly becomes vertical. Appended to this view of the world will be a set of subsidiary assumptions concerning the values which will be taken, over the forecasting period, by exogenous variables such as world demand and policy instruments themselves; for example, if a Keynesian finds that the short-term Phillips curve does not lie as 'flat' as he would like, he can 'flatten' it by assuming the government implements an incomes policy; if a monetarist finds that the link normally postulated between cuts in the growth of the money supply and inflation is threatened by the growth of social security payments in the recession, he can assume that the rate of social security benefit is flexible downwards. But once a person adopts a given view of the world, then the original element in his decision process, namely his value-judgement concerning the relative importance of different objectives of policy, is reinforced. For an individual who sees the world through 'new classical' eyes – and who therefore has constructed the underlying trade-off between inflation and unemployment as BB′ – is likely to conclude from the slope of this trade-off that any attempt to lower unemployment is futile, and *because* of this his original predisposition against treating unemployment as very important will be reinforced. As Aesop's fox demonstrated, many thousands of years ago, it is not common to put a high value on a thing one believes impossible of attainment. By contrast, an individual who sees the world through 'Keynesian' eyes, and hence sees a trade-off such as AA′, will see practical possibilities of fuller employment, and because of these perceptions will put a high value on fuller employment. Thus, on both sides of the fence, the ideology predetermines the choice of model, and the choice of model inevitably confirms the original ideology.

At present in Britain there are two complete models of the economy exhibiting a 'Keynesian' structure and 'Keynesian' recommendations about policy (Cambridge Economic Policy Group and the National Institute of Economic and Social Research), two exhibiting a broadly 'neo-classical' structure and professing 'monetarist' policy recommendations (Liverpool University and, more temperately, the London Business School) and one model rather uncomfortably bestriding the fence between the two (in HM Treasury). If there were a perfect market in economic models, then a process of competition between these rival views of the world might be expected to yield a 'winner', which produced the best forecasts, whereupon the defeated rival models would disappear from the market. Nothing of the kind appears to be happening. For one thing, the competition between models is spread across a large number of 'events' (that is, possible target variables of policy for which a prediction is required) and no one model is best at all of them: crudely speaking, the 'monetarist' models have been predicting better on inflation and the 'Keynesian' models have been predicting better on unemployment. But more fundamentally, the different models, as above noted, use different assumptions regarding exogenous variables, so that their different predictions are not really conformable – for example, a 'Keynesian' model might conclude that a £10 bn boost to the economy in the budget would have substantial effects on real output over four years and a 'monetarist' model deny this, but since both would be operating with quite different assumptions regarding complementary government policy, they would not be comparing like with like. Hence, the different available views of the world do not converge, or eliminate one another: they coexist, in a somewhat unstable oligopoly.[9] And because they coexist, the question of what is the 'right' economic policy cannot be answered. The medical analogy has now broken down almost completely.[10] There is no agreement among economists concerning the nature of the diseases that Western economies suffer from; nor is there any agreement concerning the type of macro-economic intervention which is appropriate to cure any of those diseases; nor, therefore, to return to the main theme of this book, is it possible to forecast with any sort of accuracy what direction macro-economic policy will take over the next few years.

However, let us have a try. In what follows I wish to concentrate attention on the proposals of the most coherent representatives of the two main alternative points of view. The most perceptive Keynesians realise that some form of social control must be instituted to deal with the problem of inflation at high levels of employment[11] and propose some new sort of incomes policy, often of the tax-based type; the most consistent monetarists see the deflation of the past three years as merely the prelude to a period of 'order' in which the rate of growth of the money supply and/or the budget deficit are restricted by the insertion of explicit norms for these variables into the national constitution. Let us explore these two positions a little further.

Tax-based incomes policy[12] is a logical sequel to the attempts made in the middle 1970s to relate the annual budget handout to the rate of increase of wages:[13] it makes the connection automatic. By comparison with previous incarnations of incomes policy it offers the advantage of allowing employers and workers to bargain freely without legal or governmental interference, and also of allowing relative pay to respond over long time-periods to relative changes in the productivity and scarcity of different groups of workers. The case in its favour is that if effective it could deliver a given quantum of inflation reduction at less cost in terms of lost output, lost employment and human misery than the monetarist alternative. The case against it is that it has administrative costs and may discourage productivity deals.

The proposal for imposing publicly announced limits on the budget deficit and the growth of the money supply[14] is also an evolutionary growth, but this time out of the medium-term financial strategy of the last three years rather than out of the Keynesian paradigm. Supporters of this proposal argue that it is necessary because

> the present British fiscal constitution contains a bias towards persistent budgetary deficits, and permits the manipulation of the economy for short-term political profit. The economic consequences are unremitting and volatile inflation, unending growth of government expenditure, and a continuous erosion of the effective functioning of the price system. If these conditions persist, the ultimate survival of British democracy itself will be at stake.[15]

It thus aims, like the tax-based incomes policy proposal, to get inflation down; it also promises to end the kind of 'short-term manipulation of the economy for political profit' described in our previous chapter. Unlike the Keynesian approach, it makes no proposals whatever concerning unemployment, and by implication assumes that it should be left to find its own level without the interference of government macro-economic policy.

It will be apparent from our previous discussion that there is no point in trying to offer a preference for one or other of these approaches on 'objective' or 'technical' grounds, after the manner of a doctor pronouncing on how best to cure a disease. Nor is such prescription any part of the purpose of this book. But it may be worth speculating on the future course of policy. For the last ten years or so macro-economic policy in Britain and America has been dominated by one objective, the desire to reduce inflation. There is something irrational about this. For the costs of *moderate* and *steady* inflation – namely the need to make more frequent trips to the bank, the need to change price-tags more frequently and an arbitrary redistribution of income away from those whose incomes are fixed in money terms[16] – are, to this observer at least, fairly trivial when compared with the costs of reducing inflation, particularly since the redistributive effect can be reduced by formal indexation of wages, savings and pensions. *Unsteady* inflation creates more uncertainty than steady inflation and may depress investment[17], but this is not a cost of inflation as such. There is little doubt, on the evidence of Chapter 2, that inflation has become more unpopular with the electorate of recent years, and administrations have faithfully responded to this movement; but the element of rationality in the original movement of public opinion is rather difficult to determine. Not only the popular media which we discussed in Chapter 2,[18] but also highly respectable academic commentators, have sought to whip up fear of inflation as such, not by an objective discussion of the trouble which it does cause, but by linking it quite without evidence to the risk of hyperinflation, a breakdown of the market economy and even a breakdown of moral standards.[19] Governments have now become involved in this sort of thing as well, of course, and so strident has the whole chorus become that it would not be surprising if many people had now moved from 'money illusion' – unawareness of inflation – to what we may call 'inflation illusion' – belief that if there were no inflation they could have converted their last *nominal* pay increase of say 10 per cent into a *real* increase of 10 per cent. Sooner or later this kind of illusion, like its predecessor, is bound to collapse, and when it does people's eyes are likely to focus less sharply on inflation itself and still more sharply on the loss of output and the unemployment that have been incurred in reducing it. When this happens governments would be wise to respond, as is already beginning to happen in the US.[20] The consequences of not doing so could be grave. It was not the memory of the hyperflation of 1923 which brought the Nazi Party to power in Germany ten years later, but the unemployment of the time, and the electorate's perception that only one party was capable of dealing with it. We therefore judge that an attempt to try and reduce unemployment whilst keeping inflation steady, such a tax-based incomes policy[21] has more chance of political success in Britain and America in the next five years than the anchoring of the budget and the money-supply to a rigid 'rule' which would allow no possibility of discretionary governmental response to recession.

There is a further fallacy in the 'balanced-budget rule' proposal, a fallacy which has coloured many discussions of the 'failures' of economic policy in past years. This is the belief voiced by Buchanan *et al.*,[22] Stewart,[23] Oppenheimer[24] and Brittan[25] amongst others, that those failures are due to the intrusion of too much 'politics' into the making of economic policy, and that if those political influences could somehow be reduced economic policy would be better done. The belief seems to me to be fallacious first of all because, as discussed earlier, economics is not like engineering or medicine; there is no consensus concerning what the 'right' economic policy is which would be implemented in the absence of 'political' influences.[26] For each individual there is an interrelated package consisting of his personal ethical preferences, and his view of how the economic world works, leading to an economic policy which is 'right' for him. The 'balanced-budget rule' is just one of these packages, and there is no *a priori* case for preferring it to all the others which are available. Simple rules are attractive to those who wish to make sense of a complex world but they can only be justified if some citizens are made happier than they otherwise would be by the application of this rule, and if those who suffer by it are compensated for their suffering.[27] There is little evidence that the application of a balanced-budget rule, which would put very many *additional* people out of work at a time when the rate of inflation is below 5 per cent, would do that.

But this particular rule is only a special case. The general point is that there is *no* fixed rule for the guidance of economic policy which commands sufficiently general assent to warrant its being enshrined in the constitution above the reach of political argument. It is only possible to remove an instrument of policy from 'politics' – that is, from competition between citizens to influence the way it is used – either by building a consensus or by exercising dictatorial power over the use of that instrument. Since whatever consensus there was during the 'Butskellite' years, possibly even up to 1974, has now broken down, it is in my view pointless to expect that the sequence of frequent policy reversals over the last 35 years, including the 'political business cycle', will be interrupted so long as our government stays democratic. It is possible for groups of experts who are semi-detached from the policy-making process, such as the UK Treasury's Policy Analysis Division, the US Congressional Budget Office and most of all the Sachverstaendigenrat in West Germany, to set out their view of the range of policy options, but no amount of expertise concerning the *technical* relationships involved can create a public choice. That can only be done by the ministers concerned, and we have argued that it will invariably be done, not by any continuous optimisation process but rather by an intuitive judgement concerning whether things are 'satisfactory' or not in relation to the major target variables at the time. Planning figures such as the medium-term financial strategy's targets for the money supply may appear to impose a constraint on this process, but in fact they should be seen more as an additional instrument, designed to influence expectations, than a constraint, since their 'limits' have been relaxed whenever, as in 1982, they conflicted with other economic objectives. The setting of loose medium-term targets such as this, reflecting the current government priorities, for some one 'leading target' variable – such as was done once before for the growth rate by the National Plan of 1964–66 – is about as far as it is possible to go by democratic means, I believe, in smoothing out the rate of change of government policy instruments. To go further is to deny or to suppress the diversity of opinion which exists concerning how the modern capitalist economy works and concerning what government can do to make it work better.

Notes

1 James Callaghan, introducing the 1967 Budget: *Hansard,* 11 April 1967, col. 1010.
2 R.A. Butler, introducing the 1952 Budget: *Hansard,* 17 March 1952, col. 2050.
3 Denis Healey, see epigraph to Chapter 3 above.
4 Anthony Barber: *Hansard,* 30 March 1971, cols. 1368–9.
5 Hugh Gaitskell: *Hansard,* 27 October 1955, col. 399.
6 In British central government there were only one or two in the inter-war period (Cairncross (ed.) (1981), pp. 7–8); in 1980 there were over six hundred *(Government Economic Service Directory).* For more detail and a discussion of the supply and demand for economists see the essay by Sir Alec Cairncross in Cairncross (1982).
7 Tomlinson (1982), pp. 21 and 22.
8 This prevailing philosophy of monetarism consists of the combination of a value judgement (the reduction of inflation should be the central goal of economic policy) with a technical judgement (there is a direct link between the rate of increase of the money supply and the price level). This present-day meaning of monetarism should not be confused with the old meaning, which related to the latter proposition only.
9 As might be expected in an oligopoly, there is a good deal of bumping and banging between the different competitors in their attempt to establish their claims, and since most of them depend on public money to survive, there are also allegations of political bias in the way this money is allocated. For a claim that this bias has recently worked to the detriment of the Cambridge modellers, see the essay by Weir (1982).
10 See Ian Kennedy, *Unmasking Medicine* (Reith Lectures, 1980; Paladin, 1982), Chapter 4.
11 The problem originally acknowledged by the Employment Policy White Paper of 1944: see p. 88 above.
12 For alternative expositions see United States, *Economic Report of the President and Annual Reprt of the Council of Economic Advisers* (1980), pp. 49 ff. and Layard (1982).
13 For Mr Healey's attempts to make a 'budgetary bargain' with unions and employees along these lines, see pp. 128–129 above. The Carter administration in the US would clearly have introduced a tax-based incomes policy of its own had it been re-elected in 1980; see reference cited in previous footnote.
14 See Buchanan, Burton and Wagner (1978), pp. 81 sq.
15 Buchanan, Burton and Wagner (1978), p. 81.
16 See Higham and Tomlinson (1982).
17 See memorandum by H.M. Treasury to Treasury and Civil Service Committee, United Kingdom (1981), vol. III, pp. 68–85.
18 Chapter 2 above, pp. 34–40 and especially Figure 2.4.

19 Here are two fairly typical examples of this idiom:

(1) We do not need to become full-blown Hegelians to entertain the general notion of *zeitgeist,* a 'spirit of the times'. Such a spirit seems at work in the 1960s and 1970s, and is evidenced by what appears as a generalised erosion in public and private manners, increasingly liberalised attitudes towards sexual activities, a declining vitality of the Puritan work ethic, deterioration in product quality, explosion of the welfare rolls, widespread corruption in both the private and the governmental sector, and, finally, observed increases in the alienation of voters from the political process. We do not, of course, attribute all or even the major share of these to the Keynesian conversion of the public and the politicians. But who can deny that inflation, itself one consequence of that conversion, plays some role in reinforcing some of the observed behaviour patterns. Inflation destroys expectations and creates uncertainty; it increases the sense of felt injustice and causes alienation. It prompts behavioural responses that reflect a generalised shortening of time horizons. 'Enjoy, enjoy' – the imperative of our time – becomes a rational response in a setting where tomorrow remains insecure and where the plans made yesterday seem to have been made in folly. (Buchanan and Wagner (1977), pp. 64–5)

(2) Inflation, and the spirit which nourishes it and accepts it, is merely the monetary aspect of the general decay of law and respect for law. It requires no special astuteness to realise that the vanishing respect for property is very intimately related to the numbing of respect for the integrity of money and its value. In fact, laxity about property and laxity about money are very closely bound up together; in both cases what is firm, durable, earned, secured and designed for continuity gives place to what is fragile, fugitive, fleeting, unsure and ephemeral. And that is not the kind of foundation on which the free society can long remain standing. (Wilhelm Röpke, *Welfare, Freedom and Inflation* (University of Alabama Press, 1964), p. 70. Cited in Buchanan and Wagner (1977), p. 65)

20 See Chapter 3, pp. 73–75 above.

21 If the Labour Party came to power it would be something slightly different from a tax-based incomes policy; it would probably be an 'agreement' with the unions, not enforceable by law, after the manner of 1975–8, possibly reinforced by a pact in which some trade unions would voluntarily abrogate strike action in return for index-linked pay rises (see *Financial Times,* 1 February 1983).

22 Buchanan, Burton and Wagner (1978), *passim* but especially pp. 81–4.

23 Stewart (1977), especially pp. 1–5.

24 In Harrod (1978), 54.

25 Brittan (1977), part IV.

26 This lack of consensus was well exposed in Britain in March of 1981. In that month the Chancellor of the Exchequer imposed tax increases of over £2 billion in his budget at a time when output was still falling; 364 economists in universities, or about half the total, signed a letter opposing the government's monetary policy; and the House of Commons Treasury and Civil Service Committee, on which the ruling Conservative party was in a majority, claimed (United Kingdom (1981), vol. 1, pp. xciv–xcv) that that policy lacked a sound theoretical and empirical basis. In their own words,

although over the long term the money supply and price level have moved together we have not been convinced by evidence of the direct causal relationship from growth in the money supply to inflation ... In the light of (this) experience, the view that monetary policy can work directly through expectations to reduce inflation without significantly affecting output is not valid. Emphasis in original.

27 This is the conventional welfare-economics principle of 'strict Pareto optimality'.

Appendices

Appendix I: A Formal Statement of 'Satisficing' Theory

This appendix sets out in full the basic propositions of 'satisficing' theory which, we argue in Chapter 1, is a good model for capturing the essentials of governmental decision-making in macro-economic policy. The exposition is heavily indebted to Simon (1952) and Downs (1967) but in making a distinction between 'routine' and 'non-routine' crises under (3) and (4) below we deviate from Simon's exposition. There are six basic postulates.

(1) Decision criteria

There are *acceptable-level* goals or aspiration-levels, that is, levels of targets which are not optimised, but set at a fixed level. Such goals are, in the case of a business firm, profit, inventory, or sales; in the case of an economics ministry such as the UK Treasury, unemployment, the rate of price inflation, or the level of foreign-currency reserves. The utility function for possible outcomes of policy exists, but it only has two values: good enough and not good enough. Formally, if $V(S)$ is the utility function attached to the set of possible policy outcomes S, then $V(S)$ splits into two parts, one of which, V', takes the value 1 and the other of which takes the value 0.

(2) Decision-making methods in normal times

At any given time, a set of rules of thumb for policy instruments will be in operation, whose application is thought to have a high probability of ensuring satisfactory outcomes for the target variables. These rules of thumb define the operating procedures of the organisation. Hypothetical examples of such rules of thumb are, for a business firm, 'set the wholesale price of the product by imposing a 20 per cent mark-up on normal ex-factory cost', and for a Treasury chief secretary (see pp. 46–47 above) 'confine the real growth of authorised spending in any government department to the expected real growth in the economy'. These rules of thumb are, as Wildavsky has emphasised (1964, p. 12; see also Heclo and Wildavsky (1979), pp. 21–29) *aids to calculation* in the face of uncertainty and limited resources with which to reduce it.[1] Formally, the set of policy actions A is scanned for a set of procedures A' which lead to outcomes in V', and one of the procedures in A', A^*, is put into operation.

(3) Response to 'routine crises'

If a crisis arises – that is, the application of the decision rule A^* does not lead to an outcome within V' – this does *not* automatically lead – at first – to search behaviour. (Here, we part company from Simon.) Rather, the standard rule of thumb continues to be applied. For example, if the standard rule A^* is 'reflate when unemployment is excessive, and deflate when the balance of payments deficit is excessive', then this rule will continue to be applied through the crisis, as it was during the 1950s. The greater the 'performance gap' between actual and desired values of the target variable, the stronger the variation, following the governing rule of thumb, in the prevailing instruments of policy. In a time of 'routine crisis' search behaviour *may* be initiated to prevent the crisis from recurring – for example, the attempts at quicker and more automatic stabilisation in the early 1960s. But this is not a necessary or predictable response.

(4) Response to 'major' or 'non-routine crises'

We define a *major* or non-routine crisis as a crisis which cannot be intelligently tackled by means of the prevailing decision rule; for example, a situation of rising unemployment and a deteriorating balance of payments, with both variables outside their tolerance limits, cannot be intelligently tackled by the rule of thumb 'deflate when the balance of payments is in crisis, and reflate when unemployment is in crisis'. Such non-routine crises stimulate search behaviour, usually resulting in the invention of new policy instruments (for example, the successive vintages of incomes policy). In general the changes explored with greatest intensity are those which cause the least disturbance to the bureau's operating procedures. The greater the time available for search before a decision has to be taken (for example, before the Budget has to be presented), the larger the number of new instruments and instrument-setting procedures that will be considered. If these new instruments fail to achieve their desired result, then one or more of the targets of policy must be jettisoned (for example, unemployment progressively through the middle to late 1970s).

(5) Determination of the 'desired level'
The desired levels of targets are reached by the resolution, usually through a compromise, of a *conflict* between different components of the organisation with different basic goals. The 'satisficing' inventory level, in a firm, can be seen as the compromise outcome of a bargaining process between a conservative stores manager and an expansionist sales director; likewise the 'satisfactory' levels of particular targets of economic policy can be seen as compromises between groups in the policy-making circle pushing in opposite directions: the target level of unemployment, in the 1960s, as a compromise between the Bank of England, concerned to preserve a margin of unused resources, and the economic ministers, fearful of their standing in Parliament and in the country; the target level of reserves, in the same period, as a compromise between the Finance department of the Treasury, which is directly responsible for the welfare of sterling, and the National Economy department. If the actual level of a target is stable, the 'satisfactory' or 'desired' levels of that target can be expected to remain stable also, unless the relative bargaining strength of one of the parties in such a conflict changes for an extraneous reason. If, however the actual level of the target is subject to a trend, we may expect to notice a movement in the 'desired' level. If the actual level is above the desired level for a considerable period, the desired level will move up; if the actual level is below the desired level for a long time, the desired level will move down. In other words there are

(6) Flexible targets

These are 'acceptable levels' of goals which are not rigid, but are revised in an upward or downward direction according as performance exceeds or falls short of aspiration. Sales in a given period greater or less than the target level fixed for that period will lead to higher or smaller targets, respectively, for the next period; likewise, unemployment which in any period exceeds the desired level of unemployment after the available instruments have been applied may be expected to lead to a less optimistic unemployment *target* next period, which indeed seems to reflect the attitude of British chancellors facing successively deeper unemployment troughs, and successively more severe periods of inflation, over the period 1951–71: see p. 102 above.

The essential differences between this approach and standard 'optimising' theory are, therefore:

(i) the adoption of a welfare function with only two values rather than an infinite number;
(ii) the persistence of 'rules of thumb' even though they are not consistent with optimisation;
(iii) the assumption that knowledge about the shape of the constraint is limited;
(iv) the assumption that search behaviour will take place if and only if the organisation's operating procedures are exposed as being unable intellectually to cope with a prevailing crisis;
(v) the assumption that the organisation's notion of what is attainable adapts to discrepancies between performance and achievement.

Notes

1 It has so often been stated that satisficing procedures are a response to uncertainty and limited information-processing resources that those terms must be defined here:

Uncertainty means ignorance concerning (1) whether instrument variables (for example, the public sector borrowing requirement) can be moved to their desired levels, and concerning (2) what, if they do attain their desired levels, the effect of this on the target variables will be. Characteristically a variety of predictions will be available on (2) from different model-building teams, but it will not be possible to say what is the probability that each of these predictions will come true.

Limited information-processing resources means, essentially, limited facilities for *evaluating* the information that comes in, rather than a shortage of raw material. Downs puts the general point in this way:

> The radar supervisor in Hawaii whose subordinate picked up returns from unidentified aircraft on the morning of December 7, 1941 knew that fact, but he did not grasp its significance. The number of facts gleaned every day by any large organisation is immense. In theory, (a) screening process . . . transmits only the most significant facts to the men at the top, and places them in their proper context along the way. But . . . considerable distortion occurs in this process. Each part of the organisation tends to exaggerate the importance of some events and to minimise that of others. This naturally produces a healthy scepticism among officials at the top of the hierarchy.
>
> An inescapable result of this situation is a rational insensitivity to signals of alarm at high levels. This may have disastrous consequences when these signals are accurate. (Downs (1967), p. 189).

Compare Sir Alec Cairncross' testimony on policy-making in the UK Treasury, Chapter 3, note 40, above.

Appendix II: When is an instrument not an instrument? Fiscal and monetary marksmanship, 1951–83[1]

We have consistently defined an instrument as a variable, having some influence on the economy, which is under the government's control. Commentators have often cited the government's fiscal deficit and the money supply as examples of policy instruments. In fact, as demonstrated for example on pp. 70–72 above, these variables are not directly under the government's thumb at all, since the demand for money and the elasticity of the tax base with respect to tax rates cannot be precisely forecast. In this appendix we consider whether there is anything systematic about the errors which the British government has made in forecasting the value of these 'instruments'.

Table A.1 sets out the value of the budgetary errors made in Great Britain between 1951/52 and 1981/82. It reveals

TABLE A.1 United Kingdom: public expenditure and taxation: out-turn in relation to official forecast

Fiscal year	(1) *Taxation*[1] *(£ million)*			(2) *Expenditure*[2] *(£ million)*			(3) = (2) − (1) *Fiscal 'deficit'*[3] *(£ million)*			
	Expected revenue	*Actual revenue*	*Difference between actual and expected (% of actual) in brackets)*	*Planned expenditure*	*Actual expenditure*	*Difference between actual and expected (% of actual) in brackets)*	*Planned deficit (-: surplus)*	*Actual deficit*	*Difference between actual and expected deficit (£ million)*	*(as a % GNP)*
1951/52	4015	4190	174 (4.1)							
1952/53	4498	4281	−216 (5.0)	3605	3805	200 (5.5)	−893	−476	417	2.7
1953/54	4229	4177	−51 (1.2)	3586	3809	223 (6.2)	−640	−368	275	1.2
1954/55	4242	4491	249 (5.5)	3855	3891	36 (0.9)	−600	−387	213	1.1
1955/56	4486	4639	153 (3.2)	3862	3957	95 (2.4)	−624	−682	−58	−0.3
1956/57	4929	4896	−33 (0.2)	3959	4087	128 (3.2)	−970	−809	161	0.8
1957/58	5020	5106	85 (0.6)	4069	4215	146 (3.5)	−951	−891	60	−0.3
1958/59	5263	5314	50 (0.9)	4215	4452	237 (5.6)	−1048	−862	186	0.8
1959/60	5400	5773	373 (6.4)	4494	4597	103 (2.2)	−906	−1176	−270	−1.1
1960/61	5795	5728	−67 (1.2)	4907	4989	82 (1.6)	−888	−739	149	0.6
1961/62	6263	6381	118 (1.8)	5187	5368	181 (3.4)	−1076	−1013	63	0.2

TABLE A.1 (*Contd.*)

Fiscal year	(1) *Taxation*[1] *(£ million)*			(2) *Expenditure*[2] *(£ million)*			(3) = (2) − (1) *Fiscal 'deficit'*[3] *(£ million)*			
	Expected revenue	*Actual revenue*	*Difference between actual and expected (% of actual in brackets)*	*Planned expenditure*	*Actual expenditure*	*Difference between actual and expected (% of actual in brackets)*	*Planned deficit (-: surplus)*	*Actual deficit*	*Difference between actual and expected deficit (£ million)*	*(as a % GNP)*
1962/63	6192	6572	380 (5.6)	5612	5695	83 (1.4)	−580	−877	−297	−1.0
1963/64	6621	6649	28 (0.4)	6929	6817	−112 (1.6)	308	168	−140	0.4
1964/65	7169	7431	262 (3.5)	6549	6480	−69 (1.1)	−620	−951	−331	1.0
1965/66	8199	8324	125 (1.5)	7134	7140	6 (0.0)	−1065	−1184	−119	0.3
1966/67	9626	9371	−255 (2.7)	8023	8108	85 (1.0)	−1603	−1263	340	0.8
1967/68	10679	10770	101 (0.9)	9549	10000	451 (4.5)	−1130	−770	360	0.8
1968/69	12475	12888	413 (3.2)	10725	10810	85 (0.1)	−1750	−2078	−328	0.8
1969/70	14464	14733	289 (1.9)	11800	12016	216 (1.8)	−2664	−2717	−53	0.1
1970/71	15582	15313	−269 (1.7)	12933	13450	517 (3.8)	−2649	−1863	786	1.5
1971/72	16217	16247	30 (0.2)	14149	14800	651 (4.6)	−2068	−1447	621	1.0
1972/73	16212	16449	237 (1.4)	15849	16750	899 (5.3)	−363	301	664	0.9
1973/74	16754	17250	496 (2.8)	17756	18500	744 (4.1)	1002	1250	248	0.2

1974/75	22277	22132	−145 (0.6)	21107	25605	4498 (17.5)	−1170	3473	4643	5.5
1975/76	26851	28116	1265 (4.4)	28729	34070	5343 (15.6)	1878	5916	4078	3.9
1976/77	31960	32470	510 (1.5)	34568	37072	2504 (7.2)	2608	4602	1994	1.6
1977/78	36332	36436	104 (0.3)	37940	40043	2103 (5.51)	1608	3607	1999	1.4
1978/79	41205	40942	−263 (0.6)	42328	45763	3435 (8.1)	1123	4821	3698	2.0
1979/80	48940	50172	1232 (2.4)	52658	53600	942 (1.7)	3718	3428	−290	−0.2
1980/81	61780	60523	−1257 (2.1)	64765	68358	3593 (5.5)	2985	8015	5030	2.2
1981/82	70537	70523	−14 (0.0)	73741	74727	986 (1.3)	3204	4204	1000	0.4

Notes

1. 'Taxation' is defined as the sum of Inland Revenue (broadly, taxes on income and wealth), Customs and Excise (broadly, taxes on expenditure) and miscellaneous items such as the sale of licences on motor cars.
2. The expenditure included in this table is the total expended by government departments i.e. defence, education, health, social security, etc. under the heading of 'Supply Services'. It *excludes* payments in respect of the national debt and also payments to the European Communities.
3. This is simply the difference between column 1 and column 2. It should not be equated with the public sector financial deficit or borowing requirement appearing in the official statistics.

Source H.M. Treasury, *Financial Statements* (since 1967/68, *Financial Statement and Budget Report*), Her Majesty's Stationery Office, London, annual.

average absolute errors over the thirty-year period of 2.1 per cent in forecasting tax revenue, 3.2 per cent in forecasting expenditure and 1.1 per cent of GNP in forecasting the difference between the two; the reader should note, however, that this difference excludes several categories of public income and expenditure – in particular, repayments of the national debt – and is thus not equivalent to the public sector borrowing requirement (PSBR) discussed in Chapter 5. In both categories, overshoots are more common than undershoots: tax revenue was higher than expected in 20 cases out of 31, and expenditure was higher than expected in 24 cases, or three-quarters. The overshoots are sometimes very large, and in three fiscal years, 1974/75, 1975/76 and 1980/81, they resulted in miscalculations of the budget deficit of a magnitude larger than the *intended* value of tax changes announced by any Chancellor of the Exchequer in any budget. Research reported elsewhere (Mosley, 1983) suggests that on the expenditure side, the forecast errors are greatest in the area of housing and social security, whereas on the tax side they are greater in the area of company taxation, death duties and other taxes on capital. There is a negative correlation, in general, between estimate and outturn: planned large surpluses tend to lead to an overshoot in the surplus, and planned small surpluses or deficits lead to an excess of the planned over the actual reflationary effect.

An analytical distinction can be made between two kinds of forecast errors. On the one hand, there are errors which are *exogenous* to the economic system since they are due to factors which were quite impossible to foresee when the budget is drawn up: for example, the hot dry summer of 1976 which swelled revenues from alcohol taxation and the Falklands war of 1982 which caused an unexpected jump in defence expenditure. On the other hand, there are endogenous causes of error: failure to see how the changes introduced in the budget may affect the price level or the physical volume of ecomomic activity, and hence the exchequer's revenue and expenditure. There is not much that can be done about errors of exogenous origin. But there is a good deal of evidence that many of the errors noted in Table A.1 are of endogenous origin. In particular, the

TABLE A.2 United Kingdom: fiscal and monetary marksmanship, 1976–82

	Fiscal deficit			*Growth of sterling M_3*		
	Planned	*Actual*	*Difference*	*Planned*[1]	*Actual*	*Difference*
1976–7	4968	4600	*−368*	11	7.7	*−3.3*
1977–8	3817	3607	*−210*	11	16.0	*5.0*
1978–9	4973	4821	*−152*	10	10.9	*0.9*
1979–80	3718	3428	*−290*	9[2]	10.3[2]	*1.3*[2]
1980–1	2985	8015	*5030*	9	22.2	*+13.2*
1981–2	3204	4204	*1000*	8	13.5	*+5.5*

Notes
1 Mid-point of range.
2 June 1979 to April 1980.

Sources Fiscal deficit, Table A.1; growth of sterling M_3, Table 5.2.

negative correlation between estimate and out-turn suggested above implies that when governments are planning to increase the level of demand (that is, run a deficit) they fail to forecast the extent to which income will increase, and hence the buoyancy of tax revenue (for example, 1972/73); conversely, when governments are planning to reduce the level of demand they fail to foresee the extent to which tax revenue will fall (or social security expenditure will rise) and hence underestimate the size of the deficit: for example 1980/81.

We now explore the connection between fiscal and monetary marksmanship: between the fiscal errors noted in Table A.1 and the errors in forecasting the growth of money supply previously set out in Table 5.2. Table A.2 demonstrates that since the time when monetary targets began to be published in the middle 1970s these two types of error have had a loose, but positive relationship to one another.

Some of the monetary overshoots, no doubt, represent 'Goodhart's Law', named after an adviser to the Bank of England, which states that when the authorities attempt to control any monetary aggregate, be it M_1, M_3 or whatever, the activities of the financial system in creating substitutes for the form of asset being restricted will so affect its demand and supply that its behaviour will cease thenceforth to reflect the course of banking business. For example, between 1973 and 1980 banks were required to hold non-interest-bearing deposits at the Bank of England if the growth in the interest-bearing element of their deposits exceeded defined levels (a scheme known as the Supplementary Special Deposits Scheme or 'corset'). But banks found it possible to evade this restriction by encouraging customers to borrow from them through windows which were not restricted, in particular their overseas subsidiaries. The result of this experience has been to force the Treasury and the Bank of England to watch a larger range of monetary aggregates than sterling M_3 which served as the initial guiding light.

However, it is doubtful whether Goodhart's law explains all of the discrepancies between planned and target levels of money supply. We have seen that in the period 1980–81 a much larger than expected fiscal deficit was associated with a very high rate of increase of the money supply, as had earlier happened in 1974–75. It seems extremely likely that the monetary overshoot of these years was in large part a simple and automatic response to the fiscal overshoot. Such growth of the money supply might to some degree have been prevented by allowing nominal interest rates to rise still further, but by 1981 they were already at postwar record levels.

These interconnected sources of slippage between actual and desired levels of instruments introduce obvious inefficiency into the mechanism of economic policy-making, and it is natural to ask how the inefficiency might be reduced. There are obvious options. One is to step still further back from activist policy-making and only to announce targets for the things which really can be controlled – tax rates and the monetary base. The other is to allow more frequent changes to be made, particularly in taxation, so as to allow for the correction of errors as they become manifest rather than waiting for the next Budget by which time the error may have become very large. The ideology of the Conservative party would appear to dictate the adoption of the first alternative. Its actual behaviour would appear to indicate a shift in the direction of the second: for example, the Chancellor has now committed himself to making an 'Autumn Statement' on the economy, and in the first of these, in November 1982, he carried out certain discretionary adjustments including a reduction in the employers' National Insurance surcharge. This represents a modest return towards 'fine-tuning' although it is no doubt treasonable to actually use the term within the earshot of Treasury ministers. The central paradox remains: the most powerful economic instruments, in a democracy, are those over which the government has least control.

Notes

1 The discussion in this appendix owes a good deal to the pioneering article by Allan (1965).

Appendix III: Reaction functions using forecasts of targets instead of actual values

In Chapters 4, 5 and 6 we used a simple reaction function to model the making of economic policy. This implied that policy instruments would be altered in proportion to the gap between the actual and the desired value of some policy target. Formally, where x_i is the instrument, y_i the target to which it responds and y^*_i its desired value, we predict that

$$\Delta x_i = \alpha + \beta (y_i - y^*_i)_{t-k} \tag{3.1}$$

where α and β are fixed numbers and k is an empirically determined lag.

In the analysis of the text we have interpreted y_i, the 'actual' value of the target to which policy responds, as the *most recently observed* value of that variable. This would be reasonable if policy were simply a reaction to past events in the economy. To some degree, it is. But policy is also framed in anticipation of future trends in the economy. This suggests that it would be logical to interpret y_i, in the basic

TABLE A.3 Unemployment, inflation and the balance of payments: actual and forecast values, 1963–82[1]

	Unemployment (thousands; final quarter of year)		*Balance of payments (£million; current account; calendar year)*			*Inflation (retail price index all items; in %; year-on-year unless otherwise stated)*		
	Actual (ex post) *value published* by Economic Trends *in May of year following year stated*	*Forecast* (ex ante) *value as published by National Institute in February of year stated*	*Actual* (ex post) *value for calendar year as published* by Economic Trends *in May of year following year stated*	*Forecast* (ex ante) *value as published by National Institute in February of year stated*	*Forecast* (ex ante) *value as published by Treasury* in Financial Statement *(March of year stated)*	*Actual* (ex post) *value published* by Economic Trends *in May of year following year stated*	*Forecast* (ex ante) *value as published by National Institute in February of year stated*	*Forecast* (ex ante) *value as published by Treasury in Financial* Statement *(March of year stated)*
1963	486	*500*	121	*−65*				
1964	367	*360*	−374	*−75*				
1965	350	*290*	−136	*−128*				
1966	503	*500*	−61	*150*				
1967	596	*550*	−514	*0*				
1968	578	*585*	−419	*200*	−325[5]			
1969	602	*675*	366	*825*	−51[5]	5.4		
1970	641	*750*	631	*600*	433[5]	6.4	4.0	
1971	911	*870*	952	*900*	−177[5]	9.4	7.5	
1972	780	*800*	18	*−1625*	−331[5]	7.1	4.9	

1973	512	*575*[4]	−1468	*−4680*	−675[5]	9.2	5.8	
1974	650	*850*[4]	−3828	−2737	−960[6]	16.1	*14.9*	
1975	1201	*900*[4]	−1702	−2000	1375[6]	24.2	*18.0*	
1976	1371	*1325*[4]	−1423	366	1226[6]	16.5	*10.4*	
1977	1481	*1500*	−35	1300	3276[6]	15.8	*14.2*	
1978	1364	*1400*	254	1500	3000[6]	8.1[3]		*7*[3]
1979	1355	*1400*	−2437		−3540[6]	16.0[3]		*16*[2]
1980			2737			15.3[3]		*16.5*[3]
1981						11.9[3]		*10*[3]

Notes
1 The figures in *italics* are the forecasts used in the regressions (see Table A.3)
2 Third quarter of preceding year to third quarter of year stated.
3 Fourth quarter of preceding year to fourth quarter of year stated.
4 Mid-point of forecast range.
5 Given in 1963 prices and revalued to current prices.
6 Given in 1970 prices and revalued to current prices.

Sources Actual values for all variables: *Economic Trends* for month of May following year stated. National Institute forecasts: *National Institute Economic Review* for February of year stated. Treasury forecasts: *Financial Statement and Budget Report* for the year stated.

Table A.4 United Kingdom: Reaction functions, using both forecast and actual levels of target variables as independent variables

(a) Period 1964 (I) to 1973 (IV) (40 observations)

Constant	*Regression coefficients on independent variables:*				*'Pre-election dummy'*[2]	r^2	*DW*
	Unemployment, actual difference from average value of last three years (thousands)	*Unemployment,* forecast[1] *difference from average value of last three years (thousands)*	*Balance of payments, actual difference from average value of last three years (£million)*	*Balance of payments,* forecast *difference from average value of last three years (£million)*			
Dependent variable: budget change in taxes (£ million)							
22.4		–0.56**		0.35*	3.18	0.2804	0.3153
(0.32)		(2.52)		(2.32)	(0.37)		
5.1	–0.74*		0.22		–34.7	0.1591	0.3125
(0.10)	(2.32)		(1.43)		(0.43)		
Dependent variable: change in public investment (£ million)							
46.9*		0.099*		–0.32**	12.00	0.8195	0.6325
(5.10)		(2.01)		(9.12)	(1.06)		
34.2	0.071		–0.19**		34.43*	0.5510	0.7456
(3.30)	(1.01)		(5.65)		(2.12)		
Dependent variable: change in bank rate (%)							
0.29		–0.00031		–0.0012*	–0.31	0.1370	1.3102
(1.15)		(0.23)		(2.26)	(0.23)		
0.17	–0.00030		–0.0021**		–0.040	0.3861	1.5505
(1.14)	(0.28)		(4.29)		(0.15)		

(b) Period 1974 (I) to 1982 (II) (34 observations)

Constant	*Regression coefficients on independent variables:*		*'Pre-election dummy'*[2]	r^2	*DW*
	Inflation, actual difference from average value of last three years (%)	*Inflation,* forecast[1] *difference from average value of last three years (%)*			
Dependent variable: budget change in taxes (£ million)					
92.5		49.6**	–196	0.5234	0.7651
(1.41)		(5.68)	(1.65)		
34.1	35.77**		–31	0.3484	0.7499
(0.44)	(3.91)		(0.21)		
Dependent variable: change in public investment (£ million)					
18.7		14.0**	97.4*	0.3929	0.6912
(0.69)		(3.89)	(1.97)		
–23.7	14.18**		158.5**	0.4710	0.7986
(0.93)	(4.69)		(3.36)		
Dependent variable: change in bank rate (%)					
–0.28		–0.034	0.61	0.0538	1.4470
(0.90)		(0.82)	(0.56)		
–0.19	–0.022		0.50	0.0440	1.3885
(0.63)	(0.60)		(0.86)		

Notes

1 Forecasts used are Treasury forecasts, as published in the annual *Financial Statement* where possible, and in all other cases forecasts by the National Institute as published in the *National Institute Economic Review*. The figures used are printed in *italic type* in Table A.3.

2 Pre-election dummy takes the value 1 during the four quarters before an election, 0 at other times.

equation, as a *forecast* of the policy target, and to model policy changes as a response to *forecast* discrepancies between the actual and the desired value of, say, unemployment, inflation or the balance of payments, according to the time period being considered.

This is the approach which we take in this appendix. However a problem which we immediately encounter is that the forecasts of policy variables made by the policy-making body, the Treasury, are to a considerable degree unpublished and inaccessible to research workers. Before the 1968/69 financial year the Treasury published no forecasts. From 1969/70 onwards the Treasury did publish forecasts of the main components of demand – consumption, investment, exports and so on – but no forecasts of unemployment or of the balance of payments, which we have identified as the targets of the time. In the middle seventies the major policy target became the level of price inflation, but no Treasury forecasts of this variable were published until 1978. Hence it is not possible to re-estimate equation (3.1) on the basis of *Treasury* forecasts of target variables, as we would like. As a poor second best, however, it is possible to substitute into that equation the forecasts of policy variables made by a non-governmental body, the National Institute of Economic and Social Research. Since the National Institute maintained, at least until the change of government in 1979, a great deal of intellectual influence on Treasury thinking and a substantial interchange of personnel with the Treasury, the National Institute forecasts may not be too bad a substitute for those made by the Treasury.

The relationship between the published *ex post* values and the forecasts published by these two bodies is set out in Table A3. The broad tendency is for peaks and troughs in the balance of payments – and also the inflation peak of 1975 – to be under-forecast. But there was no such tendency for unemployment, in respect of which the National Institute forecasts, except in 1974, were rather good.

Now let us see what difference it makes to put forecast rather than actual values of target variables into the reaction functions estimated in Chapters 4 and 5. The results of this exercise are set out in Table A4. For the brief period

1964–1973 – which is, of course, only a small slice of the period surveyed in Chapter 4 – the predictive power and the significance of the response co-efficients increase a great deal for public investment and for the budget change in taxes when forecasts are used instead of *ex post* values. They decrease in the case of bank rate. For the period 1974–82 the use of forecast values of inflation again provides an improvement in the fit in the case of budget tax changes, but not in the case of the other two instruments considered. Overall, therefore, the use of forecast rather than actual *ex post* values of target variables fails as often as not to improve the fit of our regressions. Before jumping, however, to the conclusion that policy-making was a reactive rather than an anticipatory process in the years under consideration, it would be necessary to re-run the above equations with Treasury forecasts in lieu of National Institute surrogates as independent variables throughout. Official restrictions on the dissemination of economic information make this impossible at the present time.

Appendix IV: Complete specification of the models used in Chapter 6

The variables in the model: definitions and sources

The principal sources used are:
BoEQB – Bank of England Quarterly Bulletin
DoE – Department of Employment Gazette
ETAS – Economic Trends Annual Supplement (1981 Edition)
FS – Financial Statistics
MDS – Monthly Digest of Statistics
UN – United Nations Monthly Bulletin
FSBR – Financial Statement and Budget Report
The data used have been modified to include all revisions and updates as available in August 1981. For some series, recent figures must be considered to be provisional.

Variable name	Definition	Prime source	Equation
C:D	Consumers' expenditure, durable goods	ETAS	B.1
C:ND	Consumers' expenditure, nondurable goods	ETAS	B.2
CBAL	Current balance of payments	ETAS	I.1
CEGG	General government final consumption	ETAS	exogenous
CG	Current grants	MDS	exogenous
CONS	Total consumers' expenditure	ETAS	I.2
DEF:GG	Financial deficit of general government	ETAS	I.3
DEF:PC	Financial deficit of public corporations	ETAS	exogenous
DI	Debt interest	ETAS	exogenous
E	Index of average earnings (production industries and some services)	ETAS	B.3
E:GG	Expenditure of general government	ETAS	I.4
EC	Employers' contributions to national insurance, etc.	MDS	B.4
EMP	Employees in employment	ETAS	B.5
ER	Exchange rate	BoEQB	exogenous
EXPT	Exports of goods and services	ETAS	B.6
FCFG	Fixed capital formation, public sector	ETAS	exogenous
FCFG:GG	Fixed capital formation, general government	ETAS	exogenous ('raw' model); B. 27 ('modified' model)
FCFG:PC	Fixed capital formation, public corporations	ETAS	exogenous
FCFP:DW	Fixed capital formation, private sector, dwellings	ETAS	B.7
FCFP:ND	Fixed capital formation, private sector, non-dwelling	ETAS	B.8
FDEF:G	Financial deficit, public sector	ETAS	I.5
FP	Forces' pay	MDS	exogenous
FT:G	Financial transactions of the public sector (net receipts)	ETAS	exogenous

Variable name	*Definition*	*Prime source*	*Equation*
GDP	Gross domestic product at factor cost	ETAS	I.6
GDPINV	GDP net of inventories	transformed	GDP-INV
GTS:GG	Gross trading surplus, general government enterprises	ETAS	exogenous
GTS:PC	Gross trading surplus, public corporations	ETAS	exogenous
H	Average hours worked per operative in manufacturing	ETAS	exogenous
IMP	Imports of goods and services	ETAS	B.9
INV	Value of physical increase in stocks and work in progress (i.e. inventories)	ETAS	B.10
ITR	Indirect tax rate	transformed	I.7
IWP	Index of world production	UN	exogenous
KT	Capital transfers from general government	ETAS	exogenous
LC	Labour costs	transformed	I.8
M1	Money stock, M1	BoE	B.11
MIPD	Invisible debits, interest profits and dividends	ETAS	exogenous
MLR	Minimum lending rate, true weighted average	ETAS	exogenous ('raw' model); B.28 ('modified' model)
MT:G	Invisible debits, transfers, general government	ETAS	exogenous
MT:PS	Invisible debits, transfers, private	ETAS	exogenous
NIC	National insurance, etc. contributions by employees	MDS	B.12
NL:G	Net lending by public sector to private sector and overseas	ETAS	exogenous
NPRF	Company profits, net of tax	transformed	I.9
OC	Other grants	transformed	exogenous
OPY	Other personal income	MDS	B.13
P	Deflator of consumers' expenditure	transformed	B.14
PADJ	Deflator of adjustment to factor cost	transformed	B.15
PC:GG	Deflator of government current expenditure	transformed	B.16

PDY	Personal disposable income	ETAS	I.10
PF:GG	Deflator of government investment	transformed	B.17
PM	Deflator of imports of goods and services	transformed	exogenous
PNDW	Price index of new dwellings	MDS	exogenous
PRF	Gross trading profits of companies	ETAS	I.11
PSBR	Public sector borrowing requirement	ETAS	I.12
PW	Price of world exports deflated by exchange rate	transformed	PWTX/ER
PWTX	Price of world exports	UN	exogenous
PX	Deflator of exports of goods and services	transformed	B.18
PY	Total personal income	MDS	I.13
R:GG	Receipts of general government	ETAS	I.14
RELPM	Relative prices, domestic and imported goods	transformed	F/PM
RELPX	Relative prices, domestic and exported goods	transformed	PX/PW
RES	Residual error in GNP	ETAS	exogenous
RL	Long rate of interest – yield on 2½% consolidated stock	FS,BoEQB	B.19
RS	Short rate of interest – 3 month local authority rate	FS, BoEQB	B.20
SA	Stock appreciation	ETAS	exogenous
SB	Subsidies	ETAS	exogenous
SELT	Selective employment tax, net payments	DoE	exogenous
TIRI	Trading income, rent, interests etc., received by general government	ETAS	exogenous
TX	Taxes on expenditure	ETAS	B.21
TXK	Taxes on capital etc.	transformed	exogenous
UN	Numbers unemployed	DoE	I.15
UR	Unemployment rate	transformed	exogenous
UVOMF	Unit volume index of imported fuels	MDS	exogenous
W	Basic wage rates	ETAS	B.23

(*Contd.*)

Variable name	*Definition*	*Prime source*	*Equation*
WR	Real earnings	transformed	E/P
WS	Wage and salary payments	ETAS	B.24
XIPD	Invisible credits, interest, profits and dividends	ETAS	exogenous
XT:GG	Invisible credits, transfers, general government	ETAS	exogenous
XT:PS	Invisible credits, transfers, private	ETAS	exogenous
YRSE	Income from rent and self-employment	MDS	exogenous
YTAX:CFI	U.K. taxes on income paid by commercial and financial institutions	ETAS	exogenous
YTAX:PS	U.K. taxes on income paid by personal sector	MDS	B.25
BCITX	Estimated value in a 'full year' of budget change in taxes	FSBR	B.26 ('modified' model only)
TRENDUR	Value of a linear trend (1960:I to 1980:II) on unemployment (UR)	transformed	B.26, B.27, B.28 ('modified' model only)
TRENDBAL	Value of a linear trend (1960:I to 1980:II) on current balance of payments (CBAL)	transformed	B.26, B.27, B.28 ('modified' model only)
TRENDP	Value of a linear trend (1960:I to 1980:II) on consumer price inflation (P)	transformed	B.26, B.27, B.28 ('modified' model only)
TRENDM	Value of a linear trend (1960:I to 1980:II) on money supply (M)	transformed	B.26, B.27, B.28 ('modified' model only)

Dummy variables

ARMCD – anticipation of removal of import controls
BLG, CU2, LP2B – incomes policy, other interventions in the labour market
CCC – competition and credit control period
DIVAT – introduction of value-added tax
D3DW – three-day week
D6812 – anticipation of 1968 budget
MSTD, STD – dock strikes
Q1, Q2, Q3, Q4 – quarterly seasonal intercept dummies
S1, S2, S3 – legislation affecting inventories
TGP – Barber's 'go-for-growth' policy
VAT – value-added tax period
ELDUM – 1 for three quarters prior to a general election, 0 at other times

Dl – 1 during period 1960 (1) to 1979 (2) (i.e. the period during which unemployment was seen as a target variable), 0 at other times
D2 – 1 during period 1960 (1) to 1971 (4) (i.e. the period during which balance of payments was seen as a target variable), 0 at other times
D3 – 1 during period 1972 (1) to 1976 (6) (i.e. the period during which inflation was seen as a target variable), 0 at other times
D4 – 1 during period 1976 (1) to 1980 (2) (i.e. the period during which money supply was seen as a target variable), 0 at other times

Discrepancy terms

In some of the identities, there is a discrepancy between the total and the sum of the components. These are handled by exogenous discrepancy terms:

AGE, PAGE – GDP identity, real and nominal
ERP – PDY identity
XMDE – CBAL identity

Equations and identities

All equations are estimated for the period 1965 (i) – 1980 (ii), a total of 62 observations. Estimation is by ordinary least squares or by auto-regressive least squares. The equations are given as estimated in the 'modified' model, that is, the version which *includes* policy reaction functions. The value of coefficients in the 'raw' model are of course different from these – by a large amount in the case of some equations. See Smith (1980) for a statement of estimated parameter values in the 'raw' model, as estimated in 1979.

t-values are quoted in parentheses below coefficients for the behavioural equations. Equations and identities are quoted in alphabetical order of left-hand side variable, not in the order in which they appear in the model. The estimated values of seasonal dummies are not quoted for economy of space.

Note In all that follows, the 'raw' model (that is, the model with all policy instruments exogenous) consists of behavioural equations B.1 to B.25 and identities I.1 to I.15, and the 'modified' model (that is, the model with policy instruments endogenous) consists of behavioural equations B.1 to B.28 and identities I.1 to I.15. This involves the creation of three extra feedback loops, each of them turning an exogenous into an endogenous variable. For a diagrammatic representation of the 'raw' and 'modified' models see Figure 6.1 above.

Behavioural equations

(B.1) to (B.25) Relationships occurring only in the 'raw' model.

(B.1) *Consumers' expenditure on durable goods*

$$
\begin{aligned}
75C{:}D_t = {} & \underset{(3.66)}{0.106}\ 75PDY_t + \underset{(2.88)}{0.061}\ 75PDY_{t-1} - \underset{(2.88)}{23.55}\ RS_{t-2} - \underset{(2.44)}{955.6}\ (P_t - P_{t-4}) \\
& - \underset{(1.62)}{147.3}\ D3DW + \underset{(2.41)}{134.1}\ D6812 + \underset{(2.89)}{161.7} DIVAT \\
& + \text{seasonals}
\end{aligned}
$$

s.e.e. = 87.8 $\bar{R}^2 = 0.8942$ D.W. (1) = 2.0503

(B.2) *Consumers' expenditure on nondurable goods*

$$
\begin{aligned}
\Delta \ln 75C;ND_t = {} & \underset{(5.61)}{0.37}\ \Delta \ln 75PDY_t + \underset{(3.48)}{0.23}\ \Delta \ln 75PDY_{t-1} \\
& - \underset{(0.06)}{0.0005} T - \underset{(2.22)}{0.029}\ D3DW + \underset{(1.02)}{0.005}
\end{aligned}
$$

(B.3) *Earnings*

$$\ln E_t = \underset{(3.69)}{0.431} \ln H_t + \underset{(27.39)}{0.798} \ln W_t + \underset{(6.58)}{0.0063}\, T + \text{seasonals}$$

s.e.e. = 0.0103 $\bar{R}^2 = 0.9997$ D.W. (1) = 1.7690

(B.4) *Employers' contributions to national insurance etc.*

$$EC_t = \underset{(48.86)}{0.17}\, WS_t - \underset{(2.63)}{3.55}\, T - \underset{(9.28)}{323.2}$$

s.e.e. = 64.5 $\bar{R}^2 = 0.9967$ D.W. (1) = 0.4328

(B.5) *Employment*

$$\triangle EMP_t = \underset{(2.01)}{0.054} \triangle\, 75GDP_t = \underset{(1.30)}{0.036} \triangle\, 75GDP_{t-3} + \underset{(1.13)}{0.015} \triangle\, EMP_{t-4} + \underset{(0.39)}{0.28}\, T + \text{seasonals}$$

s.e.e. = 99.8 $\bar{R}^2 = 0.4790$ D.W. (1) = 1.4174

(B.6) *Exports*

$$\ln 75EXPT_t = \underset{(1.79)}{0.34} \ln IWP_t + \underset{(3.92)}{0.71} \ln IWP_{t-2} - \underset{(1.15)}{0.07} \ln RELPX - \underset{(4.41)}{0.079}\, STD + \underset{(165.5)}{8.89}$$

s.e.e = 0.036 $\bar{R}^2 = 0.9799$ D.W. (1) = 1.5076

(B.7) *Private investment in dwellings*

$$75FCFP{:}DW_t = \underset{(1.82)}{0.019}\, 75PDY_{t-1} + \underset{(1.02)}{0.015}\, 75PDY_{t-4} + \underset{(0.12)}{0.0014}\, 75PDY_{t-6} - \underset{(3.40)}{131.4}\, PNDW_{t-2} - \underset{(4.38)}{14.9}\, RS_{t-2} + \underset{(0.29)}{0.36}\, T + \underset{(1.94)}{0.23}\, 75FCFP{:}DW_{t-1} + \text{seasonals}$$

s.e.e. = 36.1 $\bar{R}^2 = 0.6596$ D.W. (1) = 1.9387

(B.8) *Private investment (other than dwellings)*

$$75FCFP{:}ND_t = \underset{(3.62)}{0.069}\, 75GDP_t + \underset{(3.66)}{0.058} \triangle\, 75GDP_{t-4} + \underset{(2.00)}{0.027}\, 75\, NPRF_{t-2} - \underset{(3.03)}{26.3}\, RL_{t-4} - \underset{(1.15)}{21.3} \triangle\, RL_{t-2} + \underset{(3.41)}{10.9}\, T + \underset{(2.60)}{0.27}\, 75FCFP{:}ND_{t-1} - \underset{(0.90)}{265.7}$$

s.e.e. = 88.7 $\bar{R}^2 = 0.9543$ D.W. (1) = 1.8608

(B.9) *Imports*

$$751MP_t = \underset{(1.82)}{0.15}\, 75GDPINV_t + \underset{(3.25)}{0.25}\, 75GDPINV_{t-2} + \underset{(2.68)}{0.31}\, 75INV_t + \underset{(4.10)}{1718}\, RELPM_t - \underset{(1.24)}{167}\, UVOMF_{t-4} + \underset{(4.39)}{0.407}\, 75\, IMP_{t-3} - \underset{(1.89)}{5261}\, ARMCD - \underset{(4.86)}{989}\, MSTD + \text{seasonals}$$

s.e.e. = 254.9 $\bar{R}^2 = 0.9639$ D.W. (1) = 1.1895

(B.10) *Inventory changes*

$$75INV_t = \underset{(0.11)}{0.007}\, 75GDPINV_{t-4} + \underset{(0.62)}{14.2} \triangle\, RS_{t-1} + \underset{(1.97)}{46.4} \triangle\, RS_{t-3} + \underset{(2.58)}{0.28}\, 75INV_{t-1} + \underset{(0.74)}{137.1}\, SI + \underset{(3.16)}{536.7}\, S2 - \underset{(3.09)}{439.8}\, S3 + \text{seasonals}$$

s.e.e. = 228.5 $\bar{R}^2 = 0.5103$ D.W. (1) = 2.0141

(B.11) *Money stock*

$$\ln M1 = \underset{(5.00)}{0.24} \ln 75PDY_t - \underset{(6.92)}{0.058} \ln RS_t + \underset{(4.56)}{0.15} \ln P_t + \underset{(19.48)}{0.81} \ln M1_{t-1} + \text{seasonals}$$

s.e.e. = 0.014 $\bar{R}^2 = 0.9988$ D.W. (1) = 2.0516

(B.12) *National Insurance Contributions*

$$NIC_t = \underset{(86.0)}{0.13} WS_t + \text{seasonals}$$

s.e.e. = 81.8 $\bar{R}^2 = 0.9918$ D.W. (1) = 2.4912

(B.13) *Other personal income*

$$OPY_t = \underset{(10.51)}{0.22} WS_t + \underset{(5.39)}{0.33} PRF_t - \underset{(0.84)}{0.054} SA_t + \underset{(1.68)}{6.93} I + \text{seasonals}$$

s.e.e. = 176.9 $\bar{R}^2 = 0.9938$ D.W. (1) = 1.9905

(B.14) *Prices*

$$\Delta \ln P_t = \underset{(2.85)}{0.085} \Delta \ln PM_{t-2} + \underset{(2.56)}{0.077} \Delta \ln PM_{t-4} + \underset{(3.72)}{0.245} \Delta \ln LC_{t-2} + \underset{(3.13)}{0.23} \Delta \ln LC_{t-4} + \underset{(0.54)}{0.024} \Delta \ln ITR_{t-2} - \underset{(5.08)}{0.163} \Delta \ln 75GDP_t + \underset{(1.25)}{0.0004} T - \underset{(0.29)}{0.0033} \ln P_{t-3} - \underset{(0.69)}{0.0126}$$

s.e.e. = 0.0094 $\bar{R}^2 = 0.7145$ D.W. (1) = 1.8417

(B.15) *Adjustment to factor cost – deflator*

$$PADJ_t = \underset{(2.70)}{0.22} P_t + \underset{(12.45)}{0.88} PADJ_{t-1} - \underset{(1.67)}{0.039}$$

s.e.e. = 0.082 $\bar{R}^2 = 0.9768$ D.W. (1) = 2.0772

(B.16) *Government current expenditure – deflator*

$$PC;GG_t = \underset{(42.59)}{1.02} P_t + \text{seasonals}$$

s.e.e. = 0.08 $\bar{R}^2 = 0.9675$ D.W. (1) = 1.9069

(B.17) *Government investment – deflator*

$$PF{:}GG = \underset{(76.61)}{1.01} P_t - \underset{(6.63)}{0.082}$$

s.e.e. = 0.043 $\bar{R}^2 = 0.9898$ D.W. (1) = 0.1373

(B.18) *Export prices*

$$\ln PX_t = \underset{(3.01)}{0.17} \ln P_t + \underset{(9.51)}{0.15} \ln PW_t + \underset{(12.01)}{0.67} \ln PX_{t-1} + \underset{(11.23)}{0.14}$$

s.e.e. = 0.0105 $\bar{R}^2 = 0.9995$ D.W. (1) = 1.4354

(B.19) *Long rate of interest*

$$RL_t = \underset{(2.15)}{0.069} RS_t + \underset{(3.13)}{0.17} \Delta RS_t + \underset{(1.64)}{0.0002} \Delta 75PDY_t$$

$$+\ 0.92\ RL_{t-1} + 0.13$$
$$(28.06)\qquad (0.50)$$
s.e.e. = 0.54 $\bar{R}^2$ = 0.9644 D.W. (1) = 1.6829

(B.20) *Short rate of interest*

Before Competition and Credit Control:

$$RS_t = 1.313\ MLR_t - 1.567$$
$$(7.56)\qquad (1.32)$$

After Competition and Credit Control:

$$RS_t = 1.02\ MLR_t - 0.0001\ 75PDY_{t-1} + 0.41\ \triangle\ Ml_{t-1}$$
$$(10.53)\qquad (0.40)\qquad (0.07)$$
$$-\ 4.59\ \triangle\ Ml_{t-2} + 8.65\ \triangle\ P_t - 21.8\ \triangle\ P_{t-4}\ 15.6$$
$$(0.78)\qquad (0.87)\qquad (2.19)\qquad (1.32)$$
s.e.e. (pooled) = 0.6916 R^2 = 0.9522 D.W. (1) = 1.0991

(B.21) *Taxes on expenditure*

$$75TX_t = 0.02\ 75CONS_t - 0.078\ 75CONS_{t-1} + 0.083\ (75CONS*VAT)_t$$
$$(2.34)\qquad (0.67)\qquad (2.58)$$
$$-1079\ VAT + 0.66\ 75\ TX_{t-1} + \text{seasonals}$$
$$(2.02)\qquad (7.37)$$
s.e.e. = 133.1 $\bar{R}^2$ = 0.9310 D.W. (1) = 2.1780

(B.22) *Unemployment rate*

$$UR_t = 0.029\ \triangle\ WR_{t-1} - 0.03\ \triangle\ WR_{t-2} + 0.0002\ T$$
$$(1.48)\qquad (1.44)\qquad (4.77)$$
$$+\ 0.72\ UR_{t-1} - 0.006\ TGP + \text{seasonals}$$
$$(12.03)\qquad (4.89)$$
s.e.e. = 0.002 $\bar{R}^2$ = 0.9763 D.W. (1) = 1.7986

(B.23) *Wage rate*

$$\triangle\ \ln\ W_t = 0.060\ \triangle\ \ln\ P_{t-1} - 0.029\ \ln\ P_{t-3} + 0.080\ \ln\ WR_{t-2}$$
$$(0.42)\qquad (1.55)\qquad (0.78)$$
$$-\ 0.017\ \ln\ WR_{t-3} - 0.019\ \ln\ UR_{t-4} + 0.001\ T$$
$$(0.01)\qquad (1.98)\qquad (1.35)$$
$$+\ 0.025BLG - 0.015\ LP2B + 0.06\ CU2 - 0.105$$
$$(2.51)\qquad (2.66)\qquad (4.82)\qquad (1.28)$$
s.e.e. = 0.0159 $\bar{R}^2$ = 0.6778 D.W. (1) = 2.0105

(B.24) *Wages and salaries*

$$\ln\ WS_t = 0.43\ \ln\ EMP_t + 0.99\ \ln\ E_t + \text{seasonals}$$
$$(1.95)\qquad (197.01)$$
s.e.e. = 0.013 $\bar{R}^2$ = 0.9995 D.W. (1) = 2.0717

(B.25) *Personal Income Tax*

$$YTAX{:}PS_t = 0.15\ PY_t + \text{seasonals}$$
$$(40.99)$$
s.e.e. = 316.1 $\bar{R}^2$ = 0.9651 D.W. (1) = 1.8702

(B.26) to (B.28) *'Reaction functions' added to the 'raw model' to make up the 'modified model'*

(B.26) *Budget change in taxes*

$$BCITX = -1.09\ - 0.39\ URTD,$$
$$(0.83)\quad (3.71)$$
$$-0.12\ CBALTD_2 + 39.2\ PTD_3$$
$$(0.59)\qquad (3.82)$$
$$+8.36\ MTD_4 - 32.9\ ELDUM$$
$$(0.62)\qquad (2.20)$$
s.e.e. = 188.2 R^2 = 0.387 D.W. (1) = 1.5066

(B.27) *Fixed capital formation, general government*

$$\triangle FCFG{:}GG = \underset{(1.8)}{68.9} + \underset{(2.70)}{0.16}\ URTD_1 - \underset{(1.29)}{0.15}\ CBALTD_2 - \underset{(3.44)}{10.3}\ PTD_3 - \underset{(0.32)}{1.29}\ MTD_4 + \underset{(1.91)}{91.8}\ ELDUM$$

s.e.e. = 133.4 $\bar{R}^2 = 0.5978$ D.W. (1) = 1.0281

(B.28) *Minimum lending rate*

$$\triangle MLR = \underset{(0.59)}{0.31} - \underset{(1.47)}{0.0011}\ URTD_1 - \underset{(2.32)}{0.002}\ CBALTD_2 - \underset{(0.98)}{0.41}\ PTD_3 + \underset{(1.97)}{0.052}\ MTD_4 - \underset{(0.33)}{0.21}\ ELDUM$$

$\bar{R}^2 = 0.1181$ D.W. (1) = 1.4852

Identities

(Note: the asterisk* is used to denote multiplication)

(I.1) to (I.15) Identities occurring only in 'raw model'

(I.1) $CBAL = PX^{*}75EXPT + XIPD + XT{:}GG + XT{:}PS - (PM^{*}75IMP + MIPD + MT{:}GG + MT{:}PS) + XMDE$

(I.2) $75CONS + 75C{:}D + 75C{:}ND$

(I.3) $DEF{:}GG = E{:}GG - R{:}GG$

(I.4) $E{:}GG = PC{:}GG^{*}75CEGG + PF{:}GG^{*}75FCFG{:}GG + CG + OC + SB + KT + DI$

(I.5) $FDEF{:}G = DEF{:}GG + DEF{:}PC + NL{:}G$

(I.6) $75GDP = 75CONS + 75CEGG + 75FCFP{:}DW + 75FCFP{:}ND + 75FCFG + 75INV + 75EXPT - (75IMP + (75TX - 75SB)) + AGE$

(I.7) $ITR = (75TX - 75SB)/75CONS$

(I.8) $LC = WS + EC + SELT$

(I.9) $75NPRF = (PRF - TXK - YTAX{:}CFI)/P$

(I.10) $75PDY = (PY + EC + ERP - (YTAX{:}PS + NIC + XT{:}PS - MT{:}PS))/P$

(I.11) $PRF = GDP - WS - EC - FP - YRSE - GTS{:}PC - GTS{:}CG - SA - RES$

(I.12) $PSBR = FDEF{:}G - FT{:}G$

(I.13) $PY = WS + OPY + FP + CT$

(I.14) $R{:}GG = YTAX{:}PS + YTAX{:}CFI + PADJ^{*}75TX + NIC^{*}TXK + TIRI$

(I.15) $UN = UR^{*}\ EMP/(1 - UR)$

(I.16) to (I.19) Identities added to the 'raw model' to make up the 'modified model'

(I.16) $URTD_1 = (UR - TRENDUR)^{*}D_1$ iff $UR \geq TRENDUR$

(I.17) $CBALTD_2 = (CBAL - TRENDCBAL)^{*}D_2$ iff $CBAL \leq TRENDCBAL$

(I.18) $PTD_3 = (P - TRENDP)^{*}D_3$ iff $P \geq TRENDP$

(I.19) $MTD_4 = (M - TRENDM)^{*}D_4$ iff $M \geq TRENDM$

Appendix V: Variations over time in the officially published value of economic policy targets

In Chapters 4 and 5 above we noted that it was quite common for the published macro-economic statistics to vary quite considerably over time as errors were uncovered and new

TABLE A.5 Percentage annual growth of real GDP (at factor cost): estimates appearing in successive years' issues of *Economic Trends*

In respect of real GDP growth in the year:	*Value published in July:*																						*Range of variation, lowest to highest value*
	1960	*1961*	*1962*	*1963*	*1964*	*1965*	*1966*	*1967*	*1968*	*1969*	*1970*	*1971*	*1972*	*1973*	*1974*	*1975*	*1976*	*1977*	*1978*	*1979*	*1980*	*1981*	*1982*	
1960				4.5	4.8	5.1										4.6	5.7	5.5		5.3	5.6	5.6		4.5 to 5.7
1961				2.6	3.2	3.4	3.3									3.5	2.5	2.6		2.5	2.5	2.5		2.5 to 3.2
1962					0.2	0.4	0.7	0.8								0.9	1.3	1.2		1.2	1.1	1.1		0.2 to 1.3
1963						3.6	3.9	4.0	4.1							4.0	3.7	3.8		3.6	3.7	3.9		3.6 to 4.1
1964						5.6	5.4	5.8	5.9	5.1						5.2	5.6	5.7		5.5	5.4	5.6		5.1 to 5.9
1965							2.4	2.5	2.6	2.4	2.6					2.5	2.7	2.9		3.0	2.9	2.9		2.4 to 3.0
1966								1.4	1.8	1.6	1.9	2.0				2.0	1.9	1.7		1.8	1.8	1.8		1.4 to 2.0
1967									1.1	1.2	1.7	1.8	1.8			2.5	2.1	2.1		2.0	2.1	2.0		1.1 to 2.1
1968										3.0	2.9	3.2	3.1	3.3		3.6	4.0	4.0		4.2	4.3	4.5		2.9 to 4.5
1969											1.2	1.6	1.7	2.6	1.4	1.4	2.1	2.4		2.4	2.3	2.4		1.2 to 2.4
1970												1.5	1.6	2.1	1.5	1.8	1.9	1.9		1.8	2.0	2.0		1.5 to 2.1
1971													1.1	1.4	2.0	1.9	2.3	1.5		1.5	1.5	1.5		1.1 to 2.3
1972														1.3	1.5	2.2	1.7	1.5		2.4	2.4	2.6	2.7	1.3 to 2.7
1973															5.8	5.3	5.4	6.0	7.3	6.9	6.9	7.2	7.2	5.3 to 7.2
1974																0.5	0.4	0.1	−1.3	−1.6	−1.4	−1.9	−1.7	0.5 to −1.9
1975																	−1.7	−1.9	−2.2	−1.8	−0.8	−0.9	−1.1	−0.8 to −2.2
1976																		1.4	3.1	3.5	3.6	3.8	3.6	1.4 to 3.8
1977																			−0.1	1.5	0.8	0.9	1.3	−0.1 to 1.3
1978																				3.0	3.1	3.5	3.3	3.0 to 3.5
1979																					0.6	1.1	1.3	0.6 to 1.3
1980																						−1.4	−1.9	−1.4 to −1.9
1981																							−2.4	

Sources Economic Trends, July issue for each year; also *Economic Trends Annual Supplement* for years after 1975.

TABLE A.6 Balance of payments on current account: estimates appearing in successive years' issues of *Economic Trends*.

In respect of current balance of payments in the year:	*Value published in July:* 1960	1961	1962	1963	1964	1965	1966	1967	1968	1969	1970	1971	1972	1973	1974	1975	1976	1977	1978	1979	1980	1981	1982	*Range of variation, lowest to highest value*
1960				− 308	− 258	− 275	− 273													− 244	− 244	− 228		− 308 to − 228
1961				− 72	10	− 22	− 14	− 5												27	27	47		− 72 to 47
1962				67	102	90	93	101	127											130	130	155		67 to 155
1963					121	96	105	107	116	111										129	129	125		96 to 129
1964						− 374	− 406	− 393	− 402	− 399	− 393					− 355	− 355	− 356		− 358	− 357	− 362		− 406 to − 355
1965							− 136	− 109	− 110	− 91	− 81	− 77				− 27	− 26	− 26		− 45	− 45	− 43		− 136 to − 26
1966								− 61	− 31	5	40	55	83			100	101	104		109	111	113		− 61 to 113
1967									− 514	− 399	− 322	− 297	− 298	− 315		− 301	− 298	− 300		− 294	− 293	− 289		− 514 to − 293
1968										− 419	− 309	− 306	− 291	− 271	− 28	− 275	− 272	− 287		− 286	− 242	− 273		− 419 to − 242
1969											366	437	443	444	45	462	460	440		463	509	471		366 to 509
1970												631	611	688	69	735	733	695		731	776	781	823	611 to 781
1971													952	1051	106	1052	1084	1058		1090	1150	1076	1124	952 to 1150
1972														18	6	82	131	131		135	208	176	247	18 to 247
1973															− 146	− 1117	− 842	− 752	− 883	− 999	− 875	− 1056	− 981	− 1468 to − 752
1974																− 3828	− 3650	− 3380	− 3515	− 3591	− 3302	− 3379	− 3273	− 3273 to − 3828
1975																	− 1702	− 1635	− 1614	− 1843	− 1732	− 1674	− 1521	− 1843 to − 1521
1976																		− 1423	− 1107	− 1137	− 1202	− 1060	− 881	− 1423 to − 881
1977																			− 35	298	− 224	− 206	− 41	− 224 to 298
1978																				254	932	707	945	254 to 945
1979																					− 2437	− 1630	− 936	− 2437 to − 936
1980																						2737	3058	
1981																								

Sources Economic Trends, July issue for each year; also *Economic Trends Annual Supplement* for years after 1975.

information became available. We argued that these statistical revisions could have considerable importance for the interpretation of policy actions since they may make policy interventions which appeared quite rational at the time look misconceived in the light of the data now at our disposal. This appendix provides data in support of that argument.

A distinction must be made between the kinds of statistics which are and are not commonly revised. Statistics of *unemployment* and of *price changes* are not often altered once collected. By contrast, statistics of *national income* and the *balance of payments* are subjected to what can only be called constant revision: the *Economic Trends Annual Supplement* estimate of the growth rate of real GDP in 1960 has been revised four times *since 1975,* as has the same publication's estimate of the 1964 balance of payments.

Tables A.5 and A.6 set out the detail of these revisions. The range of variation is wide: on average it is £268 m. for the balance of payments and 1.2% for the growth rate of GDP. Also, there is a tendency for revisions in the statistics to make our view of the economy look rosier with hindsight than it looked at the time: in 17 out of 20 years since 1960 the currently available estimate of the growth of GDP is higher than the estimate originally published, and in 18 out of those 20 years the currently available estimate of the balance of payments is more positive (or less negative) than the estimate originally published. It is likely that both these biases stem from the same cause, namely the tendency of imports to be recorded at once and exports only with a lag. But they have an important implication, namely that the overly pessimistic estimate of these target variables available at the moment of decision may provoke the government into deflationary measures which might never have been considered necessary had the 'true' value of those target variables been known at the time. A case in point is 1966, in which serious deflationary measures occurred which punctured the Labour government's hopes of achieving the growth targets of the 1964 'National Plan' (see for example Crossman 1979, pp. 228–34). The principal cause of these deflationary measures was the state of the balance of payments, which according to statistics published shortly after the end of the year was in deficit over the year to the tune of £61 m. It is now estimated to have been in overall *surplus* to the tune of £113 m. The severity of the deflations of 1965 and 1968 could also be partly attributed to an overestimate of the balance of payments deficit. Finally, the reflation of 1972 might not have been so frenetic had it been known that real GDP was growing already at 2.7 per cent (as is now estimated) rather than 1.3 per cent (as was believed at the time). Those acts of policy may appear irrational now, but we are only able to exercise such a judgement because of our access to data which was denied to the people who made the decisions. The fault lies with the machinery for collecting data and making short-term forecasts, and not with the methods of policy-making themselves.

Bibliography

Alchian, A., 1950, 'Uncertainty, evolution and economic theory', *Journal of Political Economy,* vol. 58, pp. 211–21.

Allan, C.M., 1965, 'Fiscal marksmanship, 1951–1963', *Oxford Economic Papers,* vol. 17, pp. 317–27.

Allen, R.G.D., 1967, *Macro-economic theory,* London: Macmillan.

Alt, J.E., 1979, *The Politics of Economic Decline: Economic Management and Political Behaviour in Britain since 1964,* Cambridge: University Press.

Alt, J.E. and K.A. Chrystal, 1981, 'Endogenous government behaviour: overture to a study of government expenditure', chapter in Hibbs and Fassbender (1981).

Alt, J.E. and K.A. Chrystal, 1983, *Political economics.* Brighton: Harvester Press.

Arcelus, F. and A.H. Meltzer, 1975, 'The effect of aggregate economic variables on congressional elections', *American Political Science Review,* vol. 69, pp. 1232–9.

Barry, B., 1965, *Political argument,* London: Routledge and Kegan Paul.

Barry, B., 1978, 'Does democracy cause inflation? A study of the political ideas of some economists', unpublished paper prepared for the Brookings Project on the Politics and Sociology of Global Inflation.

Barnett, J., 1982, *Inside the Treasury,* London: André Deutsch.

Behrend, H., 1964, 'Price and income images and inflation', *Scottish Journal of Political Economy,* vol. 11, pp. 85–103.

Behrend, H., 1966, 'Price images, inflation and national incomes policy', *Scottish Journal of Political Economy,* vol. 13, pp. 273–96.

Behrend, H., 1981, 'Research into public attitudes and the attitudes of the public to inflation', *Managerial and Decision Economics,* vol. 2, pp. 1–8.

Blackaby, F. (ed.), 1979, *British Economic Policy 1960–74: Demand Management,* Cambridge: University Press for National Institute of Economic and Social Research.

Bispham, J.A., 1975, 'The New Cambridge and 'monetarist' criticisms of 'conventional' economic policy-making', *National Institute Economic Review,* vol. 17, (November) pp. 39–55.

Blinder, A., 1979, *Economic Policy and the Great Stagflation,* New York: Academic Press.

Bloom, H.S. and H.D. Price, 1975, 'Voter response to short-run economic conditions', *American Political Science Review,* vol. 69, pp. 1240–4.

Boddy, R. and J. Crotty, 1975, 'Class conflict and macro-policy: the political business cycle', *Review of Radical Political Economics,* vol. 7, pp. 1–19.

Borooah, V.K. and F. van der Ploeg, 1982, 'British government popularity and economic performance: a comment', *Economic Journal,* vol. 92, pp. 405–10.

Brainard, W., 1967, 'Uncertainty and the effectiveness of policy', *American Economic Review,* Papers and Proceedings, vol. 57, pp. 411–25.

Brittan, S., 1971, *Steering the Economy,* 2nd ed., London: Penguin.

Brittan, S., 1977, *The Economic Consequences of Democracy,* London: Maurice Temple Smith.

Brittan, S., 1982, 'Washington sounds a new note', *Financial Times,* 9 December.

Bruce-Gardyne, J. and N. Lawson, 1976, *The Power Game,* London: Macmillan.

Buchanan, J.M. and R.E. Wagner, 1977, *Democracy in Deficit: the Political Legacy of Lord Keynes,* New York: Academic Press.

Buchanan, J.M., J. Burton and R.E. Wagner, 1978, *The Consequences of Mr Keynes*, London: Institute of Economic Affairs.

Budd, A., 1975, 'The debate on fine-tuning: the basic issues', *National Institute Economic Review*, vol. 17 (November), pp. 56–9.

Buiter, W.H. and M. Miller, 1981, 'The Thatcher experiment: the first two years', *Brookings Papers on Economic Activity*, vol. 4 pp. 315–67.

Butler, D. and D. Stokes, 1971, *Political Change in Britain: Factors Shaping Electoral Choice*, London: Penguin.

Cairncross, F., 1982, *Changing Perceptions of Economic Policy,* London: Methuen.

Caves, R., 1968, ed. *Britain's Economic Prospects*, New York: Brookings Institution.

Chappell, D. and D. Peel, 1979, 'On the political theory of the business cycle', *Economics Letters*, vol. 2, pp. 327–32.

Chrystal, A., 1982, *Controversies in Macroeconomics,* Deddington, Oxford: Philip Allan.

Cohen, C.D., 1971, *British Economic Policy 1960–9,* London: Butterworths.

Collard, D., 1978, *Altruism and Economy,* Oxford: Martin Robertson.

Crosland, S., 1982, *Tony Crosland*, London: Jonathan Cape.

Crossman, R., 1972, *Inside View: Three Lectures on Prime Ministerial Government*, London: Jonathan Cape.

Crossman, R., 1979, *The Crossman Diaries: Condensed Version*, London: Methuen paperback.

Cyert, R. and J.G. March, 1963, *A Behavioral Theory of the Firm*, Englewood Cliffs, N.J.: Prentice-Hall.

Davis, O., M. Dempster and A. Wildavsky, 1975, 'Towards a predictive theory of government expenditure: US domestic appropriations', *British Journal of Political Science*, vol. 4, pp. 419–52.

Dow, J.C.R., 1964, *The Management of the British Economy 1945–1960*, Cambridge: University Press.

Downs, A., 1957, *The Economic Theory of Democracy*, New York: Harper and Row.

Downs, A., 1967, *Inside Bureaucracy*, Boston: Little, Brown.

Fair, R., 1975, 'On controlling the economy to win elections', Cowles Foundation discussion paper 397.

Fair, R., 1978a, 'The effect of economic events on votes for President', *Review of Economics and Statistics*, vol. 60, pp. 159–73.

Fair, R., 1978b, 'The sensitivity of fiscal policy effects to assumptions about the behaviour of the Federal Reserve', *Econometrica*, vol. 46, pp. 1165–79.

Feiwel, G.R., 1974, 'Reflections on Kalecki's theory of the political business cycle', *Kyklos*, vol. 27, pp. 21–48.

Feldstein, M. (ed.), 1980, *The American Economy in Transition*, National Bureau of Economic Research and University of Chicago Press.

Fisher, D., 1968, 'The objectives of British monetary policy, 1951–64', *Journal of Finance*, vol. 23, pp. 821–31.

Fisher, D., 1970, 'The instruments of monetary policy and the generalised trade-off function for Britain 1955–68', *Manchester School*, vol. 38, pp. 209–22.

Frey, B.S., 1978, 'Politico-economic models and cycles', *Journal of Public Economics*, vol. 9, pp. 203–20.

Frey, B.S. and F. Schneider, 1978a, 'An empirical study of politico-economic interaction in the United States', *Review of Economics and Statistics*, vol. 60, pp. 174–83.

Frey, B.S. and F. Schneider, 1978b, 'A political-economic model of the United Kingdom', *Economic Journal*, vol. 88, pp. 243–53.

Frey, B.S. and F. Schneider, 1978c, 'Recent research on empirical politico-economic models', Institute for Empirical Research in Economics, University of Zurich, Discussion paper 7804.

Frey, B.S. and F. Schneider, 1981, 'Central bank behaviour: a positive empirical analysis', *Journal of Monetary Economics*, vol. 7, pp. 291–315.

Friedlaender, A.F., 1973, 'Macro-policy goals and revealed preference', *Quarterly Journal of Economics*, vol. 87, pp. 25–43.

Friedman, B., 1978, 'Public disclosure and domestic monetary policy', in Richard D. Erb (ed.), *Federal Reserve Policies and Public Disclosure*, American Enterprise Institute.

Goldfeld, S.M. and A. Blinder, 1972, 'Some implications of endogenous stabilisation policy', *Brookings Papers on Economic Activity*, vol. 3, pp. 585–644.

Goodhart, C.A.E. 1975, *Money, Information and Uncertainty*, London: Macmillan.

Goodhart, C.A.E. and R.J. Bhansali, 1970, 'Political economy', *Political Studies*, vol. 18, pp. 43–106.

Goodman, S. and G. Kramer, 1975, 'Comment on Arcelus and Meltzer', *American Political Science Review*, vol. 69, pp. 1255–65.

Gordon, R.J., 1975a, 'The demand for and supply of inflation', *Journal of Law and Economics*, vol. 18, pp. 807–36.

Gordon, R.J., 1975b, 'Alternative responses of policy to external supply shocks', *Brookings Papers on Economic Activity*, vol. 6, pp. 183–206.

Hall, Sir R., 1959, 'Reflections on the practical application of economics', *Economic Journal*, vol. 69, pp. 639–52.
Ham, A., 1981, *Treasury Rules: Recurrent Themes in British Economic Policy*, London: Quartet.
Harrod, D., 1978, *The Politics of Economics*, London: BBC Publications.
Healey, D., 1981, *Managing the Economy*, City-Association Lectures, Spring 1981. Certified Accountants Educational Trust and City of London Polytechnic.
Heclo, H. and A. Wildavsky, 1979, *The Private Government of Public Money*, 2nd edition, London: Macmillan.
Hennessy, P., 1977, 'The Treasury: bank manager and probation officer rolled into one', *The Times*, 28 March.
Hibbs, D., 1977, 'Political parties and macro-economic policy', *American Political Science Review*, vol. 71, pp. 1467–87.
Hibbs, D., 1979, 'The mass public and macro-economic performance: the dynamics of public opinion towards unemployment and inflation', *American Journal of Political Science*, vol. 23, pp. 705–31.
Hibbs, D. and H. Fassbender, 1981, *Contemporary Political Economy: Studies on the Interdependence of Politics and Economics*, Amsterdam: North-Holland.
Higham, D. and J. Tomlinson, 1982, 'Why do governments worry about inflation?', *National Westminster Bank Review*, September, pp. 2–13.
Hirsch, F., 1977, *The Social Limits to Growth*, London: Routledge.
Hirschman, A.O., 1970, *Exit, Voice and Loyalty*, Cambridge, Mass: Harvard University Press.
Jackson, P.M., 1982, *The Political Economy of Bureaucracy*, Deddington, Oxford: Philip Allan.
Jay, P., 1976, *A General Hypothesis of Employment, Inflation and Politics*, London: Institute of Economic Affairs (Occasional Paper 46).
Johansen, L., 1965, *Public economics,* Amsterdam: North-Holland.
Kalecki, M., 1938, 'Lessons of the Blum experiment', *Economic Journal*, vol. 48, pp. 26–41.
Kalecki, M., 1943, 'Political aspects of full employment', *Political Quarterly*, vol. 14, pp. 322–31.
Kay, J., 1982, *The 1982 Budget*, Oxford: Basil Blackwell.
Keegan, W. and R. Pennant-Rea, 1979, *Who Runs the Economy? Control and Influence in British Economic Policy*, London: Maurice Temple Smith.
Kernell, S., 1978, 'Explaining presidential popularity: how ad hoc theorising, misplaced emphasis and insufficient care in measuring one's variables refuted common sense and led conventional wisdom down the path of anomalies', *American Political Science Review*, vol. 72, pp. 506–22.
King, A., 1975, 'Overload; problems of governing in the 1970s', *Political Studies,* vol. 23, pp. 284–96.
Kirschen, E.-S., 1974, *Economic Policies Compared: East and West*, 2 vols, Amsterdam: North-Holland.
Klein, R., 1976, 'The politics of public expenditure: American theory and

British practice', *British Journal of Political Science,* vol. 6, pp. 401–32.

Kramer, G., 1971, 'Short-term fluctuations in U.S. voting behaviour', *American Political Science Review*, vol. 65, pp. 131–43.

Lachler, U., 1981, 'The political business cycle: a complementary analysis', *Review of Economic Studies*, vol. 40, pp. 369–75.

Lachler, U., 1982, 'On political business cycles with endogenous election dates', *Journal of Public Economics*, vol. 17, pp. 111–17.

Laidler, D.E.W. and J.M. Parkin, 1970, 'The demand for money in the U.K., 1956–1967: preliminary estimates', *Manchester School*, vol. 38, pp. 187–208.

Laidler, D.E.W., 1971, 'The influence of money on economic activity – a survey of some current problems', in G. Clayton, J.C. Gilbert and R. Sedgwick (eds) *Monetary Theory and Monetary Policy in the 1970s*, London: Oxford University Press.

Laury, J.S.E., G.R. Lewis and P.A. Ormerod, 1978, 'Properties of macro-economic models of the UK economy: a comparative study', *National Institute Economic Review,* vol. 83, pp. 52–72.

Layard, R., 1982, *More Jobs, Less Inflation: the Case for a Counter-Inflation Tax,* London: Grant MacIntyre.

Lepper, Susan J., 1974, 'Voting behaviour and aggregate policy targets', *Public Choice,* vol. 18, pp. 67–81.

Lindbeck, A., 1976, 'Stabilisation policy in open economies with endogenous politicians', *American Economic Review Papers and Proceedings*, vol. 66, pp. 1–18.

Lipsey, R. and J.M. Parkin, 1970, 'Incomes policy: a re-appraisal', *Economica*, vol. 37, pp. 115–38.

Longstreth, F., 1984, 'The dynamics of disintegration of a Keynesian political economy: the British case and its implications', *Industrial Organisation*, forthcoming.

MacRae, D. Jr., 1975, 'Policy analysis as an applied social science discipline', *Administration and Society,* vol. 6, pp. 363–88.

MacRae, C.D., 1977, 'A political model of the business cycle', *Journal of Political Economy*, vol. 85, pp. 239–64.

Marris, R.L., 1954, 'The position of economics and economists in the government machine: a comparative critique of the UK and the Netherlands', *Economic Journal*, vol. 64, pp. 759–83.

Marris, R.L., 1967, *The Economic Theory of 'Managerial' Capitalism*, London: Macmillan.

Miller, M., 1981, 'The Medium-term Financial Strategy: an experiment in co-ordinating monetary and fiscal policy', *Fiscal Studies*, vol. 2, pp. 50–60.

Minford, P. and D. Peel, 1981, 'Is the government's economic strategy on course?' *Lloyds Bank Review*, April issue, pp. 1–19.

Mosley, P., 1976, 'Towards a "satisficing" theory of economic policy', *Economic Journal*, vol. 86, pp. 59–73.

Mosley, P., 1978, 'Images of the "floating voter"; or, the "political business cycle" revisited', *Political Studies*, vol. 26, pp. 375–94.

Mosley, P., 1981, 'The Treasury Committee and the making of economic policy', *Political Quarterly*, vol. 52, pp. 348–55.
Mosley, P., 1982, *The Economy as Represented by the Popular Press*, University of Strathclyde, Centre for Studies in Public Policy, Studies in Public Policy No. 105.
Mosley, P., 1983, 'Fiscal markmanship, 1953–1982', University of Bath papers in political economy no. 20.
Mosley, P., 1984, 'Popularity functions and the media: a pilot study of the popular press', *British Journal of Political Science,* vol. 14, pp. 119–31.
Mosley, P. and R. Cracknell, 1981, *Instrumental Reaction Functions in a Model of the UK Economy,* University of Bath papers in political economy no. 7.
Mosley, P. and R. Cracknell, 1984, 'Endogenous government policy in a model of the UK economy', forthcoming *Applied Economics*.
Mowl, C., 1980, *Simulations on the Treasury Model*, UK Government Economic Service Working Paper 34.
Mueller, J.E., 1970, 'Presidential popularity from Truman to Johnson', *American Political Science Review*, vol. 64, pp. 18–34.
Niskanen, W., 1973, *Bureaucracy: Servant or Master?*, London: Institute of Economic Affairs.
Niskanen, W., 1975, 'Bureaucrats and politicians', *Journal of Law and Economics*, vol. 18, pp. 617–43.
Nordhaus, W., 1975, 'The political business cycle', *Review of Economic Studies*, vol. 42, pp. 169–90.
O'Connor, J., 1973, *The Fiscal Crisis of the State*, New York: St Martin's Press.
Okun, A.M., 1970, *The Political Economy of Prosperity,* Washington, D.C.: Brookings Institution.
Olson, M., 1965, *The Logic of Collective Action*, Cambridge, Mass: Harvard University Press.
Peacock, J., and Wiseman, J., 1967, *The Growth of Public Expenditure in the United Kingdom*, 2nd ed., London: Allen and Unwin.
Phillips, A.W., 1954, 'Stabilisation policy in a closed economy', *Economic Journal*, vol. 64, pp. 290–323.
Pierce, J., 1979, 'The political economy of Arthur Burns', *Journal of Finance*, vol. 34, pp. 485–96.
Pissarides, C., 1972, 'A model of British macro-economic policy 1955–1969', *Manchester School,* vol. 40, pp. 245–59.
Pissarides, C., 1980, 'British government popularity and economic performance', *Economic Journal*, vol. 90, pp. 569–81.
Pliatzky, L., 1982, *Getting and Spending: Public Expenditure, Employment and Inflation*, Oxford: Basil Blackwell.
Poole, W., 1975, 'The making of monetary policy: description and analysis', *New England Economic Review*, March-April issue, pp. 21–30.
Poole, W., 1979, 'Burnsian monetary policy: eight years of progress?' *Journal of Finance*, vol. 34, pp. 473–84.
Portney, P.R., 1976, 'Congressional delays in U.S. fiscal policy-making:

simulating the effects', *Journal of Public Economics*, vol. 5, pp. 237–47.

Reischauer, R.D., 1981, ' "The Budget" for the United States', paper presented at Olivetti Foundation Conference on Major Budgetary Problems in the Eighties, Siena, November.

Richardson, Sir G., 1978, 'Reflections on the conduct of monetary policy', unpublished speech, excerpted in *National Institute Economic Review*, February.

Robinson, A., 1978, *Parliament and Public Spending: the Expenditure Committee of the House of Commons 1970–1976,* London: Heinemann.

Robinson, A., 1981, 'Congress and the budget: are there some lessons for Britain?' Bath University Centre for Fiscal Studies, Occasional Paper 11.

Robinson, A. and C.T. Sandford, 1983, *Tax policy-making in the United Kingdom*, London: Heinemann.

Savage, D., 1979, 'Monetary targets and the control of the money supply', *National Institute Economic Review*, August issue, pp. 44–51.

Savage, D., 1982, 'Fiscal policy 1974/5 to 1980/1: description and measurement', *National Institute Economic Review*, February issue, pp. 86–93.

Schick, A., 1975, 'The battle of the budget', in H.C. Mansfield (ed.), *Congress against the President*, Washington: Academy of Political Sciences, pp. 51–70.

Simon, H.A., 1952, 'A behavioural model of rational choice', *Quarterly Journal of Economics*, vol. 69, pp. 99–118.

Simon, H.A., 1957, *Models of Man*, New York: Harper and Row.

Simon, H.A., 1972, 'Theories of bounded rationality', in C.B. McGuire and R. Radner (eds), *Decision and Organisation*, Amsterdam: North-Holland.

Simon, H.A., 1976, 'From substantive to procedural rationality', in S. Latsis (ed.), *Method and Appraisal in Economics*, Cambridge: University Press.

Simon, H.A., 1978, 'Rationality as a process and as a product of thought', *American Economic Review Papers and Proceedings*, vol. 68, pp. 1–16.

Stein, H., J. Tobin, H.C. Wallich, A. Okun and E. Shanahan (discussion), 1974, 'How political must the Council of Economic Advisers be?' *Challenge*, vol. 17, pp. 28–42.

Stewart, M., 1977, *The Jekyll and Hyde Years: Politics and Economic Policy since 1964*, London: Dent.

Stigler, G., 1976, 'The economics of information', *Journal of Political Economy*, vol. 59, pp. 213–25.

Stigler, G., 1973, 'General economic conditions and national elections', *American Economic Review Papers and Proceedings*, vol. 63, pp. 160–7.

Tarschys, D., 1982, 'Curbing public expenditures: a survey of current trends', paper prepared for Joint Activity on Management Improvement for OECD, August, 1982.

Theil, H., 1956, 'On the theory of economic policy', *American Economic Review Papers and Proceedings*, vol. 46, pp. 260–366.
Theil, H., 1958, *Economic Forecasts and Policy*, Amsterdam: North-Holland.
Theil, H., 1968, *Optimal Decision Rules for Government and Industry*, Amsterdam: North-Holland.
Tinbergen, J., 1952, *On the Theory of Economic Policy,* Amsterdam: North-Holland.
Tinbergen, J., 1958, *Economic Policy: Principles and Design*, Amsterdam: North-Holland.
Tomlinson, J., 1982, 'Unemployment and policy in the 1930s and 1980s' *Three Banks Review*, September issue, pp. 17–33.
Tullock, G., 1976, *The Vote Motive*, London: Institute of Economic Affairs.
Toye, J.F.J., 1976, 'Economic theories of politics and public finance', *British Journal of Political Science*, vol. 6, pp. 433–48.
Tufte, E.R., 1978, *Political Control of the Economy*, Princeton, N.J.: Princeton University Press.
United Kingdom, 1944, *Employment Policy*, Cmd. 6527, London: HMSO.
United Kingdom, 1974, *Public Expenditure. Inflation and the Balance of Payments,* Ninth report from the Expenditure Committee, London: HMSO.
United Kingdom, 1978, *Report of the Committee on Policy Optimisation* (chairman R.J. Ball) London: HMSO.
United Kingdom, 1980, *The Budget and the Government's Expenditure Plans 1980–81 to 1983–84*, Second report from the Treasury and Civil Service Committee, London: HMSO.
United Kingdom, 1981, *Monetary Policy*, Third report from the Treasury and Civil Service Committee, 3 vols, London: HMSO (H.C. 163).
United Kingdom, 1982, *H.M. Treasury: Macro-economic model, technical manual 1982*, London: H.M. Treasury.
United States Congress, 1976, *The Congressional Budget Office: Responsibilities and Organisation*, Washington D.C.
United States Congress, 1977, *Budget Options for Fiscal Year 1978*, Congressional Budget Office, Washington D.C.
United States President, annual from 1947, *Economic Report of the President together with the Annual Report of the Council of Economic Advisers*, various issues.
Wagner, R.E., 1977, 'Economic manipulation for political profit: macroeconomic consequences and constitutional implications', *Kyklos*, vol. 30, pp. 395–410.
Wallich, H.C., 1968, 'The American Council of Economic Advisers and the German Sachverstaendigenrat: a study in the economics of advice', *Quarterly Journal of Economics*, vol. 82, pp. 349–79.
Weir, S., 1982, 'The model that crashed: how the Cambridge economic forecasting groups have been pushed out into the cold', *New Society*, 12 August, pp. 251–3.

Wildavsky, A., 1964, *The politics of the budgetary process*, Boston: Little, Brown.

Wood, J.A., 1967, 'A model of Federal Reserve behaviour', in G. Horwich (ed.), *Monetary Process and Policy: a symposium,* Homewood, Illinois: R.D. Irwin.

Young, H., 1983, *But, Chancellor: an inquiry into the Treasury*, Programme 3: The Budget-Makers. Programme broadcast on BBC Radio 4 on 13 March. To be published by the BBC.

Acknowledgements

Acknowledgements are made to Joel Barnett and André Deutsch Ltd., London, for permission to quote from *Inside the Treasury* (1982).

Further acknowledgements are due to *The Daily Mirror*/Syndication International Ltd. for permission to reproduce the front page of *The Daily Mirror* dated: 25 January 1963 and 15 June 1972.

Index